Advancing Gerontological Social Work Education

Advancing Gerontological Social Work Education has been co-published simultaneously as *Journal of Gerontological Social Work*, Volume 39, Numbers 1/2 2002.

T0386578

The *Journal of Gerontological Social Work* Monographic "Separates"

Below is a list of "separates," which in serials librarianship means a special issue simultaneously published as a special journal issue or double-issue *and* as a "separate" hardbound monograph. (This is a format which we also call a "DocuSerial.")

"Separates" are published because specialized libraries or professionals may wish to purchase a specific thematic issue by itself in a format which can be separately cataloged and shelved, as opposed to purchasing the journal on an on-going basis. Faculty members may also more easily consider a "separate" for classroom adoption.

"Separates" are carefully classified separately with the major book jobbers so that the journal tie-in can be noted on new book order slips to avoid duplicate purchasing.

You may wish to visit Haworth's website at . . .

http://www.HaworthPress.com

. . . to search our online catalog for complete tables of contents of these separates and related publications.

You may also call 1-800-HAWORTH (outside US/Canada: 607-722-5857), or Fax 1-800-895-0582 (outside US/Canada: 607-771-0012), or e-mail at:

docdelivery@haworthpress.com

Advancing Gerontological Social Work Education, edited by M. Joanna Mellor, DSW and Joann Ivry, PhD (Vol. 39, No. 1/2, 2002). *Examines the current status of geriatric/gerontological education; offers models for curriculum development within the classroom and the practice arena.*

Gerontological Social Work Practice: Issues, Challenges, and Potential, edited by Enid Opal Cox, DSW, Elizabeth S. Kelchner, MSW, ACSW, and Rosemary Chapin, PhD, MSW (Vol. 36, No. 3/4, 2001). *This book gives you an essential overview of the role, status, and potential of gerontological social work in aging societies around the world. Drawing on the expertise of leaders in the field, it identifies key policy and practice issues and suggests directions for the future. Here you'll find important perspectives on home health care, mental health, elder abuse, older workers' issues, and death and dying, as well as an examination of the policy and practice issues of utmost concern to social workers dealing with the elderly.*

Social Work Practice with the Asian American Elderly, edited by Namkee G. Choi, PhD (Vol. 36, No. 1/2, 2001). *"Encompasses the richness of diversity among Asian Americans by including articles on Vietnamese, Japanese, Chinese, Taiwanese, Asian Indian, and Korean Americans." (Nancy R. Hooyman, PhD, MSW, Professor and Dean Emeritus, University of Washington School of Social Work, Seattle)*

Grandparents as Carers of Children with Disabilities: Facing the Challenges, edited by Philip McCallion, PhD, ACSW, and Matthew Janicki, PhD (Vol. 33, No. 3, 2000). *Here is the first comprehensive consideration of the unique needs and experiences of grandparents caring for children with developmental disabilities. The vital information found here will assist practitioners, administrators, and policymakers to include the needs of this special population in the planning and delivery of services, and it will help grandparents in this situation to better care for themselves as well as for the children in their charge.*

Latino Elders and the Twenty-First Century: Issues and Challenges for Culturally Competent Research and Practice, edited by Melvin Delgado, PhD (Vol. 30, No. 1/2, 1998). *Explores the challenges that gerontological social work will encounter as it attempts to meet the needs of the growing number of Latino elders utilizing culturally competent principles.*

Dignity and Old Age, edited by Rose Dobrof, DSW, and Harry R. Moody, PhD (Vol. 29, No. 2/3, 1998). *"Challenges us to uphold the right to age with dignity, which is embedded in the heart and soul of every man and woman." (H. James Towey, President, Commission on Aging with Dignity, Tallahassee, FL)*

Intergenerational Approaches in Aging: Implications for Education, Policy and Practice, edited by Kevin Brabazon, MPA, and Robert Disch, MA (Vol. 28, No. 1/2/3, 1997). *"Provides a wealth of concrete examples of areas in which intergenerational perspectives and knowledge are needed." (Robert C. Atchley, PhD, Director, Scribbs Gerontology Center, Miami University)*

Social Work Response to the White House Conference on Aging: From Issues to Actions, edited by Constance Corley Saltz, PhD, LCSW (Vol. 27, No. 3, 1997). *"Provides a framework for the discussion of issues relevant to social work values and practice, including productive aging, quality of life, the psychological needs of older persons, and family issues." (Jordan I. Kosberg, PhD, Professor and PhD Program Coordinator, School of Social Work, Florida International University, North Miami, FL)*

Special Aging Populations and Systems Linkages, edited by M. Joanna Mellor, DSW (Vol. 25, No. 1/2, 1996). *"An invaluable tool for anyone working with older persons with special needs." (Irene Gutheil, DSW, Associate Professor, Graduate School of Social Service, Fordham University)*

New Developments in Home Care Services for the Elderly: Innovations in Policy, Program, and Practice, edited by Lenard W. Kaye, DSW (Vol. 24, No. 3/4, 1995). *"An excellent compilation. . . . Especially pertinent to the functions of administrators, supervisors, and case managers in home care. . . . Highly recommended for every home care agency and a must for administrators and middle managers." (Geriatric Nursing Book Review)*

Geriatric Social Work Education, edited by M. Joanna Mellor, DSW, and Renee Solomon, DSW (Vol. 18, No. 3/4, 1992). *"Serves as a foundation upon which educators and fieldwork instructors can build courses that incorporate more aging content." (SciTech Book News)*

Vision and Aging: Issues in Social Work Practice, edited by Nancy D. Weber, MSW (Vol. 17, No. 3/4, 1992). *"For those involved in vision rehabilitation programs, the book provides practical information and should stimulate readers to revise their present programs of care." (Journal of Vision Rehabilitation)*

Health Care of the Aged: Needs, Policies, and Services, edited by Abraham Monk, PhD (Vol. 15, No. 3/4, 1990). *"The chapters reflect firsthand experience and are competent and informative. Readers . . . will find the book rewarding and useful. The text is timely, appropriate, and well-presented." (Health & Social Work)*

Twenty-Five Years of the Life Review: Theoretical and Practical Considerations, edited by Robert Disch, MA (Vol. 12, No. 3/4, 1989). *This practical and thought-provoking book examines the history and concept of the life review.*

Gerontological Social Work: International Perspectives, edited by Merl C. Hokenstad, Jr., PhD, and Katherine A. Kendall, PhD (Vol. 12, No. 1/2, 1988). *"Makes a very useful contribution in examining the changing role of the social work profession in serving the elderly." (Journal of the International Federation on Ageing)*

Gerontological Social Work Practice with Families: A Guide to Practice Issues and Service Delivery, edited by Rose Dobrof, DSW (Vol. 10, No. 1/2, 1987). *An in-depth examination of the importance of family relationships within the context of social work practice with the elderly.*

Ethnicity and Gerontological Social Work, edited by Rose Dobrof, DSW (Vol. 9, No. 4, 1987). *"Addresses the issues of ethnicity with great sensitivity. Most of the topics addressed here are rarely addressed in other literature." (Dr. Milada Disman, Department of Behavioral Science, University of Toronto)*

Social Work and Alzheimer's Disease, edited by Rose Dobrof, DSW (Vol. 9, No. 2, 1986). *"New and innovative social work roles with Alzheimer's victims and their families in both hospital and non-hospital settings." (Continuing Education Update)*

Gerontological Social Work Practice in the Community, edited by George S. Getzel, DSW and M. Joanna Mellor, DSW (Vol. 8, No. 3/4, 1985). *"A wealth of information for all practitioners who deal with the elderly. An excellent reference for faculty, administrators, clinicians, and graduate students in nursing and other service professions who work with the elderly." (American Journal of Care for the Aging)*

Gerontological Social Work in Home Health Care, edited by Rose Dobrof, DSW (Vol. 7, No. 4, 1984). *"A useful window onto the home health care scene in terms of current forms of service provided to the elderly and the direction of social work practice in this field today." (PRIDE Institute Journal)*

The Uses of Reminiscence: New Ways of Working with Older Adults, edited by Marc Kaminsky (Vol. 7, No. 1/2, 1984). *"Rich in ideas for anyone working with life review groups." (Guidepost)*

A Healthy Old Age: A Sourcebook for Health Promotion with Older Adults, edited by Stephanie FallCreek, MSW, and Molly K. Mettler, MSW (Vol. 6, No. 2/3, 1984). *"An outstanding text on the 'how-tos' of health promotion for elderly persons." (Physical Therapy)*

Gerontological Social Work Practice in Long-Term Care, edited by George S. Getzel, DSW, and M. Joanna Mellor, DSW (Vol. 5, No. 1/2, 1983). *"Veteran practitioners and graduate social work students will find the book insightful and a valuable prescriptive guide to the do's and don'ts of practice in their daily work." (The Gerontologist)*

Advancing Gerontological Social Work Education

M. Joanna Mellor, DSW
Joann Ivry, PhD
Editors

Advancing Gerontological Social Work Education has been co-published simultaneously as *Journal of Gerontological Social Work*, Volume 39, Numbers 1/2 2002.

Routledge
Taylor & Francis Group

NEW YORK AND LONDON

First published by

The Haworth Social Work Practice Press, 10 Alice Street, Binghamton, NY 13904-1580 USA
The Haworth Social Work Practice Press is an imprint of The Haworth Press, Inc., 10 Alice Street, Binghamton, NY 13904-1580 USA.

This edition published 2012 by Routledge
2 Park Square, Milton Park, Abingdon, Oxon OX14 4RN
Simultaneously published in the USA and Canada by Routledge
711 Third Avenue, New York, NY 10017

Advancing Gerontological Social Work has been co-published simultaneously as *Journal of Gerontological Social Work*, Volume 39, Numbers 1/2 2002.

The development, preparation, and publication of this work has been undertaken with great care. However, the publisher, employees, editors, and agents of The Haworth Press and all imprints of The Haworth Press, Inc., including The Haworth Medical Press® and The Pharmaceutical Products Press®, are not responsible for any errors contained herein or for consequences that may ensue from use of materials or information contained in this work. Opinions expressed by the author(s) are not necessarily those of The Haworth Press, Inc.

Cover design by Jennifer M. Gaska.

Library of Congress Cataloging-in-Publication Data

Advancing gerontological social work education / M. Joanna Mellor, DSW and Joann Ivry, PhD, editors.
    p. cm.
    Includes bibliographical references and index.
    "Advancing gerontological social work education has been co-published simultaneously as Journal of gerontological social work, volume 39, numbers 1/2, 2002."
    ISBN 0-7890-2064-5 (hard cover: alk. paper)–ISBN 0-7890-2065-3 (soft cover: alk. paper)
    1. Social work with the aged–Study and teaching–United States. I. Mellor, M. Joanna. II. Ivry, Joann. III. Journal of geronotological social work.
HV1461.A47 2002
362.6'071'073–dc21
                                         2002156601

Advancing Gerontological Social Work Education

CONTENTS

SECTION II. SCHOOL BASED INITIATIVES

SECTION III. MODELS FOR PRACTICE:
   CLASS AND FIELD CURRICULUM PROGRAMS

ABOUT THE EDITORS

M. Joanna Mellor, DSW, joined Lighthouse International in 1999 as Director of Connections, a volunteer outreach program. Since 2000, Dr. Mellor has held the position of Vice President for Information Services, which encompasses Lighthouse International's Information Call Center and the development of a global portal. From 1986-1997, Dr. Mellor was Executive Director of the Hunter/Mount Sinai Geriatric Education Center, a federally funded program providing geriatric education to healthcare professionals with an emphasis on interdisciplinary team-work. From 1997-1999, Dr. Mellor was Assistant Professor in the Department of Geriatrics and Adult Development at the Mount Sinai School of Medicine and Social Work Coordinator in Mount Sinai's Geriatric Interdisciplinary Team Training (GITT) program, which is funded by the John H. Hartford Foundation. She has been an Adjunct Instructor at the Hunter School of Social Work since 1984, teaching a course in social welfare policy and aging. She is a co-editor of *Geriatric Social Work Education, Gerontological Social Work Practice in the Community*, and *Gerontological Social Work Practice in Long Term Care*, and is the editor of *Special Aging Populations and Systems Linkages*.

Joann Ivry, PhD, is Associate Professor and Assistant Dean at the Hunter College School of Social Work and Co-Principal Investigator of the Geriatric Social Work Field Practicum Development Program, which is funded by the John H. Hartford Foundation. She has also been associated with the Geriatric Interdisciplinary Team Training (GITT) program, also funded by the Hartford Foundation. From 1992-1994, Dr. Ivry was Co-Project Director of the Minority Management Training Program, funded by the Administration on Aging. She served as Visiting Assistant Professor at the Boston University School of Social Work before joining the Hunter College School of Social Work faculty in 1990.

Foreword

Advancing Gerontological Social Work Education is, in my judgement, a badly needed and most welcome Special Issue of *The Journal of Gerontological Social Work*. There have been a number of articles recently in the popular media and in the journals of gerontology, geriatrics, and social work, and also in reports issued by governmental agencies providing persuasive evidence of the continuing shortage of social workers choosing careers in the field of aging. Indeed professionals in geriatrics and gerontology talk about a shortage so great that they use words like "crisis," particularly when their focus is on the years after 2011, when the "Leading Edge" of the Baby Boom generation reaches age 65.

As I write this, on my desk are my notes from a conference I attended just this morning. The speaker was Kenneth L. Davis, MD of the Mount Sinai School of Medicine, and one of the most distinguished medical educators and researchers in the country. Dr. Davis was talking about treatment approaches to Alzheimer's Disease, and he pointed out that, as I am certain the readers of this *Journal* know, the estimate is that there are four million Americans who are afflicted with Alzheimer's Disease now, with the prevalence expected to be 5.8 million in 2010, and 14.3 million by 2050, when the youngest of the Baby Boom cohort will be in their mid 80s.

I cite these prevalence statistics, because in community-based social agencies, in Alzheimer's Association chapters, in hospitals and nursing homes and other long-term care facilities, social workers are key members of the multi-professional teams providing direct service for people who have Alzheimer's and their families. Equally important, social workers are engaged in advocacy efforts, and in public policy analysis and formulation. Unless there is substantial progress in the search for effective treatment strategies, thousands of social workers will continue to be needed in agencies and organizations serving people with Alzheimer's and their families.

The same kind of analysis could be made in other fields of practice and involving other social problems and other needs of older families. Consider, for

[Haworth co-indexing entry note]: "Foreword." Co-published simultaneously in *Journal of Gerontological Social Work* (The Haworth Social Work Practice Press, an imprint of The Haworth Press, Inc.) Vol. 39, No. 1/2, 2002, pp. xxi-xxii; and: *Advancing Gerontological Social Work Education* (ed: M. Joanna Mellor and Joann Ivry) The Haworth Social Work Practice Press, an imprint of The Haworth Press, Inc., 2002, pp. xvii-xviii. Single or multiple copies of this article are available for a fee from The Haworth Document Delivery Service [1-800-HAWORTH, 9:00 a.m. - 5:00 p.m. (EST). E-mail address: docdelivery@haworthpress.com].

xvii

example, grandparents caring for the children in their families, or think about the community mental health centers and programs, which, in most areas of the country, constitute a domain in which most of the professionals are social workers, and older individuals and families constitute an important and growing group of clients and patients.

I doubt that I need to belabor this point further. The need for professionally trained social workers, knowledgeable about older people and their families, skilled in meeting the needs of these people, and committed to careers in aging is a need which will become even more urgent in the coming decades of the 21st century. Publication of this, a volume on the education of social workers to meet these needs is exquisitely timed, I think, and Dr.'s Mellor and Ivry and the authors of the papers included in this volume have done a superb job. Each chapter is worth a careful read–and re-read.

Rose Dobrof
April, 2002

Introduction

I never cease to be proud of the variety of articles that are submitted to our Editorial Board for consideration for publication in the *Journal*. Proud, not so much in my role as Editor of the *Journal*, as in my role as a professionally educated social worker of more than 50 years standing. The pride I feel is in the *number* and *variety* of settings–hospitals, long-term care facilities, home care agencies, hospices, senior centers, public agencies, "think tanks," schools of social work and other academic institutions–in which social workers are fulfilling the mission of the profession. That is, to work toward the betterment of the human condition, and to help individuals and communities in this struggle. The pride I feel is also in my reading of the articles which are submitted to the *Journal*. So many of the articles reflect the importance and the quality of work, members of our profession are doing.

The articles in this volume, as is so often the case, reflect this variety of settings and of problems social workers address, and also reflect the excellence of the work of the members of our profession. Don't misunderstand: I know of hospitals which are abolishing their departments of social work, or reducing the number of staff in the departments. I know of senior centers staffed entirely by intelligent, well-intentioned, but untrained staff, and I know of home care agencies in which the size of the worker's caseload precludes the ability of the worker to provide sustained, responsive, high quality service.

Yet the bleakness of this picture of reductions in service and cut-backs in staff is leavened in many instances in which agency board and staff join together to save and improve the quality of the social work service the agency provides. I am heartened also by the number and quality of the men and women who are applying for admission to our Schools of Social Work, and, of course, by the support of foundations, most notably the John A. Hartford Foundation, for programs designed to recruit qualified applicants to the Schools, and to improve the quality of the education provided in both classroom and field.

[Haworth co-indexing entry note]: "Introduction." Dobrof, Rose. Co-published simultaneously in *Journal of Gerontological Social Work* (The Haworth Social Work Practice Press, an imprint of The Haworth Press, Inc.) Vol. 39, No. 1/2, 2002, pp. 1-2; and: *Advancing Gerontological Social Work Education* (ed: M. Joanna Mellor, and Joann Ivry) The Haworth Social Work Practice Press, an imprint of The Haworth Press, Inc., 2002, pp. 1-2. Single or multiple copies of this article are available for a fee from The Haworth Document Delivery Service [1-800-HAWORTH, 9:00 a.m. - 5:00 p.m. (EST). E-mail address: docdelivery@haworthpress.com].

10.1300/J083v39n01_01

So I write, in my usual fashion, with optimism about the future, and also with a request to our readers, particularly those who staff the service agencies in the aging network. We have a Section of the *Journal* called "From the World of Practice," and in too many issues that section does not appear, because no submissions to it have been approved for publication. I do wish more of you who are practitioners would submit reports of your work: such reports do not require Literature Searches or extensive footnoting or references to the literature or recondite statistical analyses. Rather, what we are interested in are reports of your own work with older individuals, their families, their communities. What techniques and strategies worked for you? Even, what were your failures, and can you account for the lack of success?

If you scan the last several years of *Journals,* you will see, I think, why I make this plea. Academics, obeying the "Publish or Perish" injunction of our world, are the most frequent authors of articles in the *Journal,* and as valuable as I think the works of the academics are, how I wish they could be balanced by reports from you in the field. How about it?

Rose Dobrof
Editor

SECTION I.
GERIATRICS AND GERONTOLOGY IN SOCIAL WORK EDUCATION

Introduction to Section I

M. Joanna Mellor, DSW
Joann Ivry, PhD

The four articles in this introductory section describe the growth and development of gerontological/geriatric[1] social work education, stress the importance of interdisciplinary teamwork, and provide strategies to increase student interest in gerontological social work practice. A common theme is the existence of an aging society necessitating an increased pool of well-trained gerontological social workers and the inevitable demands this has on professional education. Indeed, this theme is repeated throughout the journal volume, as each contributor identifies the demographic imperative as the overarching rationale and foundation for our concerns and hopes for gerontological social work education.

Professors Greene and Galambos offer a useful historical perspective on the development of gerontological social work education, tracing its ongoing struggle to find a place in the already crowded social work curriculum. They review the well-known tension in social work education between foundation and advanced knowledge and skills and describe the confusion between concentration and specialization. Greene and Galambos bring us to the present sit-

[Haworth co-indexing entry note]: "Introduction to Section I." Mellor, M. Joanna, and Joann Ivry. Co-published simultaneously in *Journal of Gerontological Social Work* (The Haworth Social Work Practice Press, an imprint of The Haworth Press, Inc.) Vol. 39, No. 1/2, 2002, pp. 3-5; and: *Advancing Gerontological Social Work Education* (ed: M. Joanna Mellor, and Joann Ivry) The Haworth Social Work Practice Press, an imprint of The Haworth Press, Inc., 2002, pp. 3-5. Single or multiple copies of this article are available for a fee from The Haworth Document Delivery Service [1-800-HAWORTH, 9:00 a.m. - 5:00 p.m. (EST). E-mail address: docdelivery@haworthpress.com].

http://www.haworthpress.com/store/product.asp?sku=J083
10.1300/J083v39n01_02

uation with a discussion of the CSWE/SAGE-SW Competencies Project, which identifies knowledge and skills for foundation and concentration educational levels. As Greene and Galambos correctly argue, integrating the competencies into the new CSWE Educational Policy and Accreditation Standards would greatly advance the cause of gerontological social work education.

Rosen, Zlotnick and Singer further the discussion of the SAGE-SW project. They exhort professional social work educators to prepare social work practitioners for the anticipated demographic explosion of the aged population. In this article, they provide a compelling case and guidelines for curriculum change. They recommend without qualification that all social work education should offer instruction in aging-related content. Through infusion or integration of aging content into the foundation curriculum, all social workers could be guaranteed at least basic competency in geriatrics and gerontology. The authors strongly argue that there must be "parity" for geriatrics/gerontology with other curriculum domains throughout the foundation educational year. In the advanced year, concentration/specialization in the field of aging would provide students the opportunity to deepen their knowledge and develop greater expertise. Although obstacles exist to the implementation of these guidelines, infusion, integration and specialization would ensure that the social work profession is accepting its responsibility and obligation to prepare social work practitioners for the social realities of the future.

Damron-Rodriguez and Corley underscore the importance of interdisciplinary teamwork as essential to the success of gerontological social work practice. They argue that content on interdisciplinary teams must be included as part of the standard curriculum in gerontological social work. They contend the multiple social and health care needs of frail older people require a well-managed interdisciplinary approach to treatment. Damron-Rodriguez and Corley present and review the components of a model, which form the educational basis for interdisciplinary team training. Through an understanding of organizational context, team structure, team process and team outcomes, social workers will be better able to function as interdisciplinary team members.

Unfortunately, gerontological social work continues to be an overlooked field of practice in social work education and has a poor track record in attracting students. Paramount among our activities, therefore, should be the development of strategies to bring more social work students into the gerontology field. Although gerontology is not viewed by students as glamorous a field as mental health or children's services, Kropf is on target when she states that it is urgent that the field of aging be presented as "important, challenging and rewarding." She focuses on the barriers to successful recruitment of students into the field of aging and on the need to implement aggressive and creative strategies to rectify this problem. Educators, field supervisors and practitioners will find Kropf's discussion of programmatic and collaborative approaches helpful in developing ways to bring more students into our field, enabling social work to participate and contribute in formulating and implementing a compassionate response to the care of the aged in our society.

NOTE

1. The use of the adjectives gerontological and geriatric has become muddied in recent years. In general, gerontological is used when speaking of work with older persons in relation to social environments and needs, while geriatric is employed within the medical model, describing work with older persons in health care settings. These definitional boundaries no longer suffice. It is understood that health and social needs are different but closely intertwined factors in the well-being of an older person. Gerontological care includes geriatric elements and geriatric care encompasses gerontological aspects. The purist use of gerontological/geriatric is cumbersome so, until an acceptable combining term is coined, either nomenclature in this publication is to be understood in the broader sense.

Chapter 1

Social Work's Pursuit
of a Common Professional Framework:
Have We Reached a Milestone?

Roberta Greene, PhD, ACSW
Colleen Galambos, DSW

SUMMARY. This article examines pivotal events within the social work profession that have attempted to codify social work and gerontology curriculum. Key dilemmas in developing a common base of social work practice are identified. Similar debates that have occurred within gerontology curriculum are discussed along with recent developments in

Roberta Greene is Louis and Ann Wolens Centennial Chair in Gerontology, School of Social Work, University of Texas-Austin, 1925 San Jacinto Boulevard, Room 3.130C, 1 University Station D3599, Austin, TX 78712 (E-mail: rgreene@mail.utexas.edu). Colleen Galambos is Associate Professor and Acting Associate Dean, University of Tennessee College of Social Work, 193 East Polk Avenue, Nashville, TN 37210. (E-mail: galambos@utk.edu).

The authors wish to provide special acknowledgment to the Council on Social Work Education, Anita Rosen, Director of Special Projects, CSWE, and Joan Zlotnik, Executive Director, Institute for the Advancement of Social Work Research and former Principal Investigator of the Hartford SAGE-SW initiative for their work on the SAGE-SW project and their support in writing of this article.

[Haworth co-indexing entry note]: "Social Work's Pursuit of a Common Professional Framework: Have We Reached a Milestone?" Greene, Roberta, and Colleen Galambos. Co-published simultaneously in *Journal of Gerontological Social Work* (The Haworth Social Work Practice Press, an imprint of The Haworth Press, Inc.) Vol. 39, No. 1/2, 2002, pp. 7-23; and: *Advancing Gerontological Social Work Education* (ed: M. Joanna Mellor, and Joann Ivry) The Haworth Social Work Practice Press, an imprint of The Haworth Press, Inc., 2002, pp. 7-23. Single or multiple copies of this article are available for a fee from The Haworth Document Delivery Service [1-800-HAWORTH, 9:00 a.m. - 5:00 p.m. (EST). E-mail address: docdelivery@haworthpress.com].

http://www.haworthpress.com/store/product.asp?sku=J083
10.1300/J083v39n01_03

the advancement of gerontology content within the social work curriculum. The Council on Social Work Education's (CSWE) SAGE-SW competencies are discussed and applied to the CSWE's Education and Policy Standards. Practice applications and future directions are offered. *[Article copies available for a fee from The Haworth Document Delivery Service: 1-800-HAWORTH. E-mail address: <docdelivery@haworthpress.com> Website: <http://www.HaworthPress.com> © 2002 by The Haworth Press, Inc. All rights reserved.]*

KEYWORDS. Aging competencies, generalist education, specialization, educational policy standards

This article explores the John A. Hartford Foundation funded CSWE/SAGE-SW Gerontological Social Work Competencies project and its potential influence on social work education. It describes preceding pivotal events in the profession's history that have made similar attempts to codify social work and gerontology curriculum, and asks the question: Has social work reached a milestone in establishing specializations on a generalist base? The competencies are applied to CSWE's Educational Policy and Accreditation Standards, and future directions for the project and the profession are explored. This project comes at a time when the Council on Social Work Education (CSWE) has adopted a new curriculum policy statement and the National Association of Social Workers (NASW) has developed a specialty section on aging.

COMMON BASE OF SOCIAL WORK PRACTICE

The history of social work education is characterized by a search for a conceptual definition of practice, and by the struggle to develop knowledge to support methods consistent with its professional purpose(s) (Austin, 1986; Bartlett, 1970). The interest in a holistic curriculum to guide schools of social work began as early as the 1920s when Mary Richmond, whose work was supported by the Sage Foundation, raised the central question, "Does the profession deal with social reform or technically specialized methods of casework? Scientific content or practice wisdom" (Richmond, 1930)? In fact, historical accounts are replete with such curriculum questions and task forces to address what Austin (1986) termed the professional "balance between unity and diversity" (p. 44).

Key milestones in the movement toward a common social work framework have included the 1923 through 1927 Milford Conference, which convened practitioners and educators who developed a single model for social work practice; the 1951 Hollis-Taylor study (supported by the Carnegie Foundation), which recommended that professional social work education be represented by a single combined organization, inspiring the creation of CSWE; and the curriculum study by Boehm (1959) which resulted in increased attention to the holistic nature of the curriculum and the educational objectives desirable for all social work students (Dinerman, 1984). The Boehm study also concluded that curriculum should remain broad enough to encompass work in all settings; use of all practice methods, research, ethics, and values; and field education.

However, social work training began with specialized tracks for various fields of practice: family casework, social group work, medical social work, school social work, psychiatric social work, and so forth. How would specialized practice objectives accommodate a generalist base (Brieland, 1987)? During the 1970s and 1980s, there were several major attempts to answer this question: The NASW sponsored two conferences, which resulted in the publication of *Social Work Conceptual Frameworks* (1977, 1981). The first conference publication examined social work objectives, activities, sanctions, knowledge, and skills as they applied to practice. The second conference explored specific fields of practice including the family, community mental health, schools, industry, and aging.

Progress toward defining the nature of specialization was also made during a NASW/CSWE task force in 1979, which suggested that a specialization be related to

> a population with a common condition to be altered, competence and skill within social work to serve the population, and conditions complex enough to involve a substantial body of knowledge translatable into effective interventions. (Brieland, 1981, p. 82)

The attention to a generalist foundation social work curriculum and the attempt to develop specialized fields of practice has continued (Briar, 1981; Brieland, 1995). The most recent codification is the CSWE Educational Policy and Accreditation Standards approved by the board in June 2001. The document mandates that

> The baccalaureate and master's levels of social work education are anchored in the purposes of the social work profession and promote the knowledge, values, and skills of the profession. Baccalaureate social work education programs prepare graduates for generalist professional practice. Master's social work education programs prepare graduates for advanced professional practice in an area of concentration. The bacca-

laureate and master's levels of educational preparation are differentiated according to (a) conceptualization and design, (b) content, (c) program objectives, and (d) depth, breadth, and specificity of knowledge and skills. Frameworks and perspectives for concentration include fields of practice, problem areas, intervention methods, and practice contexts and perspectives.

That is, foundation curriculum prepares students for generalist, foundation practice, while graduates of a master's social work program are prepared to be advanced practitioners who apply the knowledge and skills in an area of concentration. However, some educators believe the number of specializations continues to proliferate and the lack of definition of what constitutes a concentration threatens the unity of the profession. There remains an inner tension about social work's scope of practice–with little agreement about whether concentrations should be organized by method, field of practice, problem area, population group, methodological function, geographic area, size of target, specific treatment modalities, or advanced generalist (Hopps & Collins, 1995). The need for a definition as to what constitutes a specialization is essential if the profession is going to meet the challenge "to certify the competence of its members in society" (Bartlett, 1970, p. 53).

CORE PRINCIPLES AND GERONTOLOGY CURRICULUM

This foundation/specialization debate has also occurred within gerontology curriculum discussions. The education of professionals is increasingly understood as documenting that graduates have acquired a theoretical base and set of competencies (Curry & Wergin, 1993). Such evaluation and credentialing guarantees the public that the professional has the knowledge, skills, and personal attributes necessary to deliver competent effective service (McGaghie, 1993). However, the concern "about the organization and integrity of academic programs in gerontology" (Johnson et al., 1980) mirrors the lack of clarity about what defines social work fields of practice (Greene, 1989; Johnson, 1980; Klein, 1998; Wendt, Perterson, & Douglas, 1993).

Concern over the limited number of well-educated professionals has also prompted various projects to define essential learning for practitioners in the field of aging. In the late sixties and early seventies the need for more growth of formal education and training programs was recognized, primarily within universities and colleges. The major concern of these initiatives was to expand training, research, and services in gerontology. During this time period, the U. S. Department of Health and Human Services Administration on Aging (AOA) funded 58 programs that focused on the training of practitioners. Curriculum priorities in these programs emphasized administration, management, community coordination, planning, community organization, and community development. These curriculum areas were emphasized in anticipation of an expansion of programs under the provisions of the Older Americans Act (Tibbitts, 1970). There was a particular need to prepare practitioners to assume roles as administrators for long-term care facilities, community organizers to develop services at the community level, managers to direct multi-service senior centers, federal and state administrators to prepare for the expansion of services, specialists in aging, and teachers with specializations in aging. Professional social work education responded and seven social work programs participated in the long-term training programs funded by the AOA. Five programs provided MSW degrees in community planning and development (University of Chicago, Michigan State University/Wayne Sate University, San Diego State College, and the University of Washington). Brandeis University focused on a program of applied social gerontology and offered the MSW, DSW, and PhD degrees. The University of Wisconsin offered the MSW with an emphasis on the social work generalist (Tibbitts, 1970).

Also during this era the National Institute of Child Health and Human Development (NICHHD) Adult Development and Aging Branch funded 26 programs with an emphasis on preparing the gerontological researcher (Duncan, 1970). Social work education had less participation in this program, with only the University of Wisconsin being offered a funded program, and the University of Chicago having provisions for social work participation in its Adult Development and Aging program.

A third initiative during this era was the National Institute of Mental Health Training Programs in Aging. Fourteen of the 16 training grants were awarded to programs in social work (Boston University, University of California, University of Connecticut, Florida State University, Howard University, University of Iowa, University of Michigan, University of Missouri, New York University, University of Pennsylvania, University of Pittsburgh, University of Tennessee, Western Reserve, and University of Wisconsin). Core curriculum in these programs emphasized the generalist perspective in casework, community organization, or group work fields, and included courses in social welfare policy and services, human behavior and the social environment, and social work methods. Content on aging was included in all of these courses, and field placements emphasized work with older persons (Anderson & Blank, 1970).

Another earlier initiative was the Foundation Project conducted in 1980 by the Association of Gerontologists in Higher Education (AGHE) and the

Gerontological Society (GS), which examined the gerontology knowledge deemed necessary for practitioners (Johnson et al., 1980). The project focused on three areas of inquiry:

1. What are the components of a basic core of knowledge for people working in aging?
2. What is the knowledge essential for clusters of professions related to the biomedical sciences, human services, social and physical environment?
3. What is the knowledge essential for four professional fields: clinical psychology, nursing, nutrition, and social work?

A Delphi panel was chosen to answer these questions. The conceptual frameworks that established the parameters of the four clusters included a focus on person-in-environment interactions and a concern with biopsychosocial phenomena. The panel concluded that there is multi-disciplinary core knowledge in gerontology, and there are specific career knowledge clusters that are particular to professional curricula.

The core knowledge and cluster of topics found in the AGHE/GSA study have remained remarkably consistent with the findings of other projects over the past decades. The essential items for social work included:

- Psychology of aging (normal changes)
- Mental health & illness, e.g., depression, senility
- Marital and family relationships
- Demography of aging, e.g., age structure of society and trends
- Health care and services
- Public policy for the aged
- Economics of aging
- Legislation concerning aged, e.g., Medicare, retirement law, SSI
- Attitudes toward the aging
- Understanding aging as normal experience
- Interdisciplinary collaboration
- Planning, program development

In 1993, AOA sponsored a project to develop clearer program conceptualizations and educational outcomes for gerontological content (Wendt, Peterson, & Douglass, 1993). Participants envisioned a similar approach to the AGHE/GSA Delphi panel–a graduate professional track in gerontology with specific professional techniques. For example, all professionals should be conversant with a person-environment approach. In addition, practitioners should be able to describe biopsychosocial concepts of aging and apply that understanding to specific situations. Assessment procedures and intervention strategies were intended to maintain functional capacity and optimal levels of adaptation throughout life. The task force concluded that "professional education is rooted in a concern for the welfare of people and for the application of knowledge to solve problems on their behalf" (Wendt, Peterson, & Douglass, p. 5).

In that vein, several professional organizations have developed guidelines for instructing members of their disciplines (Barusch, Greene, & Connelly, 1990; Greene, Barusch, & Connelly, 1990). The CSWE has been the recipient of several grants from the Administration on Aging (AOA) to develop a curriculum. For example, Robert Schneider and colleagues (1984a, 1984b, 1989) compiled curriculum materials for BSW and MSW students; while Roberta Greene (1989) developed the curriculum, *Continuing education for gerontological careers.* This curriculum was based on a study that asked practitioners and employers what they thought should be included in a gerontological curriculum. The project distilled their findings into ten learning modules encompassing

1. Selected biological aspects of aging: Dementia, psychopharmacology,
2. Multifaceted gerontological assessment: Learning to evaluate the elderly client's functional capacities,
3. Intergenerational family dynamics: family development, individualization and separation,
4. Values and ethical issues on working with the aged and their families,
5. Enhancing support networks,
6. The long-term care continuum: Community living and institutionalization,
7. Cross-cultural communication with diverse ethnic and minority elderly,
8. Group processes in work with the aged,
9. Sexuality in later life, and
10. Social policy and change and the elderly: Advocacy and empowerment. (Greene, 1989)

As part of its mission to provide leadership to improve the training, distribution, utilization, and quality of personnel required to staff the nation's health care system, the Geriatrics and Allied Health Branch of the Bureau of Health Professions of the Health Resources and Services Administration (HRSA) sponsored a National Forum on Geriatric Education and Training in the spring of 1995. In response to this initiative, a series of papers were developed by identified leaders in geriatrics and health care. Referred to as the White Papers (Klein, 1995), the emphasis was on systems of care, interdisciplinary education, and the allied health profession's response to geriatric education. The findings revealed that most health profession's faculty are not prepared to teach geriatrics and gerontology; curricula at undergraduate and graduate levels of education do not include aging content; and there is little emphasis on discipline-specific research (Klein, 1995). The HRSA white paper on social work advocated for a biopsychosocial perspective, a family systems context, and a lifespan and diversity approach. The white paper also recommended that "comprehensive standards for the integration of aging curricula into all accredited schools of social work be established and adopted" (Ibid, p. 239). How can this recommendation for comprehensive standards be put into action? What will be the instrument of change?

THE COUNCIL ON SOCIAL WORK EDUCATION SAGE SOCIAL WORK PROJECT

With the baby-boomer generation approaching old age, and as the need for geriatric social workers dramatically increases, the John A. Hartford Foundation of New York City has committed itself to developing a sustained, focused, and centralized effort to strengthen the social work profession's response to the growing aging population (CSWE/SAGE-SW, 2001). To that end, The Hartford Foundation began a geriatric social work initiative, and in 1999 funded the CSWE/SAGE-SW Competencies Project. How was this project different from its predecessors?

The CSWE/SAGE-SW Competencies Project survey included sixty-five well-researched items specific to geriatric social work gleaned from earlier studies related to three domains: (1) knowledge about elderly people and their families, (2) professional skills, and (3) professional practice. The extensive literature review and discussion by an expert panel guided the survey development (CSWE/SAGE-SW, 2000).

Another important aspect of the survey was that the sample included 2,400 social work practitioners and academics. These were social workers both with and without aging interest. This sample composition was intended to obtain information on a wide range of opinion about what is needed in social work practice. Furthermore, for the first time in such a survey, respondents were asked to define which competencies *all* social workers needed to know about gerontology and which constituted *specialized* knowledge for advanced practitioners. In the analysis, the level of specialization needed was assessed through mean scores, with those closer to "1" being a competency for all, and those near "2" or higher for those with more advanced or specialized education. Ideally, these competencies can be integrated into the foundation content as indicated in Table 1. The data indicate that competencies with mean scores closer to 1 are more

TABLE 1. Integrating CSWE/SAGE-SW Gerontological Social Work Competencies with the CSWE Educational Policy and Accreditation Standards

IV. FOUNDATION CURRICULUM CONTENT
All social work programs provide foundation content in the areas specified below. Content areas may be combined and delivered with a variety of instructional technologies. Content is relevant to the mission, goals, and objectives of the program and to the purposes, values, and ethics of the social work profession.

A. Values and Ethics
Social work education programs integrate content about values and principles of ethical decision making as presented in the National Association of Social Workers Code of Ethics. The educational experience provides students with the opportunity to be aware of personal values; develop, demonstrate, and promote the values of the profession; and analyze ethical dilemmas and the ways in which these affect practice, services, and clients.
Aging Competencies
4. The diversity of elders' attitudes toward the acceptance of help. (M = 1.43)
10. The effect of generational experiences (e.g., the Depression, WWII, Vietnam War) on the values of older adults. (M = 1.72)
50. Assess one's own values and biases regarding aging, death and dying. (M = 1.08)
51. Educate self to dispel the major myths about aging.(M = 1.08)
52. Accept, respect, and recognize the right and need of older adults to make their own choices and decisions about their lives within the context of the law and safety concerns. (M = 1.10)
54. Identify ethical and professional boundary issues that commonly arise in work with older adults and their caregivers, such as client self-determination, end-of-life decisions, family conflicts, and guardianship.(M = 1.36)
55. Evaluate safety issues and degree of risk for self and older clients. (M = 1.46)

B. Diversity
Social work programs integrate content that promotes understanding, affirmation, and respect for people from diverse backgrounds. The content emphasizes the interlocking and complex nature of culture and personal identity. It ensures that social services meet the needs of groups served and are culturally relevant. Programs educate students to recognize diversity within and between groups that may influence assessment, planning, intervention, and research. Students learn how to define, design, and implement strategies for effective practice with persons from diverse backgrounds.
Aging Competencies
2. The diversity of attitudes toward aging, mental illness and family roles. (M = 1.29)
4. The diversity of elder's attitudes toward the acceptance of help. (M = 1.43)
8. The relation of diversity to variations in the aging process (e.g., gender, race, culture, economic status, ethnicity, and sexual orientation). (M = 1.58)
12. The impact of aging policy and services on minority group members. (M = 1.78)
13. The impact of aging policy and services on women. (M = 1.79)
53. Respect and address cultural, spiritual, and ethnic needs and beliefs of older adults and family members. (M = 1.24)

C. Populations-at-Risk and Social and Economic Justice
Social work education programs integrate content on populations-at-risk, examining the factors that contribute to and constitute being at risk. Programs educate students to identify how group membership influences access to resources and present content on the dynamics of such risk factors and responsive and productive strategies to redress them. Programs integrate social and economic justice content grounded in an understanding of distributive justice, human and civil rights, and the global interconnections of oppression. Programs provide content related to implementing strategies to combat discrimination, oppression, and economic deprivation and to promote social and economic justice. Programs prepare students to advocate for nondiscriminatory social and economic systems.

TABLE 1 (continued)

Aging Competencies

8. The relation of diversity to variations in the aging process (e.g., gender, race, culture, economic status, ethnicity and sexual orientation). (M = 1.58)

12. The impact of aging policy and services on minority group members. (M = 1.78)

13. The impact of aging policy and services on women. (M = 1.79)

15. Managed care policies concerning older persons and adults with disabilities. (M = 1.98)

59. Advocate for the employment and retention of professionally educated social workers in the aging network and service delivery system. (M = 1.72)

60. Keep informed of changes in theory, research, policy, and practice in social work services to older persons. (M = 1.79)

61. Educate the public, other agencies and professional staffs on the needs and issues of a growing aging population. (M = 1.85)

63. Develop strategies to address age discrimination in relation to health, housing, employment, and transportation. (M = 1.89)

64. Creatively use organizational policy, procedures and resources to facilitate and maximize the provision of services to older adults and their family caregivers. (M = 1.98)

D. Human Behavior and the Social Environment

Social work education programs provide content on the reciprocal relationships between human behavior and social environments. Content includes empirically based theories and knowledge that focus on the interactions between and among individuals, groups, societies, and economic systems. It includes theories and knowledge of biological, sociological, cultural, psychological, and spiritual development across the life span; the range of social systems in which people live (individual, family, group, organizational, and community); and the ways in which social systems promote or deter people in maintaining or achieving health and well-being.

Aging Competencies

1. Normal physical, psychological and social changes in later life. (M = 1.15)

2. The diversity of attitudes toward aging, mental illness and family roles. (M = 1.29)

3. The influence of aging on family dynamics. (M = 1.30)

5. The diversity of successful adaptations to life transitions of aging. (M = 1.45)

7. Theoretical models of biological and social aging. (M = 1.50)

8. The relation of diversity to variations in the aging process (e.g., gender, race, culture, economic status, ethnicity and sexual orientation). (M = 1.58)

9. Wellness and prevention concepts for older persons. (M = 1.67)

10. The effect of generational experiences (e.g., the Depression, WWII, Vietnam War) on the values of older adults. (M = 1.72)

11. Love, intimacy and sexuality among older persons. (M = 1.74)

17. Basic pharmacology and the interaction of medications affecting the elderly. (M = 2.31)

X-referenced for social work practice

26. Incorporate knowledge of elder abuse (physical, sexual, emotional and financial) in conducting assessments and intervention with clients and their families. (M = 1.56)

27. Assess psychosocial factors that have an effect on the physical health of older persons. (M = 1.61)

30. Gather information regarding mental status, history of any past or current psychopathology, life satisfaction, coping abilities, affect and spirituality. (M = 1.68)

34. Gather information regarding physical status such as: disabilities, chronic or acute illness, nutrition status, sensory impairment, medications, mobility, and activities of daily living (ADLs) and independent activities of daily living (IADLs). (M = 1.78)

35. Provide information to family caregivers to assist them in caregiving roles, such as information about the stages and behaviors of Alzheimer's disease and other dementias. (M = 1.83)

36. Conduct a comprehensive biopsychosocial assessment of an older person. (M = 1.89)

46. Assess short-term memory, coping history, changes in socialization patterns, behavior, and appropriateness of mood and affect in relation to life-events of those who are aging. (M = 2.14)

48. Assess for dementia, delirium and depression in older adults. (M = 2.33)

49. Conduct clinical interventions for mental health and cognitive impairment issues in older adults. (M = 2.36)

60. Keep informed of changes in theory, research, policy, and practice in social work services to older persons. (M = 1.79)

62. Engage and mediate with angry, hostile and resistant older adults and family members. (M = 1.88)

E. Social Welfare Policy and Services

Programs provide content about the history of social work, the history and current structures of social welfare services, and the role of policy in service delivery, social work practice, and attainment of individual and social well-being. Course content provides students with knowledge and skills to understand major policies that form the foundation of social welfare; analyze organizational, local, state, national, and international issues in social welfare policy and social service delivery; analyze and apply the results of policy research relevant to social service delivery; understand and demonstrate policy practice skills in regard to economic, political, and organizational systems, and use them to influence, formulate, and advocate for policy consistent with social work values; and identify financial, organizational, administrative, and planning processes required to deliver social services.

Aging Competencies

12. The impact of aging policy and services on minority group members. (M = 1.78)
13. The impact of aging policy and services on women. (M = 1.79)
14. The impact of policies, regulations, and programs on direct practice with older adults. (M = 1.94)
15. Managed care policies concerning older persons and adults with disabilities.(M = 1.98)
16. Policies, regulations and programs for older adults in health, mental health and long-term care. (M = 2.01)
44. Identify legal issues for older adults, including: advanced directives, living wills, powers-of-attorney, wills, guardianship, and Do-Not-Resuscitate (DNR) orders. (M = 2.12)
59. Advocate for the employment and retention of professionally educated social workers in the aging network and service delivery system. (M = 1.72)
60. Keep informed of changes in theory, research, policy, and practice in social work services to older persons. (M = 1.79)
63. Develop strategies to address age discrimination in relation to health, housing, employment, and transportation. (M = 1.89)
64. Creatively use organizational policy, procedures, and resources to facilitate and maximize the provisions of services to older adults and their family caregivers. (M = 1.98)

F. Social Work Practice

Social work practice content is anchored in the purposes of the social work profession and focuses on strengths, capacities, and resources of client systems in relation to their broader environments. Students learn practice content that encompasses knowledge and skills to work with individuals, families, groups, organizations, and communities. This content includes engaging clients in an appropriate working relationship, identifying issues, problems, needs, resources, and assets; collecting and assessing information; and planning for service delivery. It includes using communication skills, supervision, and consultation.

Practice content also includes identifying, analyzing, and implementing empirically based interventions designed to achieve client goals; applying empirical knowledge and technological advances; evaluating program outcomes and practice effectiveness; developing, analyzing, advocating, and providing leadership for policies and services; and promoting social and economic justice.

Aging Competencies

6. The availability of resources and resource systems for the elderly and their families. (M = 1.48)
18. Use social work case management skills (such as brokering, advocacy, monitoring, and discharge planning) to link elders and their families to resources and services. (M = 1.33)
19. Gather information regarding social history such as: social functioning, primary and secondary social supports, social activity level, social skills, financial status, cultural background and social involvement. (M = 1.34)
20. Collaborate with other health, mental health and allied health professionals in delivering services to older adults. (M = 1.42)
21. Engage family caregivers in maintaining their own mental and physical health. (M = 1.45)
22. Assist individuals and families in recognizing and dealing with issues of grief, loss and mourning. (M = 1.49)
23. Assist families that are in crisis situations regarding older adult family members. (M = 1.50)
24. Recognize and identify family, agency, community, and societal factors that contribute to and support the greatest possible independence of the older client. (M = 1.50)
25. Enhance the coping capacities of older persons. (M = 1.56)
26. Incorporate knowledge of elder abuse (physical, sexual, emotional and financial) in conducting assessments and intervention with clients and their families. (M = 1.56)
27. Assess psychosocial factors that have an effect on the physical health of older persons. (M = 1.61)

TABLE 1 (continued)

28. Use empathetic and caring interventions such as reminiscence or life review, support groups, and bereavement counseling. (M = 1.63)
29. Demonstrate awareness of sensory, language and cognitive limitations of clients when interviewing older adults. (M = 1.65)
30. Gather information regarding mental status, history of any past or current psychopathology, life satisfaction, coping abilities, affect and spirituality. (M = 1.68)
31. Develop service plans that incorporate appropriate living arrangements and psychosocial supports for older persons. (M = 1.70)
32. Assist older persons with transitions to and from institutional settings. (M = 1.73)
33. Develop service plans that include intergenerational approaches to the needs and strengths of older persons, their families or significant others. (M = 1.73)
34. Gather information regarding physical status such as: disabilities, chronic or acute illness, nutrition status, sensory impairment, medications, mobility, and activities of daily living (ADLs) and independent activities of daily living (IADLs). (M = 1.78)
35. Provide information to family caregivers to assist them in caregiving roles, such as information about the stages and behaviors of Alzheimer's disease and other dementias. (M = 1.83)
36. Conduct a comprehensive biopsychosocial assessment of an older person. (M = 1.89)
37. Set realistic and measurable objectives based on functional status, life goals, symptom management, and financial and social supports of older adults and their families. (M = 1.92)
38. Reevaluate service or care plans for older adults on a continuing basis, incorporating physical, social and cognitive changes and adjusting plans as needed. (M = 1.93)
39. Assess and intervene with alcohol and substance abuse problems in older adults. (M = 1.94)
40. Assess organizational effectiveness in meeting needs of older adults and their caregivers. (M = 1.98)
41. Conduct long-term care planning with older persons and their families to address financial, legal, housing, medical, and social needs. (M = 2.01)
45. Adapt psychoeducational approaches to work with older adults. (M = 2.14)
46. Assess short-term memory, coping history, changes in socialization patterns, behavior, and appropriateness of mood and affect in relation to life-events of those who are aging. (M = 2.14)
47. Adapt assessment protocols and intervention techniques so that they are appropriate for older, vulnerable adults. (M = 2.17)
48. Assess for dementia, delirium and depression in older adults. (M = 2.33)
49. Conduct clinical interventions for mental health and cognitive impairment issues in older adults. (M = 2.36)
56. Apply knowledge of outreach techniques with older adults and their families. (M = 1.57)
57. Ensure clarity of social work roles in providing services to older clients, their caregivers, other professionals, and the community. (M = 1.64)
58. Engage and work with older adults of varying stages of functional need within the home, community-based settings, and institutions. (M = 1.71)
60. Keep informed of changes in theory, research, policy, and practice in social work services to older persons. (M = 1.79)

G. Research
Qualitative and quantitative research content provides understanding of a scientific, analytic, and ethical approach to building knowledge for practice. The content prepares students to develop, use, and effectively communicate empirically based knowledge, including evidence-based interventions. Research knowledge is used by students to provide high quality services; to initiate change; to improve practice, policy, and social service delivery; and to evaluate their own practice.

Aging Competencies
37. Set realistic and measurable objectives based on functional status, life goals, symptom management, and financial and social supports of older adults and their families. (M = 1.92)
38. Reevaluate service or care plans for older adults on a continuing basis, incorporating physical, social and cognitive changes and adjusting plans as needed. (M = 1.93)
40. Assess organizational effectiveness in meeting needs of older adults and their caregivers. (M = 1.98)
60. Keep informed of changes in theory, research, policy, and practice in social work services to older persons. (M = 1.79)

*The level of specialization needed was assessed through mean scores, with those closer to "1" being a competency for all, and those near "2" or higher for those with more advanced or specialized education.

appropriate for inclusion in generalist training and education, and competencies with mean scores closer to two are more appropriate for inclusion in specialist education.

Application to Social Work Education and Practice

The Hartford Project provides the profession with identified competencies and guidelines on both the knowledge needed for generalist social work practice and social work practice in the specialized area of aging. This information can serve as a guideline for curriculum development in both foundation and concentration courses. To be most effective, this information should be integrated into the CSWE Educational Policy and Accreditation Standards passed by the board in June 2001 (CSWE, 2001).

The inclusion of aging competencies within accreditation standards will provide clear direction to the educator on specific aging-related topics that can be introduced to social work students when covering content areas in foundation curriculum. These competencies can be used as a base to generate lecture content, required reading assignments, and in-class exercises that will help ensure student exposure to this information. In addition, these competencies can be used to generate questions on exams and to help shape paper requirements.

They can be integrated into evaluative mechanisms that measure social work program outcomes. For instance, questions related to these competencies can be included on comprehensive examinations. Evaluations of student performance in the field should also include tasks that incorporate aging related content. Capstone experiences can also be designed to include requirements that evaluate a student's grasp of the material.

The integration of this material within the curriculum will also provide community human service agencies with guidelines on what they can expect social work graduates to know in the area of aging services. Demographic predictions indicate a growth in the aging population, and social work programs will be asked to meet the demands of this growing population. Providing these clear guidelines will help assist in meeting the future demands of human service organizations.

The application of these aging competencies can also be used in other arenas that expand beyond the scope of social work education. Regulatory boards may want to include aging competencies as a continuing education requirement to maintain licensure status. The Association of Social Work Boards and other entities that develop licensure and certification exams can also use these aging competencies to develop test questions.

Most importantly, the core professional associations need to assume a major leadership role in advocating and overseeing the adoption of these competencies within educational and practice arenas. Direction needs to be provided by practitioners on how these competencies can be emphasized in practice as well as how they can be sanctioned and integrated into organizational settings.

CONCLUSIONS AND FUTURE DIRECTIONS

The next challenge facing the social work profession is to move forward in the implementation of these competencies within education and practice arenas. In addition to the integration of these competencies within the CSWE Educational Policy and Accreditation Standards, site team members should be trained to look for aging content within the affirmation and reaffirmation process. The aging competencies should be viewed as critical content for all programs to include within their curriculum. The integration of this information in both the standards and site team reviews will provide a clear mandate by CSWE as to the importance of these competencies to professional social work education. Most importantly, it will provide clear guidance and direction for seasoned and novice social work educators on critical aging competencies as they relate to curriculum content areas.

In addition to a needed educational mandate, social work professional associations should work in tandem with educational programs to integrate this work within practice environments. Ideally, partnerships should be developed between social work programs and the practice community that move beyond the field placement experience. These partnerships can be used to increase the dialogue between education and practice arenas, which will help to maintain curriculum and practice relevancy. In addition, ongoing continuing education and training should be an integral part of these partnerships.

The historic roots of our profession center on assisting society with change, whether it be increases in immigrant populations, dealing with the trauma of postwar times, or responding to increases in poverty and unemployment. It is now the eve of a future societal change–the unprecedented growth of the aging population. This is a worldwide phenomenon, and demographic information indicates that every month, the net balance of the world's population is increasing by a million, with 70% of this increase occurring in developing countries (National Institute on Aging & the U.S. Bureau of the Census, 1993). The world is actually experiencing a demographic graying of the planet, a phenomenon not encountered previously. In America, statistics indicate that the number of persons 65 years of age and over will more than double to 80 million by the middle of the 21st Century (U.S. Bureau of the Census, 1999). As a profession, we are not prepared to meet the demands of this demographic shift (Galambos & Rosen, 1999).

The next stage of the Hartford Project is targeted for individual educators at various programs to infuse these aging competencies within their program's curricula. Although we applaud this initiative, to be more effective, this helpful initiative needs be officially sanctioned by CSWE and other professional associations.

Thus far, the emphasis has been on infusion of content, primarily at the foundation level. The project's next step could be to recommend that CSWE set up a task force to begin to look at specializations and how these competencies can be utilized within such a structure. At some level, the issue of specialization must be addressed. Additionally, the practice community needs to embrace competencies associated with aging specialization in advocacy, policy and program development, and continuing education and training areas.

The adoption of these core competencies will move us one step closer in preparing the profession to meet these future challenges. It is imperative that social work education, leadership, and credentialing take heed to help prepare the profession for this next societal change. Hopefully, the Council on Social Work Educational will see this as a gift of renewal that will help the profession come to grips with how to handle specializations. Hopefully, professional associations can use this as a guide to work in tandem with professional social work education to train and prepare students to work within the aging field. Can we handle this in such a way that it serves as a model for what constitutes a specialization? Are we prepared to take the next step?

REFERENCES

Anderson, T. E., & Blank, M. L. (1970). National Institute of Mental Health Training Programs in Aging. *The Gerontologist, 10*, 1, 153-160.

Austin, D. (1986). A history of social work education. *Social Work Education Monograph Series*. Austin, TX: University of Texas Press.

Bartlett, H. (1970). *The common base of social work practice*. New York: NASW.

Barusch, A., Greene, R., & Connelly, R. (1990). *Strategies for increasing gerontology content in social work education*. Washington, DC: Association for Gerontology in Higher Education.

Boehm, W. W. (1959). *Social work curriculum study*. New York: CSWE.

Briar, S. (1981). Needed: A simple definition of social work. *Social Work, 26* (1), 83-84.

Brieland, D. (1981). Definition, specialization, and domain in social work. *Social Work, 26* (1), 79-82.

Brieland, D. (1987). The history and evolution of social work practice. In A. Minahan (Editor-in-Chief), *Encyclopedia of Social Work* (18th Edition, pp. 739-754). Silver Spring, MD: NASW.

Conceptual Frameworks, Special Issue. (1977). *Social Work, 22* (5), 338-444.

Conceptual Frameworks II-Special Issue. (1981). *Social Work, 26* (1), 5-96.

Council on Social Work Education/SAGE-SW (2000) (www.cswe.org/sage-sw).

Council on Social Work Education/SAGE-SW (2001). *Strengthening the impact of social work to improve the quality of life for older adults and their families: A blue print for the new millennium.* Alexandria, VA: Author

Council on Social Work Education. (2001). Educational policy and accreditation standards. Alexandria, VA: Author.

Curry, L. & Wergin, J. (1993). *Educating professionals.* San Francisco: Jossey-Bass.

Dinerman, M. (1984). The 1959 curriculum study: Contributions of Werner W. Boehm. In M. Dinerman & L. L. Geismar (Eds.), *A quarter-centruy of social work education* (pp. 3-24). Washington, DC: NASW/CSWE.

Duncan, L. E. (1970). National Institute of Child Health and Human Development Training Grant Programs. *The Gerontologist, 10,* 1, 62-71.

Galambos, C. & Rosen, A. (1999). The aging are coming and they are us. *Health and Social Work, 24,* 1, 73-77.

Greene, R. R. (1988). *Continuing education for gerontological careers.* Washington, DC: Council on Social Work Education.

Greene, R. R., Barusch, A. S., & Connelly, R. (1990). *Social work and gerontology: Status report.* Washington, DC: Association for Gerontologists in Higher Education.

Hollis, E. V., & Taylor, A. L. (1951). *Social work education in the United States.* Columbia University Press.

Hopps, J. & Collins, P. M. (1995). Social work profession overview. In R. L. Edwards (Editor-in-Chief), *Encyclopedia of Social Work* (Vol. 2, 19th edition, pp. 2266-2282). Washington, DC: NASW Press.

Johnson, H. R., Britton, J. H., Seltzer, M. M., Stanford, E. P., Yancik, R., Maklan, C., & Middleswarth, A. B.(1980) Foundations for Gerontological Education. *The Gerontologist, 20* (3), 1-60.

Klein, S. (Ed.) (1995) *A national agenda for geriatric education. White papers.* Washington, DC: U. S. Department of Health & Human Services, Health Resources & Services Administration, Bureau of Health Professions.

Mcgaghie, W. C. (1993). Evaluating competence for professional practice. In L. Curry & J. Wergin. (Eds.), *Educating professionals* (pp. 229-261). San Francisco: Jossey-Bass.

National Institute on Aging & the U.S. Bureau of the Census (1993). *Wall chart on global aging.* Washington, D.C.: U.S. Department of Commerce.

Richmond, M. (1930). The need for training school in applied philanthropy. In *The long view* (pp. 99-104). New York: Russell Sage Foundation.

Schneider, R., Decker, T., Freeman, J., & Syran, C. (1984). *A curriculum concentration in gerontology for graduate social work education.* Washington, DC: Council on Social Work Education.

Schneider, R., Decker, T., Freeman, J., & Syran, C. (1984). *The integration of gerontology into social work educational curricula.* Washington, DC: Council on Social Work Education.

Schneider, R., & Kropf, N. (1989). *Integrating gerontology into the BSW curruculum: Generalist practice, human behavior and the social environment, social policy, research, and field education.* Washington, DC: Council on Social Work Education and Virginia Commonwealth University School of Social Work.

Tibbitts, C. (1970). Administration on Aging's Title V Training Grant Program. *The Gerontologist, 10*, 1, 54-61.

U. S. Census Bureau (1999). The older population in the United States: Population characteristics. Author: Washington, D.C.

Wendt, P., Peterson, D. A., & Douglass, E. B. (1993). *Core principles and outcomes of gerontology, geriatrics and aging studies instruction.* Washington, DC: Association for Gerontology in Higher Education.

Chapter 2

Basic Gerontological Competence for All Social Workers: The Need to "Gerontologize" Social Work Education

Anita L. Rosen, PhD
Joan Levy Zlotnik, PhD
Terry Singer, PhD

SUMMARY. Over the past decade, social work education has generally failed to mount a significant effort to better prepare its future practitioners to serve the needs of a growing aging population. The demographics of aging suggest a need and demand for social workers that specialize in services to older adults. However, there are insufficient programs, resources or interested students for expanding specialization opportu-

---

Anita L. Rosen is Director of Special Projects, Council on Social Work Education, and the CSWE/SAGE-SW Project Manager. Joan Levy Zlotnik is Executive Director of the Institute for Advancement for Social Work, and former Principal Investigator for the CSWE/SAGE-SW project, Phase I. Terry L. Singer is Dean of the Raymond A. Kent School of Social Work, University of Louisville.

[Haworth co-indexing entry note]: "Basic Gerontological Competence for All Social Workers: The Need to 'Gerontologize' Social Work Education." Rosen, Anita L., Joan Levy Zlotnik, and Terry Singer. Co-published simultaneously in *Journal of Gerontological Social Work* (The Haworth Social Work Practice Press, an imprint of The Haworth Press, Inc.) Vol. 39, No. 1/2, 2002, pp. 25-36; and: *Advancing Gerontological Social Work Education* (ed: M. Joanna Mellor, and Joann Ivry) The Haworth Social Work Practice Press, an imprint of The Haworth Press, Inc., 2002, pp. 25-36. Single or multiple copies of this article are available for a fee from The Haworth Document Delivery Service [1-800-HAWORTH, 9:00 a.m. - 5:00 p.m. (EST). E-mail address: docdelivery@haworthpress.com].

http://www.haworthpress.com/store/product.asp?sku=J083
10.1300/J083v39n01_04

nities. Specialization also does not address the growing realization by the profession that there is an enormous need for basic gerontological competency for all social workers. This paper presents data gathered by SAGE-SW, the John A. Hartford Foundation funded project at the Council on Social Education, that makes the case for strategic inclusion of aging education as an important consideration for social work education and teaching across the lifespan. The paper addresses numerous challenges to infusion or integration efforts aimed at restructuring the social work curriculum, and presents a model for infusing aging content into the basic BSW and MSW curricula in order to "gerontologize" the education of all students. *[Article copies available for a fee from The Haworth Document Delivery Service: 1-800-HAWORTH. E-mail address: <getinfo@haworthpressinc.com> Website: <http://www.HaworthPress.com> © 2002 by The Haworth Press, Inc. All rights reserved.]*

KEYWORDS. Aging, specialization, gerontological competencies, content infusion, social work curriculum

In 1998 the John A. Hartford Foundation began an exceptionally important, long-term geriatric social work education initiative. The focus of the initiative is directed at enhancing the preparation of social workers to meet the needs of a growing aging population. One recipient of Hartford Foundation funding was the Council on Social Work Education (CSWE) and its SAGE-SW project. Phase I of SAGE-SW, 1998-2001, sought to assess the current state of gerontological social work education, develop competencies for gerontological social work, and develop programming and resources to strengthen aging and gerontology education within social work. This paper describes a number of findings from SAGE-SW activities. These findings provide direction for Phase II that is seeking to significantly alter the way in which social work students are prepared for practice. The overall goal of this CSWE/SAGE-SW grant project is to strengthen gerontological education for all social workers in order to meet the needs of a growing aging population.

BACKGROUND

Over the past decade, social work education has generally failed to mount a significant effort to better prepare its future practitioners for a growing aging population (Scharlach, Damron-Rodriguez, Robinson & Feldman, 2000; Rosen & Zlotnik, 2001). At the same time that attention has been paid to the growth of the aging population and the potential effect of aging of baby-boomers (Administration on Aging, 2000), there are fewer gerontology spe-cialties in Masters of Social Work (MSW) programs today than ten years ago (Damron-Rodriguez, Villa, Tseng & Lubben, 1997).

Social work education has not been responsive to the demographic data that indicate a dramatic growth in the aging population. The growth of those over 65 years of age will increase from 13% of the population in 2000 to over 20% by the year 2030 (Administration on Aging, 2000). In addition, the old-old (85+ years) population has experienced rapid growth, doubling in the past 20 years (Administration on Aging, 2000). This population has a higher incidence of dependency and mental and physical disability than those of age (Adminis-tration on Aging, 2000), and requires more services. The growing aging popu-lation is increasingly diverse, and this diversity suggests the demand for more culturally competent service providers. Social work, with its comprehensive approach to the person in the environment is ideally suited to work with older adults. Yet, there is a severe shortage of those prepared to work with this popu-lation. The demographics of aging suggest a need and demand for social work-ers that specialize in services to older adults (Barusch, Greene & Connelly, 1990; NIA, 1987; Peterson & Wendt, 1990), yet professional education has not responded to these demographic realities.

In addition to the need for gerontological specialists, there also is an even greater need for basic gerontological competency for all social workers. The number of intergenerational families of three, four and five generations is in-creasing (Administration on Aging, 2000), and those social workers who work in health care provide services to a significant portion of older adults (Damron-Rodriguez & Lubben, 1997). Over 10 years ago, a National Associa-tion of Social Workers (NASW) survey of its general membership found that 62% of all respondents reported the need for gerontological knowledge (Peter-son & Wendt, 1990).

Funding from the John A. Hartford Foundation of New York City for the CSWE/SAGE-SW project enabled the assessment of the current educational climate for gerontology in social work and the move toward implementing a strategy to affect gerontological social work education. As a part of the SAGE-SW Phase I activities, staff assessed the current data and literature re-garding gerontological social work education (See annotated bibliography at *www.cswe.org/sage-sw/*). SAGE-SW staff also gathered data by conducting a survey in October 1999 of approximately 400 social work students from 17 so-cial work education programs in the Mid-Atlantic Region who were participat-ing in a daylong conference in Washington, D.C. Of the 221 respondents completing the survey, 135, or 61% percent were baccalaureate social work (BSW) students and 80, or 36% were masters of social work (MSW) students.

In addition, CSWE/SAGE-SW conducted six focus groups with BSW, MSW and doctoral students, four focus groups with BSW and MSW social work faculty and four focus groups with social work field supervisors and employers. A final component of data gathering was a national gerontological competencies survey of social work practitioners and academics, both with and without interest in aging (See accompanying article in this journal by Greene and Galambos).

One major result of the extensive data gathering by the SAGE-SW project staff was the publication, *Strengthening the Impact of Social Work to Improve the Quality of Life for Older Adults & their Families: A Blueprint for the New Millennium* (CSWE/SAGE-SW, 2001). This publication, referred to in this article as the *Blueprint*, assessed the current state of gerontological social work and provides a set of challenges to the social work profession. One of the key recommendations is the need to prepare all social work students, both BSW and MSW, to meet the needs of a growing aging population.

THE CURRENT STATE OF GERONTOLOGICAL SOCIAL WORK EDUCATION

The data gathered by Phase I of SAGE-SW suggest that the current social work educational environment has not successfully addressed the notion of education for practice with a growing aging population. For example, CSWE statistics indicate that 23 or 16% of (MSW) programs have a gerontology specialization, 7 (5%) have sub-concentrations, 17 (12%) offer aging as a specified "Field of Practice" and 6 (4%) offer a certificate in gerontology (Lennon, 1999). Only 782 (2.4%) of all MSW students in 1999 actually have chosen aging as their primary field of practice or social problem concentration (Lennon, 1999). This translates to only 4% of MSW graduates who work primarily in services to the aged (Gibelman & Schervish, 1997; Teare & Sheafor, 1995).

The limited number of MSW students in gerontological concentrations or specialties and the limited number of MSW gerontological students are the result of several factors. Among the most prominent are the inadequacy of resources and limited educational opportunities.

Inadequate Resources: Relatively few social work education programs have the trained faculty or financial resources needed to create or maintain gerontology concentrations (Damron-Rodriguez, Villa, Tseng & Lubben, 1997; Scharlach, Damron-Rodriguez, Robinson & Feldman, 2000).

The SAGE-SW national competencies study data indicate that of all groups surveyed, the population with the least amount of gerontological course work was social work faculty without specialization in aging (CSWE/SAGE-SW, 2000). Since this population comprises the majority of social work faculty, it appears likely that few faculty have much knowledge, skill or experience in social work with older people. In addition, there are limited amounts of student stipends and research monies for gerontological social work (Scharlach, Damron-Rodriguez, Robinson & Feldman, 2000).

Limited Opportunity to Specialize: SAGE-SW data, particularly those drawn from six focus groups with BSW, MSW and Doctoral students to assess the current state of gerontological social work education, indicated that, in most cases, unless students enter an MSW program with specific interest in aging, they had little opportunity to have that interest stimulated at the MSW level. The focus groups and the student survey both demonstrated that social work students have interest in acquiring knowledge in aging, even though they may have little interest in specializing in aging. However, once MSW students have determined their concentrations or specializations, there is almost no opportunity to take elective courses in another practice area, such as aging, even if the courses are available.

On the baccalaureate level, SAGE-SW data indicate that more BSW students have interest in aging than do MSW students, and about 16% of BSWs work in aging (Gibelman & Schervish, 1997; Teare & Sheafor, 1995). However, at the BSW level, CSWE accreditation standards do not allow students to specialize in the same way as MSW students can, since BSW education is generalist in nature. BSW students may choose to have an educational focus or take an elective course in aging, but the SAGE-SW survey of data indicates that there is a lack of available aging electives, minors or certificates available to BSWs.

Data from the SAGE-SW national gerontological competency survey of practitioners and academics with and without aging interest, indicate that BSW practitioners are more likely than MSWs or PhDs to have had any gerontological education (CSWE/SAGE-SW 2000). In addition, all survey respondents who had taken course work in aging or gerontology, indicate that their primary source of gerontological education was continuing education and not the social work academic curriculum.

Other important findings of SAGE-SW Phase I also were derived from the national competencies survey. The national competencies survey included 65 competency items that were developed through a thorough survey of the literature and consultation with six national expert practitioners and academics. Only items directly related to work with older people and their families were included, and items related to general social work skills, knowledge or practice were excluded.

The competency items were then arranged in a survey format which was sent to a broad national sample consisting of: social workers who have taken one of four licensing examinations (Basic, Intermediate, Advanced and Clinical) from the American Association of State Social Work Boards (AASSWB); the National Association of Social Workers (NASW) members who indicated their primary field of practice was aging; CSWE individual membership; and, all 200 members of the Association of Gerontology Education in Social Work (AGE-SW), an organization for social work gerontology educators.

Respondents were asked to indicate which of the 65 competency items were ones that all social workers–BSWs and MSWs–needed for practice; which items were needed by advanced practitioners only; and which items were needed by MSW gerontological specialists. The survey, which had an overall adjusted return rate of 51%, suggested that over one-half (35) of the gerontological competencies were needed by ALL social workers.

The thirty-five competencies deemed needed by all social workers practitioners are in the areas of knowledge, skills and professional practice. Some examples of the most often identified competencies needed by all social workers include:

- Assess one's own values and biases regarding aging, death and dying;
- Accept, respect, and recognize the right and need of older adults to make their own choices and decisions about their lives within the context of the law and safety concerns;
- Understand normal physical, psychological, and social changes in later life;
- Respect and address cultural, spiritual, and ethnic needs and beliefs of older adults and family members;
- Understand the influence of aging on family dynamics;
- Identify ethical and professional boundary issues that commonly arise in work with older adults and their caregivers, such as client self-determination, end-of-life decisions, family conflicts, and guardianship.

The competencies survey and other data gathered by SAGE-SW suggest that the current state of addressing gerontological social work education has not been successful, since the current direction does not provide all students with the opportunity to gain needed and basic gerontological knowledge or skills.

THE CASE FOR RESTRUCTURING CURRICULUM

The SAGE-SW data-gathering process suggests that there is limited activity and opportunity to bring gerontological specialization to the MSW curriculum and limited opportunity for BSWs to gain specific skill or experience with older people within the curriculum. Yet, the demographic challenges of a growing aging population strongly suggest that social work education will be derelict in its goal to educate for practice if it does not provide gerontological education in some form.

The SAGE-SW Phase I data make the case that all educational bodies should embrace some form of aging education. All helping professionals recognize the importance of the growing aging population to their entire educational content and this is especially true for social work education. Gerontological content must be configured into social work educational efforts. Strategic inclusion of aging education is an important consideration for social work education. Alternatives to the present situation might include infusion or integration of aging content into the curriculum so that all students are provided basic competence in aging (Singer, 2000).

The specialization approach is often resource intensive. Specialization may be viewed as a focused area of study that generally occurs at the graduate level, with the baccalaureate geared toward generalist practice. Though there is some confusion in social work education between the terms "specialization" and "concentration," specialization may be considered a subset of concentration. However, there are opportunities for specialization at both the associate degree and BSW levels through certification programs and minors.

Infusion comes from the Latin "infuses" or pour. Thus content is poured into the curriculum to permeate and alter that curriculum. Infusion would mean that aging content would find its "way into every aspect of the curriculum, including program and course objectives, subject areas, reading assignments, and categories for assessment of outcome. This method of bringing aging content to social work students should ensure a high level of expertise in the field" (Singer, 2000, p. 2).

Integration expects coordination or uniting of content with the rest of the curriculum. It is not as pervasive as an infused curriculum, yet indicates placing aging content in the curriculum in strategic places. The level of integration may determine the amount of emphasis a program wishes to give aging. Though there is no single model for integration, it is generally accepted that committing to an integrated model would provide extensive content in various places throughout the curriculum.

A number of authors from other professions, such as allied health and mental health professions, suggest that integration or infusion of gerontology content within the basic curriculum, combined with specialized courses, may be a more efficacious method of professional education (Hughes, 1980; Zucchero, 1998).

Social work educators also have been proponents of the integration or infusion model. In the 1980s a number of efforts were undertaken to examine the concept of integrating aging content into the basic social work curriculum. Lowy (1983) suggests that one option depending on leadership, interest and resources is that of incorporation (integration). Schneider (1984) developed a substantial amount of curricular materials for a CSWE project on gerontology. Unfortunately, for a variety of reasons, including funding and competing interests, these excellent curriculum proposals were not widely adopted. In a comprehensive article commissioned by the John A. Hartford Foundation, Scharlach, Damron-Rodriguez, Robinson & Feldman (2000) call for the development of model curricula that would integrate aging content into the foundation curriculum mandated by CSWE.

Cummings and Kropf (2000), pose an infusion model that can be used on both the baccalaureate and masters level in social work education to bring needed content about older adults with chronic mental illness to the social work curriculum so that students will be prepared to provide treatment to this growing population. Kropf (1996) also describes an infusion model for content on older people with developmental disabilities that is to be infused into the social work curricula at macro, meso and micro levels and suggests relevant content to the foundation sequence.

Andrew Scharlach and Barrie Robinson at the University of California Berkeley developed a set of social work curriculum modules for use in foundation courses, but found that use of these curriculum materials by social work faculty was variable, due to a variety of challenges (personal communication, March 1999). The modules can be found on the Internet at <*http://socrates.berkeley.edu/~aging/publications.html*>.

A variety of efforts to change the content of social work curriculum have been attempted over the past twenty-five years, but their impact has been limited. SAGE-SW has attempted an assessment of the challenges and barriers to successful infusion or integration of gerontological content into the curriculum.

CHALLENGES TO INFUSION AND INTEGRATION EFFORTS

A significant infusion model that permeates an entire curriculum was tested at McMaster University School of Social Work (Meredith & Watt 1994). This project sought to step beyond efforts of a single faculty member or a change in a single course. Rather, the concept was to infuse aging content as a departmental approach in an effort to change the entire educational structure and provide some parity of gerontological content throughout the entire foundation curriculum. The McMaster example and Singer's paper provide some insight into the elements that must be addressed to alter the way social work education prepares practitioners for a growing aging population. Some key elements for educational change are:

Organizational commitment: Unless there is commitment from the departmental or college administrators, little will be accomplished. A single faculty member with interest in aging will find it difficult to effect curricular-wide change. Administrators need to be able to see that both university and departmental mission and goal statements have some relationship to the need to build gerontological competency into the curriculum. Most mission and goal statements are general enough that imparting basic gerontological competency can be accommodated. Frequently, mission statements of universities include some "general welfare" statement or point to general themes of "education to the betterment of society" and research that "enhances the lives of others." The critical element often is not to find a "fit" between the desire to infuse gerontological competency and the social work program mission, but rather to make the case for the fit.

Incentives: If social work administrators or faculty do not perceive substantive incentives for effecting curricular change, change will not occur. Until recently, few incentives have been available to influence curricular change for gerontology. Incentives need not be solely monetary, and can be personal, mission driven or related to perception of accreditation requirements.

Competing Interests: Both the demographic imperative and numerous authors have made an excellent case for the infusion or integration of aging content into the social work curriculum. However, social work education has innumerable proponents of various special interests who wish to see their area of interest emphasized. In addition, current educational practice, whether or not it is valid and productive, is what is most familiar and comfortable to most faculty. New curricular content must compete with a substantial amount of current curricula and methods of delivering that curricula.

Faculty Comfort: As stated earlier in this paper, most social work faculty have little or no knowledge or skills in gerontological practice. They also have little knowledge of resources and curricular material to bring aging and gerontology content into general Human Behavior, Policy, Practice, Research, Diversity or Field courses. Realistically, it is difficult to expect those with few tools in gerontology to add this content to their courses.

Limited Resources: Phase I of SAGE-SW data suggest that there are resources for developing specialty courses in gerontology or geriatrics, but little in the way of easily obtained modules, projects, and materials that can be brought to a non-aging BSW or MSW course. In addition, there is a dearth of gerontological course objectives and syllabi examples for general Human Behavior, Policy, Practice, and Research, Diversity or Field courses that can be used by social work faculty.

A MODEL FOR CHANGE

The work of the first phase of SAGE-SW and the recommendations of the *Blueprint* (CSWE/SAGE-SW, 2001) has resulted in an approach in Phase II to develop a gerontological infusion model in social work education. This project includes a plan to develop needed resources and materials, opportunity for extensive technical assistance to social work educators and, planning for a number of faculty development institutes for those faculty with little gerontological knowledge who teach foundation and non-aging courses. These activities are to be conducted from the spring 2001 semester through spring of 2004.

The essence of the CSWE/SAGE-SW Phase II project activities seek to address the challenges and barriers that prevent successful infusion of aging content into the BSW, first year MSW and non-aging social work curriculum. The plan is to create a comprehensive, visible approach to infusion or integration. Phase II activities are listed below.

1. Making operational the gerontology competencies in order that they may be used in course syllabi.
2. Linking gerontology competencies to the new, 2001 Educational Policy and Accreditation Standards for social work programs as an incentive to social work education and administrators and faculty to include gerontology content in the curriculum.
3. Using a lifespan approach to infusion so that aging content becomes a part of existing curriculum, not something to be added-on.
4. Gathering, developing and disseminating educational materials and resources (e.g., case studies, projects, videos, games, curriculum modules that can be infused or integrated in BSW and first year MSW courses). Much of this work is to be conducted with identified faculty experts.
5. Delivering a series of one- and four-day faculty development institutes to help social work faculty gain the ability and interest needed so that they are able to infuse or integrate aging content into their non-aging courses. These institutes will help faculty enhance their own syllabi,

gain knowledge of curricular resources, and gain a better understanding of the range of settings and services that require gerontological knowledge and skills. The institutes also will enable faculty to appreciate the personal, academic and research benefits to infusion of aging content throughout the curriculum.

6. Seeking buy-in and support from BSW and MSW deans and directors to encourage their faculty to gain and use new gerontological knowledge and skills in overall curriculum efforts.

7. Providing on-going technical assistance and support to social work education programs and faculty who have participated in faculty development workshops. It is expected that this item and item #9 below will be conducted in collaboration with the Association for Gerontology Education in Social Work, a 20-year-old organization of social work faculty with interest and knowledge in gerontology.

8. Continually finding or developing curricular resources for integration and infusion of gerontological content, and developing effective methods of disseminating these materials through the Internet, publications and workshops.

9. Coordinating a social work and aging conference that will allow social work educators, researchers and practitioners to network and examine promising educational practices and resources to bring aging competence to social work education and practice.

Social work education has failed to prepare practitioners for meeting the needs of a growing aging population. Few social work students have been provided basic competence in aging and gerontology and for too long, needed gerontology content has not come close to gaining parity with other content across the human lifespan. The John A. Hartford Foundation has now afforded social work educators the opportunity for a more comprehensive national effort to change the preparation of all social work students. In order for this effort to be sustainable, social work faculty and practitioners with interest in aging will need to take leadership in encouraging deans, directors, educators, field practicum agencies and others that it is imperative for the profession to "gerontologize" social work education for all students.

REFERENCES

Administration on Aging [AoA] (2000). *A Profile of Older Americans* [Online]. Available: <*www.aoa.gov/aoa/stats/profile/default.htm*>.

Barusch, A., Greene, R., & Connelly, J. (1990). *Strategies for Increasing Gerontology Content in Social Work Education.* Washington, DC: Association for Gerontology in Higher Education.

Cummings, S. M., & Kropf, N. P. (2000). An infusion model for including content on elders with chronic illness in the curriculum. *Advances in Social Work, 1* (1), 93-105.

CSWE/SAGE-SW (2000). *CSWE/SAGE-SW Aging Competencies Survey Report.* [Online] Available at: <*www.cswe.org/sage-sw/competenciesreport.htm*>.

CSWE/SAGE-SW (2001). *Strengthening the Impact of Social Work to Improve the Quality of Life for Older Adults & their Families: A Blueprint for the New Millennium.* Alexandria, VA: Council on Social Work Education. [Online] Available: <*www.cswe.org/sage/sw/*>.

Damron-Rodriguez, J., Villa, V., Tseng, H., & Lubben, J. (1997). Demographic and organizational influences on the development of gerontological social work curriculum. *Gerontology and Geriatrics Education, 17* (3), 3-18.

Gibelman, M., & Schervish, P. (1997). *Who We Are: A Second Look.* Washington, DC: NASW Press.

Hughes, D. (1980). Professional training in gerontology: The case of nursing. *Educational Considerations, 8,* 1 (19-22).

Kropf, N. P. (1996). Infusing content on older people with developmental disabilities into the curriculum. *Journal of Social Work Education, 32* (2), 215-26.

Lennon, T. (1999). *Statistics on Social Work Education in the United States: 1998.* Alexandria, VA: Council on Social Work Education.

Lowy, L. (1983). Incorporation and specialization of content on aging in the social work curriculum. *Journal of Gerontological Social Work, 5,* 4, 37-54.

Meredith, S. D., & Watt, S. (1994). Gerontology development project: Infusing gerontology into social work curriculum. *Gerontology and Geriatrics Education, 15* (2), 91.

Peterson, D. A., & Wendt, P. F. (1990). Employment in the field of aging: A survey of professionals in four fields. *The Gerontologist, 30,* 679-684.

Rosen, A., & Zlotnik, J. L. (2001). Social Work's Response to a Growing Older Population. *Generations, 25* (1), 69-71.

Scharlach, A., Damron-Rodriguez, J., Robinson, B., & Feldman, R. (2000). Educating Social Workers for an Aging Society: A Vision for the 21st Century. *Journal of Social Work Education, 36* (3), 521-538.

Schneider, R. (Ed.) (1984). *Gerontology in Social Work Education: Faculty Development and Continuing Education.* Council on Social Work Education: Alexandria, VA.

Singer, T. (2000). *Structuring Education to Promote Understanding of Issues of Aging* [Online at <*www.cswe.org/sage-sw/*>].

Teare, R., & Sheafor, B. (1995). *Practice-Sensitive Social Work Education.* Alexandria, VA: Council on Social Work Education.

Zucchero, R. (1998). Unique model for training mental health professionals to work with older adults. *Educational Gerontology, 24* (3), 265-278.

Chapter 3

Social Work Education
for Interdisciplinary Practice
with Older Adults and Their Families

JoAnn Damron-Rodriguez, PhD, LCSW
Constance Saltz Corley, PhD, LCSW

SUMMARY. Training for interdisciplinary practice is integral to preparation of well-qualified gerontological social workers. Social work and other disciplines must be prepared to function in teams to achieve mutually determined therapeutic patient goals and to maintain team efficiency. A conceptual framework is presented to organize the content areas for social work education in preparation for interdisciplinary practice. Curricula tools and learning exercises are given as examples and resources for teaching in each of the four major components of the framework: context, structure, process and outcomes. Recommendations for curriculum considerations are presented. *[Article copies available for a fee from The Haworth Document Delivery Service: 1-800-HAWORTH. E-mail address: <docdelivery@haworthpress.com> Website: <http://www.HaworthPress.com> © 2002 by The Haworth Press, Inc. All rights reserved.]*

JoAnn Damron-Rodriguez is Associate Professor, School of Public Policy and Social Research, University of California, Los Angeles. Constance Saltz Corley is Professor, School of Social Work, California State University, Los Angeles.

[Haworth co-indexing entry note]: "Social Work Education for Interdisciplinary Practice with Older Adults and Their Families." Damron-Rodriguez, JoAnn, and Constance Saltz Corley. Co-published simultaneously in *Journal of Gerontological Social Work* (The Haworth Social Work Practice Press, an imprint of The Haworth Press, Inc.) Vol. 39, No. 1/2, 2002, pp. 37-55; and: *Advancing Gerontological Social Work Education* (ed: M. Joanna Mellor, and Joann Ivry) The Haworth Social Work Practice Press, an imprint of The Haworth Press, Inc., 2002, pp. 37-55. Single or multiple copies of this article are available for a fee from The Haworth Document Delivery Service [1-800-HAWORTH, 9:00 a.m. - 5:00 p.m. (EST). E-mail address: docdelivery@haworthpress.com].

http://www.haworthpress.com/store/product.asp?sku=J083
© 2002 by The Haworth Press, Inc. All rights reserved.
10.1300/J083v39n01_05

KEYWORDS. Geronotology, interdisciplinary practice, teams, social work education

Based on a dramatic demographic shift to an increasingly older population worldwide and particularly in post-industrial societies such as the United States, the anticipated demand for gerontological social workers will continue to increase to the year 2020. The percentage of older persons has tripled since 1900 (U.S. Bureau of the Census, 1992) and by the year 2030 one out of every five Americans will be over the age of 65 (U.S. Bureau of the Census, 1996). Current estimates cite a need for 60,000 to 70,000 social workers in aging by the year 2020 (Chronicle Guidance Publications, 1999). Yet it is recognized that social work education has not kept pace with the demand for gerontological social workers (Damron-Rodriguez, Villa, Tseng, & Lubben, 1997). According to national surveys of schools of social work only 5% of graduate social work students take an aging course (Damron-Rodriguez et al., 1997; Lubben, Damron-Rodriguez & Beck, 1992). About this same proportion of social workers identify their primary work as being with older adults (Giblemen & Shervish, 1997) despite the fact that U.S. News and World Report (1995) proclaims gerontological social work to be one of the top ten growing fields in the country.

Since the U.S. Bureau of Health Professions National Forum on Geriatric Education held in 1995, the social work profession has increasingly recognized this discrepancy between supply and demand for gerontological social workers. The John A. Hartford Foundation has been an impetus for providing a new level of attention to aging through its Geriatric Social Work Initiatives. For example, the Council on Social Work Education (CSWE) Strengthening Aging and Gerontology Education in Social Work (SAGE-SW) has developed competencies for social work with older adults that could be utilized in foundation and advanced curricula. Under the auspices of CSWE, funds from the John A. Hartford Foundation are also being awarded to up to 70 undergraduate and graduate social work programs under the Geriatric Enrichment in Social Work Education (GeroRich) initiative. Thus, this is a relevant juncture in social work education to discuss a key content area for gerontological social work, interdisciplinary practice.

The "graying of America" and the "worldwide age quake" have created an aging imperative for professional education. Social workers must increasingly be prepared not only to work with the growing numbers of older persons but also with the multiple other professions who increasingly will serve them. In health care and social services, as well as business and industry, teams are being increasingly utilized to address complex problems or issues (Katzenbach and Smith, 1993). Based on the needs of older persons the other disciplines that are frequently involved in geriatric interdisciplinary teams include: physicians, nurses, psychologists, dieticians, physical therapists, occupational therapists and clinical pharmacists. Psychiatrists, optometrists, dentists, audiologists, speech therapists and other specialized professionals, including chaplains, may also play a role in the geriatric interdisciplinary team, with the core team typically composed of the triad of physician, nurse and social worker (Bernard, Connelly, Kuder, Mellor, Norman & Tsukuda, 1997).

OVERVIEW: GERONTOLOGICAL SOCIAL WORK AND INTERDISCIPLINARY TEAMS

Gerontological social work is practice for or on behalf of older adults and their families. Gerontology is the interdisciplinary study of aging and is grounded in a human growth and development framework. Gerontological social work emphasizes the strengths and potential of older adults while recognizing the risks and losses in late life. Geriatric social work, a very related denotation of the field, emphasizes practice with older adults in health care settings or with persons in late life with health problems related to aging.

The following definition of gerontological social work is provided by the National Association of Social Worker's Standards for Classification of Social Work Practice:

> Gerontological social work is a professionally responsible intervention to (1) enhance the developmental, problem solving, and coping capacities of older people and their families; (2) promote the effective and humane operating of systems that provide resources and services to older people and their families; (3) link older people with systems that provide them with resources and opportunities; and (4) contribute to the development and improvement of policies that support persons throughout the lifespan. (Berkman, Dobrof, Harry & Damron-Rodriguez, 1997, p. 55)

A White Paper on Geriatric Social Work for the U.S. Bureau of Health Professions delineated the foundation knowledge for the profession in preparing to work with older adults and their families. The major knowledge arenas were cited as: (1) the biopsychosocial perspective, (2) a family systems approach, (3) the lifespan and life course development framework, (4) an advocacy approach to the recognition of ethnic diversity, special groups and underserved populations, (5) a working understanding of policy and programs of the continuum of health and social services, (6) case or care management strategies, and (7) interdisciplinary teamwork (Berkman, Dobrof, Harry & Damron-Rodriugez, 1997). These content area were related to the 1995 White House Conference on Aging and found to be related to the needs of aging adults as voiced in the conference (Damron-Rodriguez & Lubben, 1997). Further, a subsequent White Paper for the John A. Hartford Foundation provided strategies for the integration of aging into social work education (Scharlach, Damron-Rodriguez, Robinson & Feldman, 2000).

The definition and foundation knowledge of gerontological social work provide insight into the crucial role social workers play in interdisciplinary teams. Understanding the needs of older adults who require health and social services provides a further understanding why interdisciplinary teams play such a central role in geriatrics. Interdisciplinary teams are an important component in population-based practice for the elderly. In population-based practice the models of care evolve from the characteristics of the persons served. Thus the multiple problems of functionally impaired elderly require different disciplines to work together.

The biopsychosocial domains of social work practice in gerontological/geriatric social work are pictured in Figure 1. Interdisciplinary teams are those in which the biological aspects of normal aging, chronic illness and functioning interact with the psychosocial domains. Social work is the key discipline to address the social domain of role changes in late life, socioeconomic issues and most importantly, family and social support. The medical, nursing and other professions are key in the biological domain. Additionally, social work plays an important role in planning for interventions which are the result of an interaction of factors from all three domains. The team approach is required to address the interacting factors of older adult's lives, which impact their level of independence. Within each of these spheres the growing diversity of the older population must be a focus of social work education and training, as well as spiritual dimensions of aging (Corley, in press).

The majority of persons over the age of 65 function independently and do not require ongoing assistance (National Center for Health Statistics, 1990). However, the incidence of chronic illness (both physical and mental), functional deficits, and significant social losses increase with age. The older population itself is aging and persons of advanced old age (over 85 years) have even heightened needs for long term assistance in order to cope with these major challenges of later life (Jette, 1996).

Family members are overwhelmingly the source of support for older persons and yet they may themselves be aging and/or have multiple care responsibilities (National Academy on an Aging Society, 2000). Older persons are three times as likely to be hospitalized as younger age groups and have needs which require service coordination in order to most appropriately utilize both informal and formal support (National Academy of an Aging Society, 2000).

FIGURE 1. Biopsychosocial Domains for Gerontological Social Work Education and Interdisciplinary Practice

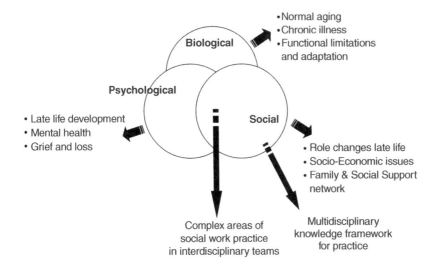

In order to address the multiplicity and interactive nature of the health and social problems of many older adults, multiple disciplines must work together (Zeiss & Steffon, 1996). Thus, the needs of vulnerable older persons and their families necessitate interdisciplinary teams (Weiland, Kramer, Waite & Rubenstein, 1996). Teamwork is a mechanism that facilitates joint action towards mutually defined goals on behalf of the older person. The following is the definition used in this chapter to define the interdisciplinary team approach:

> A group of health professionals each of whom possess particular expertise; each of whom is responsible for making individual decisions; who together hold a common purpose, who meet formally and informally to communicate, to collaborate, and to consolidate knowledge from which treatment plans are made which determine interventions and patient outcomes. (Frank et al., 1998)

A FRAMEWORK FOR SOCIAL WORK EDUCATION FOR INTERDISCIPLINARY PRACTICE

Social work and other disciplines must be prepared to function in teams to achieve mutually determined therapeutic patient goals and to maintain team efficiency. The conceptual framework developed by Saltz (1992a) is first presented to organize the content areas for social work education in preparation for interdisciplinary practice. Curricula tools and learning exercises are noted from a variety of sources in which the authors were principal contributors (Saltz & Damron-Rodriguez, 1998). These are given as examples and resources for teaching in each of the four major components of the framework: context, structure, process and outcomes. Some of these materials are derived from the Geriatric Interdisciplinary Team Managed Care Training of Trainers Program (GITMC TOT) developed by the Southern California Region of Kaiser Permanente and the University of California at Los Angeles Multicampus Program in Geriatric Medicine and Gerontology (funded by the John A. Hartford Foundation and the Garfield Memorial Fund).

As shown in Figure 2 (Saltz, 1992a), the model begins with the **context**, which includes the organizational culture in which the team operates and the relationship of the team to its environment (Sundstrom, deMeuse & Futrell, 1990). Organizational context is a crucial but often not addressed element to aid in understanding team functioning. Rewards for engaging in teamwork must be available on an organizational (and in some cases, interorganizational) basis, as well as internally among team members. Overall, team goals and objectives may be predetermined within the organization, but are sometimes (at least in part) determined by the members of specific teams. The larger organizational context is also a source of performance feedback, which influences the team's activities and is critical for the survival of the team, or may lead to its demise (McClane, 1992a).

The **structure** of a team can be predetermined, but ultimately evolves as the team begins functioning. This component is viewed in terms of both the composition of the *individuals* on the team (Rothberg, 1992) as well as characteristics of the team as a *unit* (Saltz, 1992b). The functions, training and/or professional expertise of individual team members, influence overall team functioning, including how roles are perceived/enacted. Composition, size, norms and goal setting (Scholtes, 1988) are other structural elements of the team as a unit. Understanding the stages of team development also influences the evolution of a team's structure (Saltz, 1992b).

Team **processes** are complex and multifaceted. A sizable body of literature addresses team *leadership* in terms of roles and styles, as well as types of leaders (Campbell, 1992a). *Information-sharing and communication* are process variables that are patient-focused and/or team-focused (Garner, 1992a). *Problem solving and decision making* activities include skills such as identifying and prioritizing problems, information gathering and sharing, generating and evaluating decisions (Garner, 1992b). Finally, *conflict resolution and feed-*

FIGURE 2

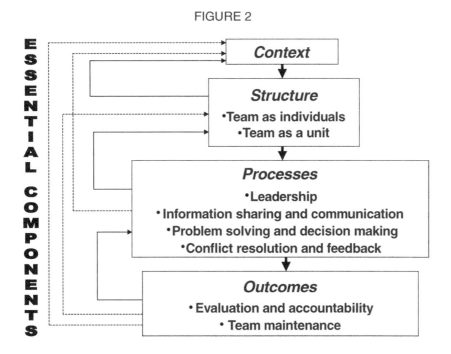

back are critical process elements (Frank and Elliott, 1992). Identifying and attempting to address sources of conflict and styles of conflict are involved here.

Outcomes are an essential, but understudied (until recently) component of team functions (Waite & Hoffman, 2001). Outcomes for the team itself are related to *evaluation and accountability* within the organizational context of practice, and also to various structural and process components as noted above (McClane, 1992b). *Team maintenance and enhancement* includes assessing individual team members as well as the team unit, along with identifying creative endeavors (Johnson & Johnson, 1991) and avenues of renewal (Campbell, 1992b).

As the arrows in Figure 2 show, the organization **context** influences the *structure* of the team, which in turn impacts on team **processes**, which ultimately determine the degree to which teams examine their **outcomes**. At the same time, changes in one component of team functioning can change another component in a non-linear fashion, as the feedback loops indicate (e.g., team outcome evaluation may reveal the consistent need for greater participation of a specific profession, which may prompt a change in team structure, which in turn may require a mandate from an administrator elsewhere in the organization context).

THE CONTEXT OF INTERDISCIPLINARY PRACTICE IN AGING

Understanding the role of social work and the functioning of interdisciplinary teams are best viewed within the organizational and societal context in which the practice takes place. The social work profession is more solidly founded in the appreciation of the interaction of professional roles and agency function than most other professions. The macro or organizational knowledge base of social work can add to the team's understanding of the influence of institutional factors on its functioning. The mission, goals, objectives and strategic plans of the organization in which the interdisciplinary team resides will influence the team's structure and process.

Gerontological social work may take place in a wide variety of settings that are most likely to have interdisciplinary teams including: hospitals, nursing homes, rehabilitation centers, health maintenance organizations, life care communities, hospice programs and multipurpose senior services. The auspices for the agencies may be public (city, county, state and federal) as well as private, for-profit and non-profit. Recent trends in healthcare delivery have resulted in larger systems of care provision through mergers and regional organization of services, i.e., management service areas. Further adding to the complexity of the context of interdisciplinary practice is that aging services must coordinate with multiple other programs in the aging network and along the continuum. Thus, education for social work interdisciplinary practice must include not only an understanding of the organization in which the worker is placed but the continuum in which the agency functions.

The continuum of care for the elderly has been viewed as linear, from most acute to lower levels of care in the community. More recent conceptualizations emphasize the interplay of services as they change over time in response to the older adult and the family, such as the community-based care model, which organizes by site of care for long term care (Damron-Rodriguez, Frank, Heck, Liu, Sragow, Cruise and Osterweil, 1998). It recognizes that home may provide as high a level of care as residential care in a nursing home. Interdisciplinary teams operating from any one of these services or a hospital will need to know the goals of these programs as evidenced in admission and discharge criteria.

State and federal policy provide broader contextual influences on the interdisciplinary team. Medicare, Medicaid and other health service reimbursement systems will produce parameters in which the team functions. Accrediting bodies (such as Joint Commission on the Accreditation of Healthcare Organizations) or external review panels may also provide guidelines or criteria for interdisciplinary team responsibilities and documentation.

These broad contextual influences include healthcare policy and legislation that may define the service eligibility of patients and clients in managed care (Frank & Della Penna, 1998). Interdisciplinary teams are frequently bound by these criteria. Utilization and resource allocation measures may evaluate the team's effectiveness within the organization (Brunner, 1995). Unless professionals understand and consider the organizational context of interdisciplinary teamwork, individuals and team process alone may be viewed as the locus of team problems.

Professional preparation for interdisciplinary practice includes understanding both the internal organizational context and relationships with the external environment. This includes an awareness of the groups with whom the team interacts and the implication for team performance. The support for teams within the organization is important as it relates to team rewards. Does the administration value teams? All of these contextual issues are an important frame for understanding team functioning.

Figure 3 depicts the multiple layers of context in which interdisciplinary teams function. Social work education can assist practitioners to understand the influence of context. A systems perspective may be used as a theoretical framework for understanding teams within the context of the organization. Some key concepts include: equifinality, synergy, positive and negative system feedback, homeostasis, and other system functions and system boundaries. An exercise from GITMC TOT which introduces the systems perspective and includes the students or participants visualizing and drawing their team by way of a network map is depicted in Figure 3.

THE STRUCTURE OF INTERDISCIPLINARY PRACTICE IN AGING

Structure is the identified order of the team. It includes the purpose and goals of the team, stages of team development, meeting rules, and roles of each member. Again, with a knowledge base of small group structure and process, social workers are prepared to understand this aspect of interdisciplinary practice. Professionals can apply knowledge of groups to this special type of group, the interdisciplinary team.

Teams in aging are structured as *multidisciplinary, interdisciplinary or transdisciplinary* (Rothberg, 1992). All teams have the characteristics of common goals, individual efforts and discipline expertise. For a team to be interdisciplinary it further requires that members are responsible for the group effort and have skills in effective group integration. In an interdisciplinary team the final product, usually a treatment plan, could not have been produced without the interaction of the team as a whole. The outcomes of the interdisciplinary team plan are interdependent on team members' interventions. In the multidisciplinary team the actions are more parallel or cumulative rather than integrated. In transdisciplinary teams, each member supports and enhances programs and activities of the other discipline. There is usually cross-training and a means for team members to substitute on certain functions while maintaining professional boundaries.

In addition to these three types of teams, team structure can vary based on whether members are core or regular, ongoing members or consultants to the team (Rothberg, 1992). Core members are expected to attend all meetings and assume ongoing responsibilities for the functioning of the team in addition to their disciplinary role. Consultant members attend based on the need for their special expertise related to a patient or team issue. To work effectively as interdisciplinary team members, the differences in these team structures must be recognized by all.

Frequently team members enter interdisciplinary practice without an understanding of what can be expected from other team members. Social workers must be able to articulate and function in a distinct role and at the same time interface and sometimes overlap with the function of other team members. Mellor & Lindeman (1998) describe the roles of social workers in teams as including assessor, care manager, group work facilitator, liaison, advocate and community resource expert.

Structure of the team flows from the goals and objectives of the team as they serve a specific population within the context of their organizational structure. Protocols for team formation are also part of the structure of the team. Meeting times, meeting space and communication guidelines (e.g., who presents what information in what order during a meeting) must be determined by the team. The clear articulation and posting of these ground rules is useful.

An additional aspect of team structure is the life cycle or stages of team development. The team as a living system moves from early stage of *forming*, to a conflictual stage of *storming*, to the development of functional expectations called *norming*, then on to optimal maintenance and functioning, or *performing* (Tuckman, 1965 in Saltz, 1992b). An exercise in identifying the stage of a team's functioning is described by Saltz (1996) which can help teams better understand their evolution.

The professional education of social workers prepares them for a leadership role based on their skill in interpersonal relationships and groupwork (Mellor & Lindeman, 1998). A social worker can have many functional roles in the team as well as the professional roles just described; these include leader, convener and facilitator. Overlapping functions may strengthen a team rather than indicate duplication and waste of resources. This is an aspect of team functioning that requires monitoring and evaluation based on team goals.

FIGURE 3

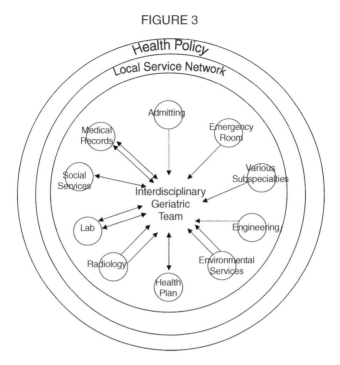

THE PROCESS OF INTERDISCIPLINARY PRACTICE IN AGING

The "process" component of team functioning is multi-faceted. Two of the components will be discussed here: leadership and communication. Team leadership is one of the most important aspects of successful teamwork. Leadership on an interdisciplinary team is not necessarily vested in any one person or discipline. The leadership role entails: defining a clear sense of purpose and scope of the team's responsibilities, tracking team achievements, being the team's link to administration, and addressing conflict and other barriers to team progress (Waite, Harker & Messerman, 1994; Zeiss & Steffon, 1996).

Leadership roles which enhance team functioning have been described as task-oriented and maintenance-oriented (Campbell, 1992). Different members of the team may be more focused on the team's tasks or outcomes, whereas others (often the social worker on the team) may bring more attention to maintenance of team process. An exercise that can help team members clarify their individual leadership style and how their styles affect the team as a whole can be found in Johnson and Johnson (1991) called "Understanding Your Leadership Actions Questionnaire." This has been adapted for use as an observational instrument in a social work research class (Saltz, 1996).

Communication on a team can be enhanced by the use of standardized instruments, which provide a common language to discuss strengths and deficits. Because each discipline has its own professional jargon, the concept of "function speak" is addressed via the common parameters measure in standardized instruments. By speaking in terms of the older adult's actual measurable functioning, professional jargon is avoided. This increases the team's client-centered goal orientation and decreases interdisciplinary team communication difficulties. *Comprehensive Geriatric Assessment* (Ouslander, Brummel-Smith & Beck, 2000) describes a number of instruments and best practices related to their use. The psychosocial assessment performed by social workers can substantially enhance the data provided by these functional measures, e.g., family and community context; values and beliefs; culture (see Figure 4).

The social worker is often called upon to represent the family in the team's communications (Saltz & Schaefer, 1996). Family members may be seen as "lay" team members at best, and in many instances are rarely present at team meetings. It is imperative that their input be present to ensure successful care and follow-up. The advocacy role of the social worker on behalf of the older adult and family members is therefore critical.

EVALUATION OF OUTCOMES IN INTERDISCIPLINARY PRACTICE IN AGING

The context, structure, and process dimensions of "Essential Components of Team Functioning" are all relevant to the fourth component of the framework, outcomes (see Figure 2). Context relates to the organizational setting, type of service, level of care and reimbursement protocols. Context also relates to the organizational culture and system of rewards for team work and team outcomes. The structure of the team can affect its efficiency and effectiveness. As an example, team size is a significant cost factor in assessing team output. An evaluation may find that a specific disciplinary representative may be rarely consulted and leads to complications in implementing a treatment plan. The problem-solving process will be required to determine if patient outcomes necessitate the ongoing inclusion of a representative of this missing team member, and if so, determine a mechanism to include his/her participation.

Social workers are essential partners in the evaluation of outcomes for patients/clients in practice settings. Yet they must also play a lead role in helping the team evaluate its own process. Elements of the "Essential Components of

FIGURE 4. Interacting Dimensions of Interdisciplinary Geriatric Assessments

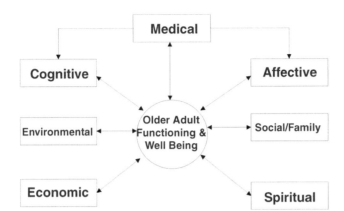

Effective Team Functioning" (see Figure 2) provide a framework for team self-assessment that has been used in a class taught by an interdisciplinary faculty team in rural Maryland. Interdisciplinary student teams designing a prevention program for participants at rural Head Start and senior center sites, are required to monitor their team functioning along the way. Individual team member assessments are combined and provide feedback to each team as a whole to target areas where team functioning would benefit from improvement (see McClane, 1992b).

Evaluation of interdisciplinary teams is an important macro-level role for social work and cannot be separated from good clinical practice. In order to evaluate team functioning in geriatrics, for example, several dimensions of team goals and objectives must be articulated. First, the *targeted patients* to be helped as well as the expected ways in which they will benefit, or *patient outcomes*, must be identified. The targeting must also include the professionals or team members who are held accountable to the outcomes of the interventions. This fundamental task of goal setting is frequently left to chance, based on assumptions rather than explicitly stated, or even based on outdated information.

Second, the goals of the team must be framed within a timeframe in order to evaluate efficiency. Both short and longer-term goals for the team outcomes need to be stated and communicated on an ongoing basis to members.

Third, the team's goals or purpose should be differentiated from tasks. Tasks may include the completion of the review of charts and treatment planning for a specified number of cases each meeting. A goal may be the increase of patient's level of independence as measured by their activities of daily living. Both task and goal orientations are necessary. However, a task orientation essential to efficiency can hamper effectiveness if patient outcomes are not clearly articulated and the focus of each meeting. A lofty goal orientation alone may sabotage team effectiveness as well.

Each of these dimensions can be related back to the systems perspective. The systems perspective assists in identifying processes for Total Quality Improvement (TQI) and Continuous Quality Improvement (CQI). These frameworks for evaluating process and outcomes in organizations are increasingly required as ongoing aspects of the system. For example, external reviewers such as the Joint Commission for the Accreditation of Healthcare Organizations (JCAHO) require that such evaluation processes are in place and that equally in place are processes to respond and implement improvements. Accomplishing this requires collaboration across disciplines. JCAHO defines quality as the degree to which patient care practices increase the probability of desired patient outcomes and decrease the undesired outcomes. This is judged within the context of the population, setting and relevant current knowledge. The positive and negative outcomes are important data collection point or feedback mechanisms for teams. Data collection is an integral part of evaluation. Sources of objective measurement for each of the dimensions of team's objectives must be established and existing instruments utilized (Waite & Hoffman, 2001). Patient's records, assessment reports, team minutes, and service utilization figures are all important data sources for measuring efficiency and effectiveness. Social work education must incorporate knowledge about these accrediting processes and promote social work leadership in the teamwork necessary for successful accreditation.

CONCLUSION AND IMPLICATIONS

The complex needs of older adults with functional challenges, and their families who provide support, require social work interventions that are founded in a firm biopsychosocial knowledge base. Social work interventions with vulnerable older people increasingly require an interdisciplinary team approach. It is essential for gerontological social workers to acquire not only the requisite knowledge and competencies to work with older adults but also to work with other health professionals who serve the elderly.

A synopsis of key knowledge areas relevant to the biopsychosocial approach to work with the elderly has been articulated, relying on recent White Papers (Berkman, Dobrof, Damron-Rodriguez & Harry, 1998; Scharlack, Damron-Rodriguez, Robinson & Feldman, 2000). These areas (see Figure 1) relate primarily to direct practice. However, macro practice skills related to advocacy, program planning, and policy are essential to practice with older adults and their families as well. These skills can be related to the organizational context depicted in Figure 3. The relevance of these social work knowledge and skill areas to those required in the comprehensive geriatric assessment, a core to interdisciplinary practice, was highlighted (see Figure 4). A definition of the disciplinary role of social workers on an interdisciplinary team was provided. Further roles for social work as delineated by Mellor and Lindeman (1998) expand the roles of social work on interdisciplinary teams. It is essential for social workers to bring to the geriatric team sound professional expertise in the field of aging. Disciplinary competence is the first requirement for effective interdisciplinary practice.

This paper asserts that beyond the knowledge areas related to work with and on behalf of older persons, social work education should be related to team practice. The framework of context, structure, process and outcomes (Saltz, 1992a) was presented (see Figure 2) in order to outline core areas of knowledge and skill essential for interdisciplinary work. Interdisciplinary practice skills are important generically to social work, thus deserving integration into the curriculum of the profession. Other client populations require interventions delivered by multiple disciplines, e.g., developmentally disabled persons (Thyer & Kropf, 1995), chronically mentally ill persons, and persons with HIV/AIDS. Thus, the integration of an interdisciplinary perspective to social work curriculum is warranted. Specific examples of older adults and persons with other complex constellations of needs could be presented in curriculum modules.

The interdisciplinary team focus groups conducted as part of a CSWE-funded Millenium Project (Saltz & Damron-Rodriguez, 1998) identified barriers to addressing interdisciplinary practice within the curriculum and in field education. These include the challenge of adding special classes in an otherwise full curriculum which has also been identified as the major barrier for curriculum change related to social work education in aging (Damron-Rodriguez & Lubben, 1997). The integration versus specialization dialog is ongoing in the profession; for the arena of interdisciplinary skills, it is recommended that content on teams be integrated into the curriculum for all students.

Related to the model presented in Figure 2, **context** may be addressed through examples from organizational development and policy classes, which can relate to teams within organizations and the impact of policy on practice with specific populations within delivery systems. **Structure** and **process** aspects of teams can be addressed in group work classes where the interdisciplinary team is seen as a special form of face-to-face group. Direct practice classes as well can assist in the professional identity issues for social workers and assist in relating this process for their profession with other disciplines. **Outcome** issues for teams are relevant for evaluation and research classes.

Increasingly, social work practice with older adults and with many multi-need populations will require work within a team practice mode. The profession must prepare new professionals not only to know who they are in relation to the client but to other disciplines as well. Social workers must bring their knowledge to interdisciplinary practice in service not only to the client and family, but to promote the optimal functioning of the team as well. Social work is particularly suited to play a major facilitating role in the effectiveness of interdisciplinary teams and to envision new models of team practice (e.g., Corley, 2001). The framework provided here is a comprehensive approach for educating social workers to recognize policy and organizational factors relevant to teams, to understand group structure and process, to intervene and advocate the best outcomes for clients and their families, and to promote optional functioning of the team itself.

REFERENCES

Berkman, B., Dobrof, R., Harry, L., & Damron-Rodriguez, J. A. (1997). White paper: Social work. In S. M. Klein (Ed.) *A national agenda for geriatric education: White papers*. New York: Springer Publishing Company, 53-85.

Bernard, M., Connelly, R., Kuder, L., Mellor, J., Norman, L., & Tsukuda, R. A. (1997). White Paper: Interdisciplinary education. In S. M. Klein (Ed.) *A national agenda for geriatric education: White papers*. New York, NY: Springer Publishing Company.

Brunner, B. K. (1995). The use of work teams: A help or hindrance to performance? *Topics in Health Information Management, 16*, 32-40.

Campbell, L. (1992a). Team leadership. In American Congress of Rehabilitation Medicine (Ed.), *Guide to interdisciplinary practice in rehabilitation settings*. Gleview, IL: Editor.

Campbell, L. J. (1992b). Team maintenance and enhancement. In American Congress of Rehabilitation Medicine (Ed.), *Guide to interdisciplinary practice in rehabilitation settings*. Glenview, IL: Editor.

Chronicle Guidance Publications (1999). Geriatric Social Workers, Brief 534, Moravia, NY: Chronicle Guidance Publications, Inc.

Clark, P. G. (1997). Values in health care professional socialization: Implications for geriatric education in interdisciplinary team work. *The Gerontologist, 37* (4), 441-451.

Clark, P. G., & Drinka, T. J. K. (Eds.) (1994). Conceptual foundations for interdisciplinary education in gerontology and geriatrics, *Educational Gerontology 20* (1).

Corley, C. S. (in press). Health, spirituality, and healing. In T. Tirrito & T. Cascio (Eds.), *Religious organizations in community services*. New York: Springer.

Corley, C. S. (2001). The spirit of teamwork and the evolution of interdisciplinary education and practice. Presented at the Annual Meeting of the Gerontological Society of America, November 2001, Chicago, IL.

Damron-Rodriguez, J. A., Frank, J., Heck, E., Liu, D., Sragow, S., Cruise, P., & Osterweil, D. (1998). Physician knowledge of community-based care: What's the score? *Annals of Long-Term Care, 6* (4), 112-121.

Damron-Rodriguez, J. A., & Lubben, J. E. (1997). The 1995 WHCoA: An agenda for social work education and training. *Journal of Gerontological Social Work, 27* (3), 65-77.

Damron-Rodriguez, J. A., Villa, V., Tseng, H. F., & Lubben, J. E. (1997). Demographic and organizational influences on the development of gerontological social work curriculum. *Gerontology and Geriatrics Education, 17* (3), 3-18.

Drinka, T. J. K. (1994). Interdisciplinary geriatric teams: Approaches to conflict as indicator of potential to model teamwork. *Educational Gerontology, 20*, 87-103.

Frank, J., and DellaPenna, R. (1998). Geriatric team training in managed care organizations. In Siegler, E. L., Hyer, K., Fulmer, T., & Mezey, M. (Eds.). *Geriatric interdisciplinary team training.* New York, NY: Springer, 149-163.

Frank, J., DellaPenna, R., Alfarich, T., Damron-Rodriguez, J., Waite, M., Meltzer, P., & Cardagan, M. (1998). Geriatric Interdisciplinary Team Managed Care Training of Trainers Program. University of California and Kaiser Permanente.

Frank, R. G. & Elliott, T. R. (1992). Conflict resolution and feedback. In American Congress of Rehabilitation Medicine (Ed.), *Guide to interdisciplinary practice in rehabilitation settings.* Glenview, IL: Editor.

Garner, H. G. (1992a). Information sharing and communication. In American Congress of Rehabilitation Medicine (Ed.), *Guide to interdisciplinary practice in rehabilitation settings.* Glenview, IL: Editor.

Garner, H. G. (1992b). Team problem solving and decision making. In American Congress of Rehabilitation Medicine (Ed.), *Guide to interdisciplinary practice in rehabilitation settings.* Glenview, IL: Editor.

Gibelman, M., & Schervish, P. H. (1997). *Who we are: A second look.* Washington, D.C.: NASW Press.

Jette, A. (1996). Disability trends and transitions. In Binstock, R. & George, L., (Eds.), *Handbook of aging and social sciences.* San Diego, CA: Academic Press, 94-117.

Johnson, P. W., & Johnson, F. P. (1991). *Joining together: Group theory and group skills.* Englewood Cliffs, NJ: Prentice Hall.

Katzenbach, J. R., & Smith, D. K. (1993). *The wisdom of teams.* New York: Harper Collins.

Lubben, J., Damron-Rodriguez, J., & Beck, J. (1992). A national survey of aging curriculum in schools of social work. *Journal of Gerontological Social Work, 18*, (3/4), 157-171.

McClane, W. E. (1992a). The context for teamwork. In American Congress of Rehabilitation Medicine (Ed.), *Guide to interdisciplinary practice in rehabilitation settings.* Glenview, IL: Editor.

McClane, W. E. (1992b). Evaluation and accountability. In American Congress of Rehabilitation Medicine (Ed.), *Guide to interdisciplinary practice in rehabilitation settings.* Glenview, IL: Editor.

Mellor, M. J., & Lindeman, D. (1998). The role of the social worker in interdisciplinary geriatrics teams. *Journal of Gerontological Social Work, 30* (3/4), 3.

National Academy on an Aging Society (2000). Caregiving: Helping the elderly with activity limitations. Washington, D. C.: National Academy on an Aging Society, No. 7, 1-6.

National Center for Health Statistics (1990). Current estimates from the National Health Interviews Survey: U. S. 1989, Vital and Health Statistics, Series 10, 197.

Ouslander, D., Brummel-Smith, K., & Beck, J. (2000). *Comprehensive geriatric assessment.* New York: McGraw Hill.

Pew Health Professions Commission & California Primary Care Consortium. (1995). Interdisciplinary collaborative teams in primary care: A model curriculum and resource guide. San Francisco, CA: Pew Health Professions Commission.

Pew Health Professions Commission (1995). Health professions education and managed care: Challenges and necessary responses. San Francisco, CA: UCSF Center for the Health Professions.

Rothberg, J. S. (1992). Knowledge of disciplines, roles, and functions of team members. In American Congress of Rehabilitation Medicine (editor), *Guide to interdisciplinary practice in rehabilitation settings.* Glenview, IL: Editor.

Rubenstein, L. Z., Stuck, A. E., Soi. A. L., & Weiland, D. (1991). Impacts of geriatric evaluation and management programs on defined outcomes: Overview of the evidence. *Journal of the American Geriatrics Society (Supplement), 30,* 85-165.

Saltz, C. C., & Schaeffer, T. (1996). Interdisciplinary teams in health care: Integration of family caregivers. *Social Work in Health Care, 22* (3), 59-70.

Saltz, C. C. (1992a). A guide to the Guide. In American Congress of Rehabilitation Medicine (Ed.), *Guide to interdisciplinary practice in rehabilitation settings.* Glenview, IL: Editor.

Saltz, C. C. (1992b). Stages and structure in team development. In American Congress of Rehabilitation Medicine (Ed.), *Guide to interdisciplinary practice in rehabilitation settings.* Glenview, IL: Editor.

Saltz, C. C. (1996). Promoting skills in evaluating interdisciplinary geriatric teams. *Gerontology and Geriatrics Education, 16* (4), 70-90.

Saltz, C. C., & Damron-Rodriguez, J. C. (1998). Interdisciplinary education: A social work sourcebook. Alexandria, VA: Council on Social Work Education.

Scharlach, A., Damron-Rodriguez, J., Roberson, B., & Feldman, R. (2000). Educating social workers for an aging society: A vision for the 21st century. *Journal of Social Work Education, 36,* 521-538.

Scholtes, P. R. (1988). *The team handbook: How to use teams to improve quality.* Madison, WI: Joiner, Assoc.

Sundstrom, E., deMeuse, K. P., & Futrell, D. 1990). Work teams: Applications and effectiveness. *American Psychologist, 45,* 120-133.

Thyer, B., & Kropf, N. (Eds.) (1995). *Developmental disabilities: A handbook for interdisciplinary practice.* Cambridge, MA: Brookline Books.

Tuckman, B. W. (1965). Developmental sequences in small groups. *Psychological Bulletin, 63,* 384-399.

U. S. Bureau of the Census (1996). Current populations reports, Special Studies, pp. 23-190, 65+ in the United States. Washington, D. C.: U. S. Government Printing Office.

U. S. Bureau of the Census (1992). Census of population. Washington, D. C.: U. S. Government Printing Office.

U. S. Bureau of Labor Statistics (1992). Current Population Survey, Annual Average Data. Washington, D. C.: U. S. Government Printing Office.

U. S. News & World Report. Twenty hot job tracks: The best 1996 career guide (1995, October 30). *U. S. News & World Report, 119* (7), 98.

Waite, M. S., Harker, J. O., Messerman, L. I. (1994). Interdisciplinary team training and diversity: Problems, concepts and strategies. *Gerontology and Geriatrics Education, 15* (1), 65-82.

Waite, M. S., & Hoffman, S. B. (2001). Team Productivity. In G. D. Heinemann & A. M. Zeiss (Eds.), *Team Performance in health care: Assessment and development.* Kluwer Academic/Plenum Publishers.

Weiland, D., Kramer, B. J., Waite, M. S., & Rubenstein, L. Z. (1996). The interdisciplinary team in geriatric care. *American Behavioral Specialist, 39*, 655-664.

Zeiss, A., & Steffon, A. (1996). Interdisciplinary health care teams: The basic unit of geriatric care. In L. Cartensen, B. Edelstein, & L. Dombrand (Eds.), *The practical handbook of clinical gerontology.* Newbury Park, CA: Sage.

Chapter 4

Strategies to Increase Student Interest in Aging

Nancy P. Kropf, PhD

SUMMARY. Due to changing demographics, all social workers will have experience working with older clients and their families within professional roles. Unfortunately, social work education continues to lag in preparing students to be effective in practice with aging clients. Several strategies are presented with the goal of increasing student interest in the field of aging. At the program level, initiatives include using experiential learning, infusing aging content into required courses, and enhancing faculty capacity in aging. In addition, social work programs can build collaborations within the university setting and practice community. Overall, the goal is to present aging as an exciting and rewarding field of practice, and ensure that all students have the knowledge and skills to be effective in practice with older clients. *[Article copies available for a fee from The Haworth Document Delivery Service: 1-800-HAWORTH. E-mail address: <docdelivery@haworthpress.com> Website: <http://www.HaworthPress.com> © 2002 by The Haworth Press, Inc. All rights reserved.]*

Nancy P. Kropf is Associate Professor in Social Work, University of Georgia, and current President of the Association of Gerontology Education–Social Work (AGE-SW).

Address correspondence to: Nancy P. Kropf, PhD, School of Social Work, University of Georgia, Athens, GA 30602 (E-mail: nkropf@arches.uga.edu).

[Haworth co-indexing entry note]: "Strategies to Increase Student Interest in Aging." Kropf, Nancy P. Co-published simultaneously in *Journal of Gerontological Social Work* (The Haworth Social Work Practice Press, an imprint of The Haworth Press, Inc.) Vol. 39, No. 1/2, 2002, pp. 57-67; and: *Advancing Gerontological Social Work Education* (ed: M. Joanna Mellor, and Joann Ivry) The Haworth Social Work Practice Press, an imprint of The Haworth Press, Inc., 2002, pp. 57-67. Single or multiple copies of this article are available for a fee from The Haworth Document Delivery Service [1-800-HAWORTH, 9:00 a.m. - 5:00 p.m. (EST). E-mail address: docdelivery@haworthpress.com].

KEYWORDS. Aging, social work education, student interest in aging, recruitment strategies

Over the next few decades, the increase in the number of older adults is expected to be dramatic. The Census 2000 reports that during the decade of 1990 and 2000, the median age for the population increased from 32.9 years to 35.3 years of age. In addition, the number of mid life adults, those individuals aged 45-54 years, increased 49% from the 1990 statistics (U. S. Bureau of the Census, 2001). By 2030, the number of adults over age 65 is expected to climb to 70 million, or one in every five people (American Association of Retired Persons, 2000).

The number of older adults is rising rapidly, yet an important part of this "aging story" is the increase in the oldest segment of the population. In 2000, the number of Americans who were 85 years or older, which equaled four million adults, was 43 times larger than that cohort group in 1900 (U. S. Department of Health and Human Services, 2001). While the number of older adults in our society has risen sharply, this trajectory is expected to be even more steep in the coming decades.

In spite of this major demographic shift, the profession of social work has been slow to prepare students to work with older clients and their families. In one of the first discussions about labor force trends, Elaine Brody (1970) admonished social work for the lack of responsiveness to the field of aging. More than thirty years ago, she described the lack of trained and sensitive gerontological practitioners as a situation of "crisis proportions." In a recent interview about the state of gerontology in social work education, these statements were echoed by Abraham Monk, a pioneer in social work education and aging. Reflecting about progress in enhancing curricula in aging, he suggests that students continue to avoid work with older adults for other "more glamorized fields of practice" (AGE-SW, Spring 2001, p. 2). Clearly, there continues to be challenges in preparing students for effective practice with the older population.

With the demographics trends being so clear and convincing, what are the reasons that few social work students receive education about and pursue careers with older adults? Several factors seem to be involved in this situation including inadequate faculty preparation (Damron-Rodriguez & Lubben, 1997; Kropf, Schneider & Stahlman, 1993; Wendt & Peterson, 1993), low student interest (Berenbaum, 2000; Kane, 1999; Mosher-Ashley, 2000; Paton, Sar, Barber, & Holland, 2001) and curriculum/organizational barriers (Lubben, Damron-Rodriguez, & Beck, 1992). To overcome these obstacles, strategies must be implemented to recruit students into aging at all curriculum levels.

The overall objective is to portray the field of aging as an important, challenging, and rewarding area for social work practice.

THE CURRENT LEVEL OF STUDENT INTEREST IN AGING

By all accounts, student interest in working with the older population continues to remain low compared to other client populations. When compared to other fields of practice, gerontological social work ranked fifth behind the other contexts of mental health, child welfare, health, and family service (Scharlach, Damron-Rodriguez, Robinson, & Feldman, 2000). In fact, only about 10% of all MSW students select an aging course during their program of study (Damron-Rodriguez & Lubben, 1997). Student interest at the BSW level is also low, with about 5% of undergraduates reporting an interest in working with older adults (Kropf, et al., 1993). Regardless of the type of social work degree held, few students complete their education with a career goal to work with older adults, or identify themselves as gerontological social workers.

After graduation, however, many practitioners become aware of the importance of understanding aging-related issues. Most practitioners do not hold roles in settings where they primarily work with older clients, as less than 5% of NASW members have expertise in gerontology (Gibelman & Schervish, 1994). A more typical experience is working with older clients in age–integrated settings such as health care, mental health and other social welfare settings (Peterson & Wendt, 1990; Reed, Beall, & Baumhover, 1992). In a survey of NASW members, 62% of practitioners who did not work with older adults specifically reported that gerontology content was needed in their jobs (Peterson, 1990). Even social workers who hold gerontology or geriatric practice roles report inadequate preparation to work with their older clients (Gleason Wynn, 1995). Taken together, these findings suggest that after graduation, most students need to have some education and experience in working with issues involving older adults and their families, yet most do not study this content during their social work programs of study.

If student interest continues to remain low, what are the factors that motivate those students who do select aging courses and careers? One significant factor appears to be close contact with older adults. Relationships with older persons seem to promote a sense of caring that leads to a decision to work with this population (Kane, 1999; Paton et al., 2001). However, the type or meaning of the experience also must be examined as increased exposure to older adults does not necessarily translate into positive impressions (Cummings, Kropf & DeWeaver, 2000; Mosher Ashley, 2000). Similar to other stereotypes, negative experiences, such as only working with the very ill or functionally impaired, may promote a distancing between younger and older cohorts.

The expertise of faculty also is a factor in recruiting students into practice with older clients. When faculty convey excitement and experience working with older adults, students may select this field of practice and become energized to work with the older population. However, most social work programs have limited faculty resources in aging. At the MSW level, 75% of programs have no faculty member who is identified with aging (Damron-Rodriguez & Lubben, 1997). A similar situation exists at the baccalaureate level, where about 50% of programs have no faculty member who has expertise in gerontology (Kropf et al., 1993). Across the curriculum, few faculty are available to work with and develop student interest in the field of gerontology.

The limited number of faculty with gerontological expertise influences the type of content that is taught within the curriculum. As few students select aging electives, the opportunity to educate students about older adults is through infusing gerontology content into required courses. Given the fact that few faculty have expertise in aging, content on older adults is often sporadically covered or omitted entirely within required course sequences (Kropf et al., 1993). A striking fact is that most practicing social workers report that they received little to no prior knowledge or skill development in gerontology during their programs of study (Klein, 1996).

In summarizing the current status of gerontology in social work education, it appears that a significant proportion of students do not receive adequate instruction about aging. Compared to other client populations, the desire to work with older clients remains low in spite of demographic trends that indicate all social workers will face issues of aging within their practice. Unfortunately, low student interest is compounded by a lack of expertise in many social work faculty. Therefore, attempts to change this situation need to address multiple factors that currently exist within social work programs.

INCREASING STUDENT INTEREST

Clearly, social work educators and administrators need to implement more aggressive and creative strategies to better prepare students to work with the increasing number of older clients. On a positive note, several encouraging changes have recently taken place. The John A. Hartford Foundation is funding several initiatives to enhance gerontology capacity-building within the social work profession. These projects are targeted toward implementing field internship experiences in aging, strengthening curriculum options, supporting mid career faculty in gerontology, and recruiting and developing doctoral students in completing dissertation research in aging. The ultimate goal is to promote faculty development and increase program resources for student learning.

These initiatives alone, however, are insufficient to meet the expected labor force needs in gerontological social work. At the program level, departments can develop student interest through curriculum innovations and teaching methodologies. In addition, faculty development can be undertaken in several possible ways. At the institution level, programs can maximize the resources that are available within the college or university, as well as seek partnerships with community agencies that serve older adults. While major funding opportunities certainly enhance the ability to increase student interest in aging, most strategies can be implemented that are not contingent upon extramural funds.

Programmatic Initiatives

Teaching methodologies. Social work programs can use various approaches to increase aging content within the department and curriculum. Since exposure to older adults can provide students with an opportunity to dispel negative stereotypes of aging, one strategy is to have assignments include contact with the older population. Examples of course assignments could be visiting an agency that provides service to older adults (e.g., senior center, adult day care) or an interview with an older clients from a different cultural background. In order to prepare students for these types of assignments, the curriculum should be assessed to determine if course content represents the broad array of issues with the older population.

Experiential learning can also increase student interest in aging. In social work education, internships are one forum where students have the opportunity to practice with older clients. Through practicum experiences in aging placements, students become socialized as geriatric social workers and learn knowledge and skills specific to the older population. An even greater number of students complete practicum experiences in age integrated settings such as adult protective services, hospitals, and hospices. Although these settings provide services to individuals of all ages, a significant percentage of clients are older adults. Even though students may not have a particular interest in gerontology, internships in placements that serve older adults can foster an appreciation for the field of aging.

Service learning is another method to provide students with opportunities to work with older adults. Although service learning has been used extensively in other disciplines, this instructional methodology is relatively rare in social work education (Forte, 1997; Kropf & Tracey, 2000). Service learning has been defined as "structured learning" (Burns, 1998), a method to "participate in organized service activities to meet community needs" (Brandell & Hinck,

1997), and an opportunity to "engage students in real life experiences" (Morton & Troppe, 1996). Service learning typically involves collective learning where students and instructor partner with agencies around real needs within the community. Examples of service learning projects might be helping organize a community conference on some issues of aging (e.g., dementia, caregiving, spirituality) through the local senior center, or structuring a program for participants of an adult day care center.

Service learning has positive outcomes for both students and faculty members. For students, the opportunity to work with classmates can provide a "safer" environment in which they can challenge the myths of aging. In an evaluation of service learning in a long term care facility, for example, 90% of students reported that this project was useful in their education. In addition, significant positive changes were found in attitudes toward older adults from pre- to post-test (Hegeman, 1999). If service learning is sequenced early in programs of study, students might be more motivated to enroll in electives, pursue a specialization, or select their internship in aging.

Technology also provides an opportunity to enhance curriculum content in aging. Some evidence exists that older students are more motivated to pursue gerontology content than younger classmates (Kropf et al., 1993). Non-traditional students often struggle with issues which can create barriers within their education, (e.g., full time employment and family responsibilities) that can delay or stall their programs of study. Web-based or distance education courses provide a flexible method to meet the needs of these students and a survey elective on social work with older clients seems especially adaptable for web-based form. In addition, this type of format may also fulfill a continuing education function for current practitioners who need to enhance their knowledge and skills in this area.

Curriculum infusion. The changing demographics of the population indicate that all students should have some understanding about older individuals and their families. Instructional methods that isolate aging into discrete content (e.g., such as electives or aging concentrations) limit the potential audience to students who enroll in those courses. Several models exist that promote infusion within the curriculum (cf. Bogolub 1998; Cummings & Kropf, 2000; Kropf, 1996) and provide all students with exposure to the content area. In addition, aging resources that are currently available can be useful for infusion initiatives. Content from syllabi on aging courses (cf. Richardson, 1999), such as readings, activities, or audio visual material, can be extracted and introduced into other courses. Infusing aging content across the curriculum promotes the principle that all students will address gerontology-related issues in their roles as social workers.

In applying an infusion strategy, aging can be conceptualized in various ways. Some infusion models highlight the diversity within the older population, such as content on older adults who have developmental or psychiatric disabilities (Cummings & Kropf, 2000; Kropf, 1996). This type of strategy provides students with an understanding of the breadth of issues that older adults present to social workers, and can broaden student's perspective on mental health issues. Other population groups that are included in the curriculum, such as persons of color, women, gay/lesbian individuals, also present an opportunity to infuse aging content as issues about older members of these groups should be included within courses.

A different strategy is to conceptualize aging as an aspect of diversity (cf., Harrison, Wodarski, & Thyer, 1996). As with other forms of oppression such as racism, sexism or homophobia, older adults experience discrimination as a result of ageism in our society. Content that highlights the negative impact of stereotypes based upon age can be included in courses, and is especially relevant for practice, policy, and human behavior content.

Faculty development. An organizational barrier in teaching aging content is the low level of expertise that many faculty possess. Research indicates that many social work departments have few, if any, faculty members with interest in gerontology (Kropf et al., 1993; Lubben et al., 1992; Scharlach et al., 2000). A factor in enhancing aging content within the curriculum is developing faculty members' abilities to teach this content.

One method to increase faculty expertise is structuring co-teaching arrangements that provide instructors with an opportunity to develop a more solid skill base. For example, agency personnel who are gerontological social workers can be invited to co-teach courses with faculty. In addition to strengthening academic and practice-based relationships, this strategy promotes an integration of aging content within the course. An alternative model is to partner with other programs that have a higher degree of aging expertise represented on the faculty. One example of this type of arrangement is the Distance Learning Partnership in Gerontology developed within the State of Georgia (Malone, Schmidt & Poon, 1998). In this program, distance learning sites are paired together between schools that have various levels of expertise. "Lead instructors," or those faculty who have a greater knowledge base, partner with schools that are beginning to develop gerontology content. As instructors teach with "master teachers," they also enhance their ability to teach content within their own programs.

Research collaborations also develop faculty competence in aging, as well as attract students to gerontology. Projects that have an intergenerational focus are especially fruitful opportunities as faculty partner with colleagues who specialize in other practice contexts. One example is the Project Healthy

Grandparent Model™ that provides support to grandparents who are raising grandchildren. This university-based intervention model brings together faculty and students to implement a legal, health, and psychosocial program within the community (Gaines, Kelley, & Spencer, 1997). In addition to being multidisciplinary, faculty with expertise in child welfare, health, and gerontology collaborate to implement and evaluate interventions with custodial grandparent families. As issues of aging are often central to the families' needs, this project expands the number of faculty and students who become involved with interventions for an older population.

Institutional support can also be provided to encourage faculty to become involved in gerontology associations. For example, the Association of Gerontology in Higher Education (AGHE) and the Association for Gerontology Education–Social Work (AGE-SW) both offer institutional memberships which allow multiple faculty from a program to join. In addition to receiving information that can enhance teaching, these organizations provide a forum for faculty to build a professional network of others who are interested in aging and education.

Environmental Modifications

Institutional collaborations. In addition to changing the internal structures of social work programs, initiatives can be mounted to expand aging education by fostering collaborations with other units within the university. University gerontology centers or departments are especially fruitful units with which to connect, as these programs often offer courses, continuing education, and faculty development opportunities. In addition, affiliated faculty may be resources and provide a network for professional development in aging.

Social work programs can evaluate various strategies that involve sharing resources with other units within the university. Building collaborations across programs can enhance course content, generate additional student credit hours, and serve as a method to recruit students into major courses or graduate programs. A fairly easy method to establish these collaborations is to cross list courses with other programs. A course on older families, for example, could be cross listed in social work and sociology. Cross listed courses are a mechanism to attract students from other departments, as well as provide a strategy to mount content that may not attract enough students from a single department.

Students may also be attracted to aging if there is some formalized "incentive" which can provide an additional advantage when pursuing jobs or graduate programs. Examples are establishing a minor or a certificate program which involves completing a series of aging-related courses. Depending on the level of support at the university, completion of these formalized courses of study may be part of a student's transcript or diploma.

Building community partnerships. Programs can also benefit by establishing partnerships with agencies in the community that have particular expertise in aging services. As already noted, service learning programs provide one opportunity to have students and faculty partner with community practitioners. Likewise, agency personnel are also valuable resources as co-teachers, adjunct faculty members, and guest presenters within social work courses.

Collaborative relationships can also create other avenues to enhance content and increase student interest in aging. Close working relationships between social work program and organizations may increase the likelihood that graduates will compete favorably in hiring decisions. Administrators that understand the curriculum and hold a favorable evaluation of the program overall, may be inclined to select job applicants who are alumni. If current students learn that graduates are obtaining jobs, they hold perceptions that jobs in aging do exist. In addition, faculty that have a grasp of service agencies can include content that is relevant to practice, and keep current with policy and practice developments that are taking place within the field.

In summary, demographics indicate that baccalaureate and graduate social work students will be faced with challenges that are a result of an increasingly older population. Unfortunately, social work continues to lag in educational preparation of students for this professional context. Although initiatives are developing that can assist in augmenting aging content, programs can be more responsive and proactive. Several methods are presented to increase the number of students and target alternative teaching methodologies, infusing content across the curriculum, and enhancing faculty expertise in aging. In addition, opportunities to partner with other university units and the practice community can stimulate both faculty and student interest in aging. Ultimately, the goal is to ensure that graduates in social work programs leave with an adequate knowledge and skill base to practice with older clients.

REFERENCES

American Association of Retired Persons (2000). A profile of Older Americans: 2000. <http://www.aarp.org>.

Association for Gerontology Education–Social Work (Spring 2001). Feature Interview with Dr. Abraham Monk. *AGEnda 19* (1), pp. 2 & 15.

Berenbaum, R. (2000). Motivating students in the helping professions to work with the aged. *Educational Gerontology, 26* (1), 83-96.

Bogolub, E. B. (1998). Infusing content about discharging legal responsibilities into social work practice classes: The example of mandated maltreatment reporting. *Journal of Teaching in Social Work. 17* (1/2) 185-199.

Brandell, M., & Hinck, S. (1997). Service learning: Connecting citizenship with the classroom. *NASSP Bulletin, 81*, (591), 49-56.

Brody, E. M. (1970). Serving the aged: Educational needs as viewed by practice. *Social Work, 15*, 42-51.

Burns, L. T. (1998). Make sure it's service learning, not just community service. *Education Digest, 64* (2), 38-41.

Cummings, S., & Kropf, N.P (2000). An infusion model for including content on elders with chronic mental illness in the curriculum. *Advances in Social Work, 1* (1), 93-105.

Cummings, S., Kropf, N. P., & DeWeaver, K. (2000). Knowledge of and attitudes toward aging among non-elders: Gender and race differences. *Journal of Women & Aging. 12* (1), 77-91.

Damron-Rodriguez, J., & Lubben, J. (1997). The 1995 WHCoA: An agenda for social work education and training. In C. Saltz (Ed.). *Social work response to the 1995 White House Conference on Aging: From issues to actions.* (pp. 65-77) New York: Haworth.

Forte, J. A. (1997). Calling students to serve the homeless: A project to promote altruism and community service. *Journal of Social Work Education, 33*, 151-166.

Gaines, S. K., Kelley, S. J., & Spencer, L. (1997). Creating health-focused academic community partnerships. *Metropolitan Universities*, 27-39.

Gibelman, M., & Schervish, P. H. (1994). Who we are: The social work labor force as reflected in the NASW membership. Washington, DC: NASW Press.

Gleason Wynn, P. E. (1995). Addressing the educational needs of nursing home social workers. *Gerontology and Geriatrics Education, 16* (2), 31-36.

Harrison, D. F., Wodarski, J. S., & Thyer. B. A. (Eds.). (1996). *Cultural diversity and social work practice.* (2nd ed.), Springfield, IL: Charles C. Thomas.

Hegeman, C. R. (1999). Service learning in elder care. Paper presented at the Gerontological Society of America Annual Conference, San Francisco, November.

Kane, M. N. (1999). Factors affecting social work student's willingness to work with elders with Alzheimer's Disease. *Journal of Social Work Education, 35* (1), 71-85.

Klein, S. (Ed.). (1996). *A national agenda for geriatric education: White papers.* Rockville, MD: Health Resources and Services Administration.

Kropf, N.P. (1996). Infusing content on older people with developmental disabilities into the curriculum. *Journal of Social Work Education, 32* (2), 215-226.

Kropf, N. P., Schneider, R. L., & Stahlman, S. D. (1993). Status of gerontology in baccalaureate social work education. *Educational Gerontology 19* (7), 623-634.

Kropf, N. P., & Tracey, M. (2000). Service learning as a transition to foundation field. Paper presented at the Annual Program Meeting of the Council on Social Work Education, New York.

Lubben, J. E., Damron-Rodriguez, J., & Beck, J. C. (1992). A national survey of aging curriculum in schools of social work. *Journal of Gerontological Social Work, 18* (3/4).

Malone, D. M., Schmidt, M., & Poon, L. (1998). The distance learning partnership in gerontology: The Georgia model for gerontology higher education. *Educational Gerontology, 24* (3), 247-265.

Morton, K., & Troppe, M. (1996). From the margin to the mainstream: Campus compact's project on integrating service with academic. *Journal of Business Ethics, 15,* 121-132.

Mosher-Ashley, R. R. (2000). Factors influencing college students to choose careers working with elderly persons. *Educational Gerontology, 26* (8), 725-736.

Paton, R. N., Sar, B. K., Barber, G. R., & Holland, B. E. (2001). Working with older persons: Student views and experiences. *Educational Gerontology, 27* (2), 169-183.

Peterson, D. A. (1990). Personnel to serve the aging in the field of social work: Implications for educating professionals. *Social Work, 35* (5), 412-415.

Peterson, D. A., & Wendt, P. F. (1990). Employment in the field of aging: A survey of professionals in four fields. *The Gerontologist, 30,* 679-684.

Reed, C. C., Beall, S. C., & Baumhover, L. A. (1992). Gerontological education for students in nursing and social work: Knowledge, attitudes, and perceived barriers. *Educational Gerontology, 18,* 625-636.

Richardson, V. (Ed.) (1999). Teaching gerontological social work: A compendium of model syllabi. Alexandria, VA: Council on Social Work Education.

Scharlach, A., Damron-Rodriguez, J., Robinson, B., & Feldman, R. (2000). Educating social workers for an aging society: A vision for the 21st century. *Journal of Social Work Education, 36* (3), 521-538.

U. S. Bureau of the Census (2001, May 15, 2001). Nation's median age highest ever. <http://www.census.gov/Press-Release/www/2001/cb01cn67.html>.

U. S. Department of Health and Human Services (2001). HHS Fact Sheet; HHS Programs and initiatives for an aging America *<http://www.hhs.gov/news>.*

Wendt, P. F., & Peterson, D. A. (1993). Developing gerontological expertise among higher education faculty. *Educational Gerontology, 19,* 59-70.

SECTION II.
SCHOOL BASED INITIATIVES

Introduction to Section II

M. Joanna Mellor, DSW
Joann Ivry, PhD

Sections II and III focus on a range of specific projects and programs designed to develop social workers for geriatric social work practice. The articles in Section II are bound by a common thread in that the programs described are all recipients of John A. Hartford Foundation funding and offer concrete examples of the vision outlined by Robbins and Rieder. Robbins and Rieder trace the history and rationale for the Hartford initiative and describe its various projects. The three following chapters represent one facet of this initiative, the Practicum Partnership Program, and provide the reader with an "up-front" image of a vision becoming reality, as well as a detailed understanding of three specific programs located at the University at Albany School of Social Welfare; University of Michigan School of Social Work; and Hunter College School of Social Work/Brookdale Center on Aging. The three other Practicum Partnership Programs, while not represented here, offer similarly targeted programs. They are administered by the University of Houston Graduate School of Social Work in partnership with the Social Work Program of Texas Southern University; the Southern California Geriatric Social Work Consortium; and the Hart-

[Haworth co-indexing entry note]: "Introduction to Section II." Mellor, M. Joanna, and Joann Ivry. Co-published simultaneously in *Journal of Gerontological Social Work* (The Haworth Social Work Practice Press, an imprint of The Haworth Press, Inc.) Vol. 39, No. 1/2, 2002, pp. 69-70; and: *Advancing Gerontological Social Work Education* (ed: M. Joanna Mellor, and Joann Ivry) The Haworth Social Work Practice Press, an imprint of The Haworth Press, Inc., 2002, pp. 69-70. Single or multiple copies of this article are available for a fee from The Haworth Document Delivery Service [1-800-HAWORTH, 9:00 a.m. - 5:00 p.m. (EST). E-mail address: docdelivery@haworthpress.com].

10.1300/J083v39n01_07   69

ford Bay Area Consortium at University of California, Berkeley. The last article in this section, by Lubben and Harootyan, addresses the shortage of doctoral leadership in gerontology/geriatrics and discusses the Hartford Doctoral Fellows Program as a means of cultivating "geriatric social work faculty to become teachers, role models and mentors" to the social work profession.

Chapter 5

The John A. Hartford Foundation
Geriatric Social Initiative

Laura A. Robbins, MS
Corinne H. Rieder, EdD

SUMMARY. This article chronicles the development and implementation of the John A. Hartford Foundation Geriatric Social Work Initiative–a grantmaking program with total funding of $22 million, as of December, 2001. The Foundation aims to improve the care of older adults by increasing the capacity of social workers to care for them. The article describes a variety of grants to improve the gerontological training of future social workers. *[Article copies available for a fee from The Haworth Document Delivery Service: 1-800-HAWORTH. E-mail address: <docdelivery@haworthpress.com> Website: <http://www.HaworthPress.com> © 2002 by The Haworth Press, Inc. All rights reserved.]*

KEYWORDS. Geriatrics, gerontology, curriculum, faculty development, philanthropy practicum

Laura A. Robbins is Senior Program Officer, and Corinne H. Rieder is Executive Director and Treasurer, The John A. Hartford Foundation, 55 East 59th Street, New York, NY 10022.

[Haworth co-indexing entry note]: "The John A. Hartford Foundation Geriatric Social Initiative." Robbins, Laura A., and Corinne H. Rieder. Co-published simultaneously in *Journal of Gerontological Social Work* (The Haworth Social Work Practice Press, an imprint of The Haworth Press, Inc.) Vol. 39, No. 1/2, 2002, pp. 71-90; and: *Advancing Gerontological Social Work Education* (ed: M. Joanna Mellor, and Joann Ivry) The Haworth Social Work Practice Press, an imprint of The Haworth Press, Inc., 2002, pp. 71-90. Single or multiple copies of this article are available for a fee from The Haworth Document Delivery Service [1-800-HAWORTH, 9:00 a.m. - 5:00 p.m. (EST). E-mail address: docdelivery@haworthpress.com].

http://www.haworthpress.com/store/product.asp?sku=J083
© 2002 by The Haworth Press, Inc. All rights reserved.
10.1300/J083v39n01_08

As of December 2001, the John A. Hartford Foundation has committed more than $22 million to the expansion of geriatric social work education in the United States. While only four years have elapsed since the Initiative's beginning, the authors were invited to write this chapter, to document the program's conceptual underpinnings and its early development.

The Hartford Geriatric Social Work Initiative (see author notes) seeks to strengthen and advance social worker's practice with older adults by enhancing school's capacity to train aging competent social workers. It is designed to build on the small cadre of geriatrically knowledgeable social workers and develop leaders for the future. It is also developing an expanded infrastructure in academic and professional organizations, which can sustain a focus on the needs of America's older adults.

THE HARTFORD GERIATRIC SOCIAL WORK INITIATIVE

Today, the Hartford Geriatric Social Work Initiative collaborates with social work education programs to prepare needed, aging-savvy social workers and improve the care and well-being of older adults and their families. Specifically, the Initiative:

1. *Cultivates faculty leaders in gerontological education and research* through a *Faculty Scholars Program,* which supports the career development and research of talented faculty, and a *Doctoral Fellows Program,* which provides dissertation support, mentorship and leadership development for promising students;

2. *Creates excellent training opportunities in real-world settings* through a *Practicum Partnership Program,* which is developing and testing innovative, aging-rich rotational field experiences for graduate students that connect communities and schools of social work; and

3. *Creates new gerontological curricula and other teaching tools* through a *Faculty Development Program,* which is strengthening the ability of social work to develop, integrate and teach aging content in new and existing courses. This is being accomplished through training, information exchange and dissemination, and through a *Geriatric Enrichment Program,* which is expanding the number and quality of aging courses and learning experiences focused on aging at both the undergraduate and graduate levels.

BACKGROUND

The John A. Hartford Foundation

The family fortune that provided the Hartford Foundation's endowment came from the Great Atlantic and Pacific Tea Company, known to generations of grocery shoppers as the A & P. The Hartford Foundation was established in 1929 by John A. Hartford, the company's president whose father had founded the A & P grocery chain in the 1850s. When John and his brother George, who served as chairman of the A & P board, died in the 1950s, the bulk of their estates were left to the Foundation. Today, the Foundation's assets are nearly $600 million, with annual grants this year totaling $27 million.

In his wisdom, John Hartford felt that future generations of Trustees should have the freedom to determine the Foundation's direction, within the overall rubric of "doing the greatest good for the greatest number." Since its founding, the Foundation has concentrated attention on the health care field, an area where its founder and subsequent Trustees felt "the greatest good" could be done for humankind.

For the past 20 years, the Foundation has increasingly focused on the challenges of caring for our country's growing population of older adults. Hartford's Trustees and staff are committed to ensuring that both current and future health professionals who treat older adults–doctors, nurses, and social workers–are well trained in geriatrics and gerontology. The Foundation is also committed to developing, evaluating, and disseminating models of improved care so that all older adults have access to effective and affordable health care services.

Understanding the Need for More Aging-Savvy Social Workers

In 1998 one of the authors [LR] was primary care giver to three frail older adults, two parents–one with Alzheimer's disease and one revolving through hospitals and rehabilitation care–and an aunt with diabetes and heart ailments who had recently lost her husband and who had no children. Though trying to meet their needs as best as possible, it was clear after Aunt Tina's third hospitalization within two months of her husband's death, that a better care system was needed. In retrospect, it is evident how lucky we were to secure the services of a geriatric social worker. From the first moment of her involvement with Aunt Tina, the social worker improved Tina's (and the author's) quality of life and spared the health system and its payers unnecessary costs. Tina's last years of life were safe and happy because of an excellent, well-trained social worker who understood the unique needs of older adults, the network of services available to apply to these needs, and who had the skills to be able to form and sustain a service plan that matched Tina's needs with what was available. The challenges and benefits reflected in this personal experience have been echoed in the Foundation's work during the last two decades.

The John A. Hartford Foundation has been supporting the development of America's geriatric care capacity since 1981. The more we have understood the complexity of services needed, financing streams employed, and the increasing diversity of the nation's older adults, the more it has become clear that older adults need professionals trained in assessment and service linkage to navigate successfully through the health and supportive service systems. Increased numbers of elderly, a move toward community-based care, earlier hospital discharges, and increased expectation of patient/family responsibilities–all have pointed to a heightened need for geriatric social workers. Further, the need for better approaches to helping older adults to maintain their independence and dignity has become increasingly clear. It was natural then, that the Foundation turned its attention to social work. After all, who knows the relationship of individuals to systems better than social workers, and who is better positioned to give a voice to older individuals?

The Foundation began to have some experience with the social work profession as part of its Aging and Health Program. Through its support of primarily medically-oriented projects over the prior twenty years, the Foundation had increasingly recognized that non-physician health professionals were key, particularly for frail elderly. The Foundation thus began funding projects that demonstrated the efficacy of partnering nurses, social workers, physician assistants, and paraprofessionals with primary care physicians in order to address the psycho-social aspects of elder patient's care. Then, in response to a need expressed by health care employers, the Foundation supported the development of new approaches to *training* health professionals on how to be effective team members for geriatric care. Through these projects, the Foundation gained an increasing appreciation for the important role of the social work professional.

What also became apparent, however, was the distance between the geriatric knowledge base of existing social workers and that which would be needed to serve the growing number of older adults. This prompted an exploration into the ways to assist the social work profession build its geriatric capacity.

The Exploration Process

Foundation staff began an exploration of geriatric social work. Literature searches led to experts, experts led to other leaders and conversations with national social work professional organizations. After six months of research, and the generous sharing of information and experience by interviews with approximately 30 experts, patterns began to emerge. While there had been a few pioneers in the field and some periodic funding to stimulate the development of a geriatric social work capacity, particularly from federal sources, little consistent and dedicated attention had been given to this field. Although there are more than 600,000 practicing social workers, few were specially trained to meet the needs of the elderly. In 1987, the National Institute on Aging projected the need for 40-50,000 geriatric social workers, yet barely 10 percent of that number existed. In the absence of a deliberate effort to increase these numbers, the projected 60-70,000 geriatrically-knowledgeable (or what we have come to call "aging-savvy") social workers needed by 2020 would not be available.

The most compelling finding from our research, however, was the apparent mismatch between the need for geriatric knowledge by practicing social workers and the training that they received in this area. The results of a survey by the National Association of Social Workers[1] found that 62 percent of social workers in practice said they needed aging information. However, research by Joanne Damron Rodriguez in 1997[2] found that less than 3 percent of social workers received training on older adults and their needs and illnesses. This profound disparity between the demand for and the current and future *aging-savvy* social workers, ultimately led the Foundation to its commitment to supporting geriatric social work development.

Once the need was clear, the Foundation set out to explore whether its limited resources coupled with its funding style and historic strengths were a good match to address this need. After more consultation with experts, an advisory committee of eleven thoughtful and experienced social work educators and providers were convened on July 30,1997 in New York City. The collective 333 years of experience represented in the room helped to narrow the scope of a potential response to three areas: enhancing geriatrics in the social work curriculum, strengthening geriatrics for current social workers in practice, and improving social work services for the elderly. Commissioned white papers in each of these areas by teams of social work practitioners and educators led the Foundation to conclude that the best starting point would be the education system. If successful, the other areas would be addressed in the future.

During this program development phase, one additional key point emerged. There was an important disconnect between social work practice and the colleges and universities that educated and trained social workers[3]. The Foundation's emerging program, would need to bridge that gap, as well.

First Phase: Testing Approaches, Building Awareness

To date, the Hartford Geriatric Social Work Initiative has included six projects, three of which were contemplated at its outset. In June 1998 the nine members of the Hartford Foundation's Board of Trustees reviewed a Program Initiative Proposal to strengthen geriatric social work. With Trustee approval, the proposed Initiative included endorsement of efforts to: (1) develop faculty members committed to research and teaching about the health and supportive needs of elders; (2) develop field training sites necessary for students to gain a true appreciation of the need for, and rewards of, geriatric social work; and (3) build consensus on standards for geriatric social work training and a clearinghouse for geriatric teaching tools. Woven throughout would be an effort to strengthen the connections between those institutions that provide care to the elderly and those that educate the professionals who will go on to provide services. With the Trustee's unanimous endorsement, the Foundation launched the Hartford Geriatric Social Work Initiative.

The three program areas delineated in the Foundation Proposal were targeted to address three obstacles to the development of geriatric social workers. These limitations and the Foundation's program responses are outlined in the following sections. In the development of these efforts, we benefited greatly from the insights provided in a white paper written for the Foundation, Educating Social Workers for an Aging Society: A Vision for the Twentieth Century (A. Sharlach et al., 1998).

Creating Awareness and Consolidating Resources

The Initiative awarded its first grant to the Council on Social Work Education (CSWE), the sole accrediting body for social work baccalaureate and master's programs. In September 1998, the Foundation's Trustees approved a $574,988 grant over two years. "SAGE-SW"–Strengthening Aging and Gerontology Education for Social Work–was created under the leadership of Joan Zlotnik, PhD, then special assistant to the president at CSWE. The project sought to (1) assess current social work education materials for aging content, (2) determine core competencies for MSW students specializing in aging as well as minimum competencies that all BSW students should acquire to help older persons maximize their potential for well-being; (3) identify and describe "best practices models" in gerontological social work education; and (4) develop a "blueprint" to move geriatric social work education from current capacities to best practices.

Project staff developed a network of interested educators, conducted focus groups of aging-interested and non-aging interested faculty, and collected geriatric education materials. In addition they commissioned a survey that resulted in a delineation of 63 aging-related competencies that all social workers should have upon completion of their education, as well as those that aging specialists should have. A Web site (www.cswe.org/sage-sw) and newsletter served to share information broadly, and project staff and others provided technical assistance to help programs interested in further developing aging content. The CSWE's Web site now has a geriatrics section, gerontological news is often in its quarterly newsletters, and the number of sessions dedicated to social work at its annual meeting have increased. In addition to the specific aging-related resources developed and gathered, the SAGE-SW project sounded a call to alert CSWE members to the need to prepare for the rapidly aging society in which their graduates will be working. The project culminated in "A Blueprint for the New Millennium," which provides an outline for an approach to significantly enhance geriatric and gerontological content into social work.

Faculty Shortage→Faculty Scholars

The second grant funded in the Initiative began to create the next generation of academic leaders to help to address the needs of the aging population.

In the absence of faculty to serve as mentors, role models, and leaders who can advance the science of caring for older adults, few students have the opportunity to experience the richness, importance and excitement of geriatric social work. Also, in the absence of geriatric faculty who can create new knowledge through their research, improvements in care for older adults have been slow to evolve. One goal of the Geriatric Social Work Initiative, therefore, is to create more such faculty leaders. The Hartford Geriatric Faculty Scholars represented the first step towards this goal. It was designed to attract and retain outstanding junior faculty committed to geriatric social work. At its inception, the Program identified four outcomes, to:

- Build the leadership development and enhance the skills of ten Hartford Geriatric Social Work Faculty Scholars poised to become the next generation of leaders in geriatric social work education;
- Increase the visibility and desirability of geriatric social work, supported by new knowledge generated and reported by the Scholars through publications, workshops and presentations at major conferences;
- Establish a network of Hartford Geriatric Social Work Faculty Scholars who will continue their development beyond the scope of the project; and
- Create a network of Hartford Geriatric Social Work Mentors as an ongoing continuing vehicle for the development of further Scholars.

In March 1999, the Board of Trustees approved a $2,304,856 grant to support the Scholars program. Designed and co-led by Barbara Berkman, PhD, Helen Rehr/Ruth Fizdale Professor of Social Work at Columbia University, and Linda Harootyan, MSW, Deputy Director of the Washington-based Gerontological Society of America, the program protected time for faculty and provided them with the skills that would enhance the likelihood of their successful emergence as leaders in the field. Each of the named Hartford Geriatric Social Work Faculty Scholars received two years of research support for a project focused on social work roles in improving geriatric outcomes, to be carried out in a community-based practice setting. They had explicit faculty development plans with local sponsors committed to the scholar's development at their own institutions. National geriatric social work mentors (chosen from among the field's current leaders) also gave direction to the scholars. The two sets of mentors provided complementary guidance, one targeted to institutional professional success, the other to national geriatric leadership development. Finally, the Scholars participated in specially-created institutes to further develop their leadership, education, research skills, as well as networking. A national solicitation and an able selection committee led to the selection of 10 highly talented faculty from 10 master's programs from around the country.

During the course of the program, these committed individuals have begun to emerge as leaders of the future, and have collectively coalesced as a group charged to create change. (A list of these Hartford Geriatric Social Work Faculty Scholars and their projects can be found in Appendix A.) In 2000, the Trustees approved an expansion of this program, as described later in the chapter.

Aging-Rich Practicum Shortage→Practicum Partnership Program

Because where social work students do their practica is a predictor of what kind of job they seek, it is no surprise that in the absence of gerontologically-oriented practica, limited numbers of students opted for careers in geriatric social work. The goal, therefore, of the Practicum Partnership Program (see Author Note) was to create more aging rich practicum sites and training experiences. During the planning process for this project, an advisory panel identified the characteristics of an excellent geriatric practicum site. These traits included exposure to elderly across the continuum of care (see Appendix B for others). In turn, a graduated process was designed to stimulate change in the master's programs' practica. First, all deans and directors of master's programs were provided with the criteria and invited to respond with a two-page letter of interest, outlining their institution's capacity to mount an aging-rich practicum program. Sixty-four programs responded, nearly half of the master's programs in the country. In retrospect, this overwhelming response was the Foundation's first indication that there was significant pent-up interest in geriatrics training that only needed a vehicle for expression. From these 64 schools, 38 were invited to submit planning proposals, and all invited schools did. In March 1999, the Foundation awarded the New York Academy of Medicine a grant, under the leadership of its Senior Vice President Patricia Volland, MSW, MBA, to serve as the coordinating center for the 11, $50,000 practicum planning projects, which were selected. The award required the creation of a consortia comprised of a master's program in social work and a minimum of five community-based service providers, at least two of which had to be new to the school. Further, the criteria required that these practica include rotations for students so that they could experience the breadth of the service network, much as the older clients in the community would, by working with a variety of providers who served the whole continuum of older adults, from well to frail elderly. After nine months of planning and development of an implementation plan and site visits by the Foundation and coordinating center staff, six of the planning sites were selected to receive awards to support full implementation.

Initially, the Foundation had planned to support two years of implementation. However, during the pre-grant site visits to what would become the implementation sites, a few things became clear. First, successful institutional change would require more than two years of support. Second, each of the 11 planning projects had developed something novel, with the potential to increase the attractiveness and competence of graduating social workers. Finally, at each site visit, there were students truly eager to participate in an aging practicum. Therefore, the Foundation amended its plans and awarded three years of support to the six implementation sites (see Appendix C) and provided a pool of funds both to support the other planning grant schools to further develop their unique features, and to allow interested students from each of these schools to receive stipends to pursue aging practica. Here again, it was required that they rotate in their field placements in order to be exposed to a spectrum of agencies and older adults. In addition to each of the sites, the coordinating center for the program was awarded additional support to reflect the changes in the program's implementation. In total, the Foundation awarded $2,854,694 to the six demonstration sites and the expansion of the coordinating center.

Almost three years later, it is still premature to describe the full scope of the models and their effectiveness. An evaluation of the program is being conducted by the New York Academy of Medicine. As of this writing, 96 students have graduated from the program, and 126 others are currently enrolled. The majority of those who graduated have either accepted or are pursuing jobs in aging services. It has also become clear that the community partners are eager and happy to be included in the academic enterprise and that influencing the graduate curriculum of their future employees is important to them.

Second Stage: Acceleration, Expansion and New Directions

The response to the Hartford Geriatric Social Work Initiative surpassed the Foundation's expectations. It became apparent that a good deal of latent interest in geriatric social work surfaced rapidly, catalyzed by the program. Even recognizing that the availability of significant new funds through the Initiative represented a considerable attraction towards the area, there were many explicit and symbolic indicators of growing interest in the field. For example, special committees or interest groups were formed within the major social work organizations including the National Association of Deans and Directors, the National Association of Social Workers, and the Baccalaureate Program Directors. In addition, more social workers began attending the annual meeting of the Gerontological Society of America meeting. Because of this vigorous national response, as well as the number of applicants for each of the programs, and many individual communications to program and Foundation staff, the Foundation accelerated its funding in this area. Beginning in 2000, Hartford's Trustees authorized a second wave of projects. The next three major projects were designed to: (1) broaden the pipeline leading to faculty development; (2) significantly expand technical assistance and faculty development capacity in geriatric social work; and (3) support the geriatric enrichment of social work programs across the country. These programs are described below.

Leadership Development: Adding Cohorts to the Faculty Scholars Program; Adding the Doctoral Fellows Program

The Foundation understood that a critical mass of leadership faculty would be needed to ensure continued strengthening of the field. To this end, two additional steps were taken. The first was a renewal of the Hartford Faculty Scholars program in September 2000, of $5,641,227, to include an additional three cohorts of ten faculty, again to be supported for two years each. While the program was refined based on process evaluations of the first cohort's activities, the basic structure remained the same. By 2005 at the grant's conclusion, we expect that 40 Hartford Geriatric Social Work Faculty will have completed the program, and a vital, national network of outstanding faculty leaders will have been created.

The second step, also in September 2000, complemented the Faculty Scholars project and sought to broaden the pipeline of talented future faculty who would become geriatric social work leaders. With a five-year, $2,445,146 award to the Gerontological Society of America, the Foundation directed its resources towards doctoral candidates with geriatric academic career goals. The Doctoral Fellows Program, in essence, was designed to interrupt a "chicken-and-egg" cycle, which had limited entry into careers as academic geriatric social work faculty. With few aging-focused faculty available to provide financial support through research and teaching assistantships to doctoral candidates, few of these graduate students pursued an interest in aging. These future faculty were then diverted towards those areas in which faculty members with financial resources were available. The result has been few new faculty in aging, and a continuing and unhelpful cycle.

The Hartford Geriatric Social Work Doctoral Fellows Program was designed to attract and support a cadre of outstanding future faculty who are interested in aging, but who, in the absence of such support might have their interests diverted to other fields. It provides two years of dissertation support for each Fellow at $20,000 per year, which is matched by the equivalent of $10,000 from the Fellow's university. The Fellow's dissertations must address ways to improve the health and well being of older persons, their families, and caregivers. Like the Scholar's program, selection is based on the quality and importance of the project proposed, the applicant's commitment to aging, their leadership potential, and their university's commitment to their development. By the program's conclusion, 24 new faculty members in aging will have received support. Again, as in the Scholars program, a deliberate network among the Fellows is being fostered. Further, program elements have been designed to overlap the Faculty Scholars activities to connect to the two cohorts of committed (and we trust future) faculty leaders in geriatric social work. The program is under the joint leadership of James Lubben, DSW, MPH, Professor of Social Welfare and Urban Planning at the University of California, Los Angeles, and Linda Harootyan, MSW, Deputy Director of the Gerontological Society of America.

Building on SAGE-SW–Training Faculty, Creating New Curriculum

Social work faculty from around the country responded strongly to CSWE's first project, SAGE-SW. They expressed a clear interest in improving their ability to include aging in their courses. The Council's *Blueprint for the New Millennium* recognized the importance of incorporating the aging competencies, particularly at the basic foundation course level. In response, in March, 2001 the Trustees again awarded a grant to the CSWE, this time for $1,480,692 for three years. The new Faculty Development project was designed with two major thrusts, to: (1) train faculty who teach the required basic courses in social work programs to infuse geriatric content into their lessons–with a particular focus on baccalaureate programs; and (2) continue to develop, collect, and support the distribution of geriatric curricular materials to social work educators across the country. By the end of this grant, under the leadership of Frank Baskind, PhD, Dean of the Virginia Commonwealth University's School of Social Work, and CSWE's President, more than 400 baccalaureate and masters level social worker faculty will have learned how they can infuse more geriatric content into the foundation courses of social work. With the assistance of master teachers, participants in the Faculty Development seminars will learn to translate at least one of the competencies developed in the initial CSWE grant into lesson plans. In addition, annual meetings open to any educator or practitioner interested in geriatric social work will reinforce the network of interested individuals and further strengthen the field. Once again, the response thus far has exceeded expectations. While each Faculty Development Institute was designed to accommodate 35 participants, several of the Institutes have been oversubscribed, with requests of up to 80 applicants for the early seminars. Doubtless, some of the demand was stimulated by the Geriatric Social Work Initiative's other projects, particularly the final new component of the Initiative, the Geriatric Enrichment Program.

The GeroRich Program

The final award in the second wave of funding our Social Work Initiative responded to social work education program's interest in strengthening the geriatric content of their programs. Again, within the social work community, there appears to have been significant pent-up demand for support in aging. Responding to this interest, the Trustees approved a three-year, $5,244,254, grant to CSWE, this time directed by Nancy Hooyman, PhD, Professor of Social Work at University of Washington. The project is to move social work education and training towards a "transformed" gerontology curriculum–one that will have altered structure, organization, and learning outcomes so that it fully incorporates gerontology into social work training. The Geriatric Enrichment Program will work to ensure that gerontological learning opportunities are embedded in all relevant learning experiences for students. Challenged to propose ways in which every student in every year of training receives exposure to geriatrics, baccalaureate schools and master's programs were invited to submit proposals for up to $30,000 per year for two years. In addition, the program required participation for a third, unfunded year. Because of the Foundation's desire to reach a broad spectrum of schools nationally, the selection process included a diverse range of programs including public/private, small/medium/large, geographic diversity(including rural sites), and a range of innovations. One hundred and three of the 611 eligible programs submitted proposals.

Two Phases: A Hopeful Start

Between 1998, when the Hartford Geriatric Social Work Initiative was developed, and December 2001, geriatric social work has become more visible within social work education, some 200 schools have some enhanced involvement in geriatric social work education, and at least 130 agencies have developed collaborations with education institutions. Further, each of the participating professional social work organizations have developed a mechanism to address aging issues. At least $4 million from non-Hartford funding has been directed by private sources to geriatric social work. For example, the Hearst Foundation has awarded a total of $2.5 million in endowments for geriatric social work stipend support to 5 schools of social work. Other Foundations, such as the Archstone Foundation in California and the Burden Foundation in New York, have also made awards for geriatric social work enrichment to social work programs.

Finally, the Trustees and staff at the Hartford Foundation greatly appreciate and want to thank all those who have dedicated significant time and care to the development and execution of the Initiative and its constituent programs–from consultants to program leaders to applicants and other funders. Your contributions have helped to create an environment in which older adults in the future will be able to have the benefit of well-trained, knowledgeable, aging-savvy social workers.

AUTHOR NOTE

We have chosen to use the term "geriatric" rather than gerontological to describe our Initiative. While we understand that some in the social work community feel these terms describe significantly different aspects of theory and practice related to older people, we prefer to use them interchangeably and do so throughout this article.

The Practicing Partnership Program was originally called the Geriatric Social Work Practicum Implementation Project.

NOTES

1. Peterson, D. A., & Wendt, P. F. (1990), Employment in the Field of Aging: A Survey of Professionals in Four Fields, *The Gerontologist*, 30 (5), 679-684.

2. Damron-Rodriguez, J., Villa, V., Tseng, H. F., & Lubben, J. E., (1997) *Demographic and Organizational Influences on the Development of Gerontological Social Work Curriculum, Gerontology and Geriatrics Education*, 17 (3), 3-18.

3. Volland, P., Berkman, B., Stein, G., & Vaghy, A., (2000) Social Work Education for Practice in Health Care: Final Report, New York Academy of Medicine.

APPENDIX A

1999-2001 Hartford Geriatric Social Work Faculty Scholars

Margaret Adamek, PhD
Indiana University School of Social Work
Research project: Barriers to Treating Geriatric Depression in Long-Term Care: A Research Update.

Denise Burnette, PhD
Columbia University School of Social Work
Research project: Self-Care of Chronic Health Conditions: The Experience of Urban, African American Elders Self-Care.

Letha Chadiha, PhD
George Warren Brown School of Social Work
Washington University in St. Louis
Research project: Beyond Coping: An Empowerment Intervention with African Americans Caregivers of Dependent Low Income Elders.

Nancy Kropf, PhD
University of Georgia School of Social Work
Research project: "Let's Talk": A Intervention for Grandparents Raising Grandchildren.

Ji Seon Lee, PhD
Fordham University Graduate School of Social Services
Research project: Social Work Services and Patient Outcomes in Home Health Care.

Philip McCallion, PhD
SUNY-Albany School of Social Welfare
Research project: An Evaluation of the FDCE Program for Spouse Caregivers of Persons with Dementia.

Matthias Naleppa, PhD
Virginia Commonwealth University School of Social Work
Research project: Evaluation of Geriatric Task-Centered Case Management.

Cynthia Poindexter, PhD
Boston University School of Social Work
Research project: HIV-Infected and HIV-Affected Elders: Experiences, strengths, and needs.

Stephanie Robert, PhD
University of Wisconsin-Madison School of Social Work
Research project: Examining changes in publicly-funded long-term care services under Family Care-Wisconsin's pilot long-term care project.

Jeanette Semke, PhD
University of Washington in Seattle School of Social Work
Research project: Community Residential Care for Older Adults with Neuro-psychiatric Disorders.

2001-2003 Hartford Geriatric Social Work Faculty Scholars

Patricia Brownell, PhD
Fordham University, New York, NY
Research topic: Evaluation of the first elder abuse shelter in the U.S.

Sandra Sue Butler, MSW, PhD
University of Maine, Orono, ME
Research topic: Evaluation of the impact of the Senior Companion Program on elders and companions.

Sherry M. Cummings, MSW, PhD
University of Tennessee, Nashville, TN
Research topic: Evaluation of an interdisciplinary geriatric mental health team.

Charles A. Emlet, ACSW, PhD
University of Washington, Tacoma, WA
Research topic: Exploration of sources of social support for older adults with HIV/AIDS.

Betty J. Kramer, PhD
University of Wisconsin, Madison, WI
Research topic: Study of providers of end of life care for frail elders in managed care.

Hong Li, MSW, PhD
University of Illinois, Urbana, IL
Research topic: Examination of the adequacy of informal and formal services used by rural demented elders.

Yat-Sang (Terry) Lum, PhD
University of Minnesota, St. Paul, MN
Research topic: Analysis of factors influencing well-being of nursing home residents.

Ailee Moon, PhD
UCLA, Los Angeles, CA
Research topic: A crosscultural study of factors that influence practice responses to elder abuse.

Michael W. Parker, DSW
University of Alabama, Tuscaloosa, AL
Research topic: A study of long distance caregiving among U.S. army officers.

Tazuko Shibusawa, MSW, PhD
Columbia University, New York, NY
Research topic: A comparative study of partner abuse experienced by older Black, Latina, and Caucasian women.

The ten Scholars were selected by a National Program Committee comprised of: Dr. Amanda Barusch, University of Utah; Dr. David Biegel, Case Western Reserve University; Dr. Nancy Hooyman, University of Washington, Seattle; Dr. Amy Horowitz, Lighthouse International; Dr. Rosalie Kane, University of Minnesota; Dr. James Lubben, University of California, Los Angeles; Dr. Deborah Padgett, New York University; and Dr. Marsha Mailick Seltzer, University of Wisconsin-Madison.

National Selection Committee

The National Selection Committee is comprised of:

Dr. Amanda Barusch, University of Utah
Dr. David Biegel, Case Western Reserve University
Dr. Ruth Dunkle, University of Michigan
Dr. James Lubben, UCLA
Dr. Deborah Padgett, New York University

APPENDIX B

Essential Components for Geriatric Field Practicum Education

Required Components:

I. Practicum sites with well developed basic and aging specific practice

    A. Readiness to provide quality educational experiences
    B. Leadership in aging services with a commitment to learning
    C. Ability to enhance student knowledge of the aging population and the aging process and to support practice skill development
    D. Ability to expose students to client experiences along the aging continuum
    E. Ability to expose multidisciplinary practice

II. Consensus between Agency/School/Student

    A. Goals of field practicum clearly defined
    B. Learning objectives that incorporate the aging continuum effectively
    C. Standards for student training with clearly defined educational outcomes
    D. Clear communication and structured links between/among consortium members

III. Competent field supervision

    A. Understanding of adult learning styles
    B. Ability to provide structured learning experiences
    C. Experience and knowledge of the aging process

Desired Components:

IV. Integrated learning opportunities that connect field/course content

    A. Coordinated by field instructor
    B. Jointly taught by field instructor/faculty
    C. Peer (student) participation
    D. Student opportunities to integrate field/course content (i.e., class reports, rounds, practice based research, case discussions in class)

V. Agency practice/course content that reflects the current needs of the aging population along the continuum

    A. Cultural diversity
    B. Aging continuum
    C. Multidisciplinary practice

VI. Commitment to innovation by Council on Social Work Education standards

APPENDIX C

Practicum Implementation Sites

Hunter College, City University of New York
New York, NY
Rose Dobrof, DSW
Joann Ivry, PhD, ACSW
$325,000, Three Years

State University of New York, Albany
Albany, NY
Ronald W. Toooland, PhD
Anne E. Fortune, PhD
$323,640, Three Years

University of California, Berkeley
Berkeley, CA
Barrie Robinson, MSSW
Andrew Sharlach, PhD
$475,000, Three Years

University of Houston
Houston, TX
Virginia Cooke Robbins, LMSW, ACP
Ellen Stevens-Roseman, MSW, DSW, ACSW
$325,000, Three Years

University of Michigan
Ann Arbor, MI
Ruth Dunkle, PhD
Lily Jarman-Rhode, MSW
$325,000, Three Years

Partners In Care Foundation
Burbank, CA
W. June Simmons, LCSW
JoAnn Damron Rodriguez, PhD
$475,000, Three Years

Coordinating Center

New York Academy of Medicine
New York, NY
Patricia J. Volland, MSW, MBA
$606,054, Three Years

Chapter 6

Student Pioneers
and Educational Innovations:
Attracting Students to Gerontology

Abigail R. Lawrence, PhD, MSW
Lily Jarman-Rohde, MSW
Ruth E. Dunkle, PhD
Ruth Campbell, MSW
Harriet Bakalar, MSW
Lydia Li, PhD

SUMMARY. Recruitment of students into gerontological social work is an increasingly important issue as the population of older adults grows. This article describes one initiative designed to aid in the promotion of geriatric social work: the University of Michigan's Geriatric Fellowship Program. Using qualitative in-depth interviews with 13 MSW Fellows as well as survey data of 219 MSW students, the authors examine the moti-

Abigail R. Lawrence, Lily Jarman-Rohde, Ruth E. Dunkle, Harriet Bakalar, and Lydia Li are affiliated with School of Social Work, University of Michigan, 1080 South University Avenue, Ann Arbor, MI 48109. Ruth Campbell is affiliated with Turner Geriatric Clinic, University of Michigan Hospitals.

This project is supported by the John A. Hartford Foundation.

[Haworth co-indexing entry note]: "Student Pioneers and Educational Innovations: Attracting Students to Gerontology." Lawrence et al. Co-published simultaneously in *Journal of Gerontological Social Work* (The Haworth Social Work Practice Press, an imprint of The Haworth Press, Inc.) Vol. 39, No. 1/2, 2002, pp. 91-110; and: *Advancing Gerontological Social Work Education* (ed: M. Joanna Mellor, and Joann Ivry) The Haworth Social Work Practice Press, an imprint of The Haworth Press, Inc., 2002, pp. 91-110. Single or multiple copies of this article are available for a fee from The Haworth Document Delivery Service [1-800-HAWORTH, 9:00 a.m. - 5:00 p.m. (EST). E-mail address: docdelivery@haworthpress.com].

vating factors that led students to specialize in geriatric social work and to apply for a geriatric fellowship. Family exposure to aging issues, "accidental" exposure through volunteer work, enthusiastic role models, job opportunities, and recognition of a social problem frequently instigated student's interest in gerontological social work. Incentives for application to the Geriatric Fellowship Program include: the unique field placement rotation model, financial support, individualized attention, group learning opportunities, and assistance with job placement. Directions for future recruitment efforts are discussed. *[Article copies available for a fee from The Haworth Document Delivery Service: 1-800-HAWORTH. E-mail address: <docdelivery@haworthpress.com> Website: <http://www.HaworthPress.com>* © *2002 by The Haworth Press, Inc. All rights reserved.]*

KEYWORDS. Recruitment, geriatric social work, fellowship, education, field work

INTRODUCTION:
THE NEED TO RECRUIT STUDENTS
TO GERIATRIC SOCIAL WORK

Statistics concerning the rapidly rising population of older adults are cited frequently by educators and advocates for the elderly, and yet a concurrent rise in the population of geriatric social workers remains to be seen (National Institute on Aging, 1987). Projections of the need for health professionals through the year 2020 call for 20,000 additional social workers who understand the needs of older people, especially in the areas of prevention and management of disease and disabilities (NIA, 1987). Yet 21% of all MSW and BSW programs listed in the CSWE 1987 directory had no classroom faculty with aging expertise and 53% had no field faculty in aging. Only 4% of all MSW students even took an aging course during their graduate program (Lubben, Damron-Rodriguez & Becker, 1992).

In fact, social work students may actively avoid work with older people or provide fewer services to them. In examining the factors affecting the willingness of social work students to work with elders with Alzheimer's disease, Kane (1999) found that practice with that population was ranked last of 15 different practice areas. Rohan et al. (1994) discovered that oncological workers admitted that they were more likely to provide care to their younger patients than to their older ones. Even more discouraging, many social work students believe that the field of social work views the elderly negatively (Kane, 1999).

Without an adequate pool of professionals trained in geriatric social work, haphazard troubleshooting and makeshift solutions will come to replace appropriate and well-planned strategies for addressing the needs of the elderly population. The increasingly dire need for more geriatric social workers is clear.

The John A. Hartford Foundation is attempting to address this need for geriatric social workers through the development of four geriatric social work initiatives: The Hartford Scholars Program, which supports the development of junior faculty in gerontology; The CSWE-SAGE initiative, a clearinghouse for information on social work education in gerontology; the Doctoral Fellows Program; and the Geriatric Social Work Field Practicum Development Program, which is currently in place at six U. S. graduate schools of social work, including the University of Michigan.

In this paper we describe one initiative designed to aid in the promotion of geriatric social work: the Hartford Initiative as it is implemented through the University of Michigan School of Social Work Geriatric Fellowship Program. Preliminary evaluation of this program identified the motivating factors that led students to study geriatric social work and identified what attracted students to a geriatric fellowship.

THE UNIVERSITY OF MICHIGAN SCHOOL OF SOCIAL WORK GERIATRIC FELLOWSHIP PROGRAM

With funds from a Hartford Foundation planning grant in 1999-2000, the University of Michigan School of Social Work developed a consortium of 16 agencies that serve the elderly in Greater Detroit, Washtenaw County, and in Michigan's state capitol, Lansing. These sites represent diverse populations of older people, methods of intervention, professional disciplines, and services along the continuum of care. Planning grant funds allowed the School and the Consortium to develop the Geriatric Fellowship Program that was launched in April 2000.

The purpose of the Geriatric Fellowship Program is to attract more graduate students to the field of gerontology and health, and to train more MSWs to work on behalf of older people and their families. Designed to benefit both students and field instructors, the Program consists of seven special features:

- A Consortium that embodies the "Spiral Concept of Care." The Spiral Concept refers to the non-linear path by which an older person moves among formal and informal services in an effort to maintain optimal health along the continuum of care.

- A Consortium that helps us reach older people of color, especially African-Americans and Latinos, who are traditionally underserved and the fastest growing populations of elders in the United States. The diversity within the Consortium helps us train students in culturally competent practice with these populations.
- Fieldwork rotations designed to expose students to a continuum of services, multidisciplinary care, and a range of practice interventions on behalf of older people. Each student is placed in an "anchor" site within the Consortium for two terms, then rotates through two or three "satellites" during a third term. Selection of the anchor placement is determined by the student's intervention method (Interpersonal Practice, Management, Community Organization, or Policy and Evaluation); satellite placements are designed to build on and complement the student's learning in the anchor site. Together, anchor and satellite placements expose students to programs at six types of sites in three environments: the living environment (nursing home, assisted living, retirement community, home); health care environment (hospital, outpatient clinic, adult day care, hospice); and community environment (religious setting, senior center, community agency). Prior to beginning fieldwork, Fellows conduct group visits to each agency in the Consortium for socialization to geriatric social work, exposure to the continuum of services for elders, and selection of anchor and satellite preferences.
- A three-term, integrative seminar in geriatric social work taught by practitioners and faculty from social work, nursing, medicine, and public health. The seminar occurs concurrently with fieldwork. Practitioners are given honoraria for lecturing on selected seminar topics. We hope to eventually involve other faculty and students from three Michigan schools of social work in the seminar.
- Honoraria and discounts at University of Michigan Continuing Education workshops for Consortium field instructors who help plan fieldwork rotations, assignments, and provide student supervision. Consortium members also receive free agency web hosting and technical support offered by the School, individualized training in student supervision, and publicity through the dissemination efforts of the Fellows Program.
- Support for 13 incoming students per year for four terms. Support consists of stipends, funds to attend professional conferences, and assistance with job placement.
- A comprehensive evaluation component will evaluate all educational objectives as well as the student's gerontological knowledge and intervention skills, the extent of gerontological content in all courses offered by

the School, and the placement quality and how agency productivity were impacted by the Fellows Program.

The Consortium played a central role in the development of every aspect of the Fellows Program. They assisted in the development of educational goals and objectives for the Program, which state that upon completion of the Program, each student should demonstrate knowledge of the continuum of care; demonstrate knowledge of coping and support systems; apply multiple interventions to promote health; evaluate effectiveness of practice; demonstrate skill in working with diverse populations; participate in interdisciplinary collaborations; develop preventive strategies; examine mortality and morbidity trends; and examine national and international policy issues. To shape a program that allows students to meet these goals, Consortium members assisted in the development of the spiral concept of care, seminar topics, design of the fieldwork rotations, agency evaluation instrument, recruitment and job placement strategies, and participated in the selection of applicants to the Program. On an ongoing basis, Consortium members attend monthly meetings of the Consortium, instruct students, lecture in the integrative seminar, develop fieldwork assignments, and help arrange rotations.

Our first cohort of Fellows (who began in September 2000) consisted of 13 students. Though all the Fellows are female, they represent diverse ages, backgrounds, and levels of knowledge and skill in gerontology. Two Fellows are students of color.

This fellowship program provides the opportunity to examine two significant aspects of geriatric social work training: the trajectory for the development of an interest in gerontology, and the aspects of a fellowship program in geriatric social work that were incentives for recruitment of students.

METHODS AND ANALYSIS

Our investigation of the motivating factors for student's choice of gerontological social work entails the examination of data from four sources. First, a focus group was conducted during the planning stages of the Geriatric Fellowship Program. Current University of Michigan M.S.W. students were invited to discuss their reasons for choosing concentration areas (Children and Youth, Community and Social Systems, Mental Health, Health, or Adults and Elderly). A total of 15 student volunteers participated. These students were asked to consider what factors influenced their choice of concentration area, as well as what incentives might be needed to attract more students into the Adults and Elderly concentration. Second, the application essays from the first cohort of

Geriatric Fellowship applicants (n = 26) were examined for content related to motivational factors for working with the elderly. In particular, written responses to the question "Please identify any previous work, volunteer, or life experiences you have had that contributed to your interest in gerontology" were analyzed. Third, a baseline survey with closed-ended questions regarding student's reasons for applying or not applying to the Geriatric Fellowship Program was administered to 318 incoming M.S.W. students at the start of the 2000-2001 school year (n = 211 completed surveys). Finally, in-depth semi-structured qualitative interviews were conducted with each of the 13 Fellows during their first two months in the Geriatric Fellowship Program. Students were asked questions regarding their reasons for applying to the Fellowship, origins of their interest in geriatric social work, their initial experiences in the program, and their expectations for the Fellowship program (including field placements, seminar, and post-Fellowship outcomes). Qualitative data were transcribed and coded inductively using grounded theory methods.

FINDINGS:
WHAT FACTORS INFLUENCE THE DECISION
TO STUDY GERONTOLOGICAL SOCIAL WORK?

In most cases, the development of an interest in elderly populations could best be identified as a process beginning years before the actual decision to enter the field of study. Furthermore, many respondents cited not one but several influential reasons for their interest in geriatric social work. Of the initial 26 applicants to the Geriatric Fellowship Program, 15 mentioned a family experience with an elder, 20 described a work or volunteer experience that influenced their decision to pursue geriatric social work, seven cited an academic research project that sparked their interest, seven mentioned an influential undergraduate internship, and three discussed the growing recognition of a social problem in need of addressing. Still others noted the predicted expansion of the job market in gerontological services. Most applicants cited more than one influential force, suggesting those experiences can "add up" to promote an interest in working with elders.

One of the most frequently cited reasons for developing an interest in social work with the elderly was family exposure to aging issues, either through a close and positive relationship with an elderly relative or through a more difficult experience with a relative's aging process. Explains Annette[1], a returning student in her early 50s,

> I would say . . . the seed [of my interest in gerontology] had its germination in my childhood because I had a wonderful grandmother who . . .

was really more like my mom. . . . I learned so much from her that it just always implanted in my head the fact that there's so much to learn from older people.

Said Allison, 27, "I came to be interested in gerontology . . . really through my grandfather. . . . I've always been really close to him and . . . he's always just been a really important part of my life." Nancy, age 52, felt that because she was an only child of older parents and grew up surrounded by older individuals, "it was natural for me to have those sort of interactions, and have older people in my life as opposed to kids. So this was . . . a natural progression for me to come to this point." Sheryl, 46, explained that "my mother is in her 70s, and just watching her go through the aging process is making me have more of an attraction for [gerontological social work]."

Other Fellows articulated the process of finding it difficult to watch an elderly relative face the challenges of old age. Joan, 49, was the caretaker of her grandmother "and helped her get through the process of dying," which illuminated "how difficult that is, how emotional it is for the person dying and the people who participate." Likewise, Carol, 52, explained, "I was interested in gerontology because I witnessed my parents growing older and I felt very helpless because they had a lot of problems. I thought that there should be someone who could help people get through this transition . . . that's what inspired me in the first place. . . . I felt helpless and I wanted to be able to do more." It is important to note at this point that of the 13 Fellows, five (38.4%) are returning students in their mid-40s or older. This is statistically significant, as only 7.9% of the full-time University of Michigan M.S.W. student body is over age 41. It is possible that gerontological social work as a second career choice for returning students may be facilitated by their increased exposure to aging parents and older friends, as well as the awareness of their own aging and its concomitant issues.

A heartfelt passion for working with the elderly was another frequently cited reason for studying gerontological social work. As Sheryl stated, "[it was] where my passion was and where my heart was . . . a lot of it is just following my heart." Sheryl explained that initially she was not sure whether she wanted to work with children or with older adults. After trying a B.S.W.-level field placement with each population, she knew that she felt more comfortable with elderly individuals. "I did the . . . kid experience, and it didn't seem like there was much change I could do [because they were going home to environments out of my control] . . . I'm hoping to see more [effects of my work] when I'm working with older adults." Several other Fellows described a similar choice between working with children and working with elders, and a salient theme emerged from their responses: they felt helpless working with youngsters, while working with the elderly produced feelings of efficacy for them. Tina, 22, articulated this phenomenon well:

> The big difference I found with working with kids . . . was I had a hard time looking at them and saying "I don't know what your future's gonna look like . . . I can only do so much for you." I felt really helpless. And with the elderly sometimes I feel helpless, but at the same time I can make their last years comfortable and nice for them. . . . So that's what I enjoy more.

Several Fellows found that their interest in older adults was sparked almost accidentally, through an undergraduate field placement or through a job in a field only tangentially related to seniors. Mona, 23, did an undergraduate internship with female inmates at a county jail, many of whom were older women. She found that there were "a lot of similarities in the sense of things I was passionate about in working with children, a lot of it still applied [to the older inmates]," particularly around minority issues. The opportunity to work with elders of color was a large factor in her initial interest in gerontology. Liza, age 30, took a job coordinating volunteers for United Way. Although her background experience was in maternal and child health, she found that her new job exposed her both to senior service agencies and to active and healthy older adults who were eager to volunteer their time. "There's this whole population of people that have so many resources to offer," she noticed, "and how are they involved in their families and communities? How are they going to be able to continue offering the skills that they have and continue to be valued in the community?"

Several Fellows highlighted the role of enthusiastic mentors and supervisors as well. Rachel was placed at an Adult Day Care facility for her undergraduate internship, and found that "the supervisors there were definitely people that I struck a chord with and they were very enthusiastic about what they were doing, and from [that time on] . . . I always came back wanting to be . . . my supervisor from that first experience." Stacey, 26, worked alongside a geriatric psychiatrist who "really advised me to go into geriatric social work . . . he felt like it would be a good thing for me, that I would like it and that I would be good at it and that there would be good opportunities in the field, so he encouraged me to do it." Enthusiastic and influential professors, colleagues, and supervisors can guide potential students into a given field.

Many Fellows spoke of particular social problems that captured their attention and drew them to the field of gerontological social work. Tina found it troublesome that institutionalized older adults are frequently overlooked by society. Annette explained that,

One of the greatest problems in our society is that we value beauty and attractiveness so much that the person's older-looking body becomes a wall for many people being able to hear what they have to say. . . . I think it's critical to our society. . . . There are just a number of places where so much is being missed because their voice isn't getting heard.

Rebecca, 24, was particularly moved by an undergraduate class discussion in which she heard students using "horribly patronizing" language to discuss their work with elderly individuals. She explains,

I just remember thinking [that] if I can recognize that there is an insensitivity or this misunderstanding, or if I feel that there should be another approach to elderly care, that my responsibility [was] to be in elderly care, and it was the first time I really felt like I wanted to concentrate on this population.

Having grown up in Trinidad, Stacey found the cultural lack of respect for elders in the U. S. to be disturbing. She explained, "I always thought older people were . . . just so deserving of respect. . . . I never thought of old people as . . . sickly . . . and I never got this whole concept of old people as decrepit and . . . a burden on society . . . until I moved to America." Her own cultural views on aging led her to be dissatisfied with the predominant American cultural attitudes towards the elderly.

The instigation for entering geriatric social work may also come in part from the increasing awareness of the expanding job market in elder services. Several Fellows made reference to the strength of geriatric social work as an expanding field. Said Nancy, "I thought gerontology was a good area to look into for practice in social work. I didn't know what the opportunities were, but it just seemed to me, if you looked at the demographics, that would be a good area in which to practice." Focus group participants who had not chosen to concentrate in Adults and Elderly, too, mentioned wishing that they had known early on about the plenitude of social work positions with elderly individuals and service agencies.

Because one of the foremost goals of the Fellowship Program is to increase the number of well-trained geriatric social workers, of particular interest to the Consortium are the reasons why an individual's interest might specifically change from something other than elderly populations to working with older adults. While more research is needed in this area, several suggestions can be gleaned from the interview and focus group data. Two Fellows discussed a marked change of heart from being uncomfortable around elderly individuals to wanting to work with seniors. Rebecca admitted that "I never felt very comfortable with geriatrics; I did not feel very comfortable around the elderly. Most people do tend to have a squeamishness [about some aspects of older adults]." She was initially motivated to work with elders out of her recognition of a social problem (the patronizing treatment of elders), but she found that while working in a hospital setting with older adults, her "squeamishness" faded:

> I think every time you see a catheter you kind of cringe at first a little . . . [but] when I'm with the people, I guess knowing them as people . . . knowing that your sole job as a social worker in that setting is to be their advocate and to be their voice for them . . . the squeamishness doesn't really fit in, so I guess it wasn't really an issue once I started working there.

Rebecca was not alone in her initial feelings of "squeamishness." Other Fellows, too, acknowledged the difficulty of working with frail older adults:

> The only thing that scared me, or that pushed me away a little bit, was when my own grandparents were deteriorating. And a lot of people ask me, "How could you want to work with older adults? It's so depressing." And I totally understand where they're coming from. . . . I can totally empathize with people who are scared because I have had that feeling too. (Rachel)

Rachel overcame her own fears by separating her feelings about clients from her feelings about family members. Sheryl wondered aloud why gerontological social work "isn't an area that people are interested in. For me . . . as I'm doing it, what I'm finding is that it gets a little scary for me to think about growing older . . . [that] this is what I'm getting close to." However, despite her fears about her own aging, she finds it helpful to know that she is able to make the aging process more pleasant for others.

FINDINGS: WHAT FACTORS INFLUENCED THE DECISION NOT TO STUDY GERONTOLOGICAL SOCIAL WORK?

Two possible deterrents were suggested from the data gathered from students not interested in working with older people: fears about aging and the elderly, and lack of awareness about opportunities to work with diverse elderly populations. For some students, fear came from exposure to elders in poor health. One focus group participant described a summer job she had had at age 15 working as a feeding aide for impaired residents of a nursing home, which she found extremely overwhelming and "depressing." She vowed never to do that type of work again.

A lack of awareness about opportunities to work with a variety of elderly individuals may also prevent students from focusing on gerontological social work. Liza explained that when she asked herself why she had not thought of working with the elderly, she realized that her only perceptions of gerontological social work involved nursing homes. She said, "I thought, well, you get older and you go in a nursing home, and I don't want to manage a nursing home or be a nursing home [employee], so, what would I do? And I think society doesn't encourage us to think very much about really creative and interesting ways that you could work with the elderly." A widespread aversion to doing nursing home work, coupled with a lack of knowledge of other opportunities, may very well hinder an individual from choosing to pursue social work with elders.

For those students who do choose to specialize in gerontological social work, the interest in working with older adults almost invariably develops in a process-like fashion rather than as a sudden decision, regardless of whether the interest is a marked contrast from a previous interest or a life-long passion. All of the Fellows referred to multiple factors that "added up" to ignite their full-fledged interest in pursuing geriatric social work. Family experiences, recognition of a social problem, or "accidental" exposure to elders were often supplemented with volunteer work or academic research that provided an opportunity for individuals to further explore the field. "For me it was just–it was kind of a process, an unfolding as I went through," said Sheryl. Jokes Tina,

> I can't think of a specific moment where I was like, "I wanna work with old people" . . . I mean . . . half the people tell me–my grandmother was the first to tell me, "Don't go into this field, it's depressing. All my friends are getting old, they're dying . . ." And then everybody else is like, "oh, I think that's wonderful," you know, someone-has-to-do-it type of attitude. I guess I've always, not always wanted to. I mean, as a child, I wasn't like "Oh, I want to be a gerontologist when I grow up!" That definitely wasn't my dream job, but I think over the past few years, it's sort of become what I enjoy.

FINDINGS:
WHAT ATTRACTS STUDENTS
TO THE GERIATRIC FELLOWSHIP PROGRAM?

What are the best ways to attract applicants from among students with both a longstanding interest in geriatric social work and those with a newer interest? Once a student's interest in geriatric social work has been ignited, what will ensure that s/he remains engaged in the field?

Due to time constraints, recruitment efforts for the first cohort of Geriatric Fellows were directed only towards students who had already applied and been accepted to the School of Social Work. A letter of invitation, a fact sheet about the Fellowship, and a brochure about careers in gerontological social work were sent to all admitted students. A web site detailing the Geriatric Program was created and linked to the University of Michigan School of Social Work web page. In addition, admissions and field instruction staff were encouraged to promote the Fellowship program to any appropriate incoming students.

Of the 26 applicants, 20 heard of the Fellowship through the letter of invitation distributed to all applicants accepted into the M.S.W. Program, one read about it on the web site, and five heard about it from an admissions or field instruction staff member or a colleague at their workplace. A similar proportion of non-applicant students heard about the Fellowship through each method: 80.7% heard of it through the invitational letter, 10.4% heard about the Fellowship through a personal contact with someone in the School of Social Work, and 7% heard about the Fellowship through the web site designed to provide detailed information on the fellowship. The method of recruitment did not seem to affect a student's decision to apply.

The results of the interviews with the Fellows emphasize the importance of personal contacts with staff in the School of Social Work. "A lot of encouragement" from staff members in the Office of Field Instruction as well as from a faculty member led Rachel to apply. Three other Fellows mentioned specific conversations they had had with staff members, which influenced their decision to apply.

Baseline survey data illuminate reasons for applying or not applying among the entire incoming M.S.W. student body. Of those who did not apply for the Fellowship, 54.1% indicated that they were "not interested in gerontology or older adults," 22.4% indicated that they "did not want to be a 16-month student," 12.6% had not heard about it at all, 8.2% only heard about it after the application deadline, and 13.6% did not apply for "other" reasons. Of those who did apply, their top three incentives for applying included a tie between the stipend money and the individualized attention (each receiving 15 weighted points), followed by assistance with job placement (13 weighted points). Other incentives (in order of preference) included: the seminar, close coordination of field and classroom experiences, and the field placement rotations (an option not available outside the fellowship program).

Interview data with Fellows presents a fuller–and slightly different–picture of the reasons why applicants were interested in the Fellowship. Fellows articulated their views of the potential benefits of involvement in the Fellowship program and suggested that while the stipend money was important, it was most certainly not the most important factor involved. The field rotation model and the Consortium were frequently cited as strong attractions to the Fellowship, as were the seminar, the general knowledge and focus on the elderly that Fellows would receive personal attention, opportunities for group work, post-Fellowship job opportunities, and the prestige/honor of the Fellowship.

"Quite frankly, the $12,000 was a godsend," admitted Nancy, "but that wasn't the main, or the only reason for doing this," she concluded. Annette explained that "I really wanted to come to the School of Social Work, but given my age . . . I was very worried about the money that I might have to borrow and the debt that I would incur." The Fellowship provided an opportunity for her to attend the School of Social Work without incurring as large a debt. Carol explained that the stipend money "had a lot to do with" her decision to switch from enrolling as a 20-month student (where she would have her summer off from school) to a 16-month student (entering in September and continuously being in the program for 16 months): "I knew that if I got the Fellowship then I could afford to quit my job and go in the program for 16 months." Perhaps the most powerful example of the fact that the tuition reimbursement is no more important, and possibly less so, than the other components of the Geriatric Fellowship is the example of Larissa, who was offered full tuition from one of the five schools that did not receive the full Hartford Foundation implementation grant but did receive some Hartford Foundation money to provide stipends to students. Although the other school offered her a better financial package than the University of Michigan did, she chose to attend the University of Michigan because "they had an actual [Geriatric Fellowship] program, over just the money."

What about the Fellowship program attracts students as much as or more so than the tuition reimbursement? The Fellows repeatedly mentioned the field experience as a highly attractive aspect of the program. Comments centered on both the rotational model as well as on the quality of placements. Explained Sheryl,

> I like the rotating field placement . . . having a satellite and a regular anchor site, because just being part of two different atmospheres I think can make a difference by . . . concentrating in two different ways or being with a different group of people. . . . It just [allows me to] see something from a different perspective. . . . So this will give me a bigger picture of what is out there.

Tina, too, said that one of the "big keypoints" in her decision to apply to the Fellowship was the agency rotations: "I liked the fact that we would . . . have a choice of a couple [agencies], like the anchor and satellite sites . . . [in my undergraduate placement] it seemed so stagnant being in the same place . . . it was frustrating because you can only do so much and then you want to learn something else." She hoped to get a clearer sense of her career goals by experiencing two or more agencies. "I think that's one of the great things about the Fellowship, is hopefully seeing a lot of different environments and being exposed to a lot of different things and finding out about things that I don't know exist," said Allison.

As important to the Fellows was the quality of field placements. Because each field placement site or agency had been hand-selected by the Office of Field Instruction to participate in the Consortium, Fellows felt that this "specialized group of agencies" would provide them with a unique and high-quality field experience. "The fact that the agencies were selected . . . to give us the ultimate experience of learning about the aging process" was very attractive to Tina. "I'm excited about the fact that these agencies are . . . part of the Hartford consortium, so they know what we're trying to advance," she added. Mona also saw the Consortium of agencies as an influential benefit of the Fellowship, in that Consortium members were well apprised of the Fellowship program and of the Fellows themselves: "To have agencies that already know that this is a group of people [specializing in aging] and so they're seeking out the group . . . that's an advantage [of the Fellowship]." Rebecca found it particularly exciting to "have this package of opportunity to be involved [and] have these links to [the] geriatric social work community" through the Consortium. She does, however, acknowledge one drawback to the Consortium model: fewer options from which to choose her field placement. Because Fellows must be placed at Consortium agencies, they are limited to 16 different sites rather than several dozen.

The field placement experience included agency site visits prior to the Fellow's selection of placement preferences, which was also mentioned by several Fellows as a wonderful opportunity. "Nobody [else] gets to go and look at these places [before choosing where they'd like to be placed], and talk to the people before and then make a choice. I feel very, very privileged because of that," said Carol. Especially because she does not come from a gerontology background, Stacey said that "just to be able to see [each] place and get an overview of how that place is run, is going to give me a richer experience of [understanding] aging services in general."

Several Fellows selected the seminars as the potentially "best part of being a Fellow." "The most specialized part of it I think is the seminar, and being able to have that kind of forum . . . that specialized time to talk about elderly issues and . . . that direct interaction with different elderly care workers," explained Rebecca. "It seemed like [the seminar] was covering so much . . . I was looking at the [syllabus] and I thought, this just expands so much on what I learned in [other] courses," noted Sheryl.

The focus on aging and the elderly in general was also cited by many Fellows as the most attractive part of the Fellowship. Stacey explained, "I don't have a large . . . prior experience with the geriatric population, and I applied for [the Fellowship] because I really felt like it would help me to get some base knowledge and contacts . . . that I would need to do what I wanted to do." Agreed Joan, "I think I'll think a lot more about the elderly than I could have possibly in any other situation, which is one of the reasons that I found that I wanna do this, that I wanted all that valuable information. . . . It'll give us, I think, overall understanding." Liza remembered receiving the letter of invitation and thinking how "that would be great to be able to really focus on that with people who have experience already, that are going to be in the program, and have a seminar that really focuses on aging issues, and a field placement that could be aging specific." Particularly in an environment in which most M.S.W. students do not concentrate in Adults and Elderly (only 14% of the student body concentrates in Adults and Elderly), the Fellowship would allow her to connect with other students and classes that she otherwise might not encounter: "I think I would feel like getting a solid foundation in geriatrics and gerontology would be harder if I wasn't a Fellow," she said. Most importantly, the Fellowship is geared towards keeping Fellows focused on a particular career track. Explained Carol,

> I expect that [the Fellowship] will shape [my M.S.W. experience] in the way that I wanted it to . . . and that is, by keeping me focused on adults and elderly. . . . I mean, I don't care if you're 21 or 51, sometimes you still don't know what you wanna do. And this has really helped me focus on going in the direction that I wanted to go in originally. . . . This has given me an additional boost.

Slightly more surprisingly than their interest in the tuition reimbursement, field experience, and classroom experiences, Fellows placed an overwhelmingly strong emphasis on the attractiveness of the personalized and individual attention implicitly offered by the Fellowship program. This may be in part due to the fact that the University of Michigan School of Social Work is relatively large, at over 600 full-time students. At least eight of the 13 Fellows discussed the benefits of individual attention at length. "One of the biggest problems with school systems is that they are very impersonal and they're a process that may not be so easy to get through for most people. . . . The larger the organization, the less personal attention you get. . . . That was attractive to me, that I would get some individual attention," said Joan. Larissa, who moved to Ann Arbor from a small Midwestern town, admitted that "I really like the idea of being part of a smaller group within the bigger school . . . the thought of Ann Arbor in itself was overwhelming. . . . So I really like the idea of . . . having a smaller group to go through it with." Receiving more individualized attention from the Consortium provides Fellows with several advantages. Because she has "closer relationships with the advisors and field instructors," Stacey feels that "if I had a problem . . . I'm not just a number. . . . People are looking out for me." As a result, problems may be solved more efficiently and any questions she has may be answered in a more timely manner. Carol poignantly describes her feelings about the benefits of receiving personal attention from faculty and staff through the Geriatric Fellowship:

> I don't feel isolated as one might feel when they come to a program. . . . I feel very confident that there's somebody here that I can talk to if I have real problems . . . It's just nice to have that sort of safety net. . . . You're not just one of 600 people out there just trying to swim to shore. . . . Somebody's out there with a little boat in case you wanna get in, and that's how I feel! It's like a real life line.

Moreover, Carol felt that the increased contact with gerontology faculty and staff in the school of social work would provide her with a better understanding of the field and "what are good things to go into. . . . I think this will be beneficial because I'll be steered in the right [career] direction."

Perhaps the most frequently discussed benefit of all is the opportunities afforded by being part of a group of Fellows. From providing tangible support to a more abstract sense of belonging, there were numerous ways in which the group aspects of the Fellowship were highly attractive to Fellows. These results suggest that a promising direction for recruiting students into geriatric social work might include a stronger emphasis on group formats for learning.

First, the "group" nature of the Fellowship provides support for a "minority" group of sorts within the School of Social Work–Adults and Elderly concentrators. "I have a sense of belonging to something where I don't get that sense in my regular classes, being the only Adults and Elderly person in so many of them . . . I feel anchored to something," said Nancy.

Second, the group format facilitates an expanded learning process, as Fellows can learn from one another. "I guess the only real expectation that I had [of the Fellowship] was that in some way all of us would be together learning rather than just being spread out in classes," explained Larissa. "I think just having the 13 of us, that's what excites me the most. . . . I think that makes it easier for us to learn from each other," she added. In particular, learning from a group of women of diverse ages was attractive to her, and she felt that the small group format facilitated learning from people with different perspectives. Tina anticipated discussing field placement experiences and thereby learning about "12 other jobs that are out there that you could do rather than just learning about yours," as well as having a forum in which to share suggestions or strategies for dealing with problems that arise in placement.

Third, group learning environments can provide tangible support for individuals. Joan discussed sharing articles and books on gerontological subjects with her fellow Fellows, while Nancy described the ways in which Fellows are "looking out for each other" through sharing rides to class at night or in the rain. Allison mentioned her satisfaction in knowing that if she's ill and must miss a class, her fellow Fellows will take good notes for her.

Less tangible is the sense of belonging and emotional support provided by the group format. One returning older student explained that "I can feel like a misfit because of the age thing, and sometimes I feel like sort of an odd thumb. . . . [But] being a Fellow and being part of the group . . . that alone has been extremely helpful." Being part of the Fellowship group provides a buffer from the stresses of entering a large graduate program and a new environment. Said Allison, "Really getting to know a small group of other students rather than being thrown into a group of 300 students . . . it's nice being kind of gently introduced." Several Fellows mentioned the feelings of strong camaraderie that were already developing, perhaps because Fellows share "the same passion, the whole commonality, the interest that drew us all to apply for it in the first place" (Sheryl) and perhaps because Fellows simply know one another better. Feeling "understood" by others was valued highly among the Fellows as they discussed the group experience.

Lastly, the group nature of the Fellowship facilitates the establishment of long-term ties and networks between future geriatric social work professionals. Said Sheryl,

> I can picture myself, years from now, still being in contact with some of these people, finding out what they're doing . . . being able to [learn from these people], knowing somebody that's in the same field . . . having an already established network.

Agreed Rachel,

> It will be nice to have that cohort now and to hopefully continue those ties so when we all leave we have this group [to network with]. Just to have that network will . . . be something I wouldn't have gotten otherwise. If it was just me doing this program, I definitely wouldn't get that, but now I feel like I'm part of a group that will be able to give and to receive from each other, which is really nice.

The benefit of increased post-Fellowship job opportunities cannot be over-looked. Several Fellows spoke explicitly about their hopes that the Fellowship would make them better job candidates after graduation. "I think it's going to make a difference when I'm looking for a job," explained Sheryl, because of the additional knowledge she will have as well as the additional networks and contacts she will have established through the Consortium and the site visits. Mona elaborated:

> I can see long-term advantages [of the Fellowship] in terms of upon graduation and looking for jobs. . . . I [will] have had a more focused experience . . . and hopefully within the job market be able to market that . . . I really hope that this provides me with some kind of edge and . . . quality that prospective employers will look at and say, "Wow, this is really something distinctive and noticeable."

In the end, in fact, it appears that the benefits of participating in the Fellowship were enough to combat the several barriers to application that a few Fellows expressed. Two or three of the Fellows had wanted to concentrate not in Adults and Elderly, but in Mental Health, although they intended to work with older adults. The benefits of the Fellowship program were enough to change their minds, especially once they were assured that mental health issues would be covered in the seminar. Similarly, those Fellows who had intended to follow the 20-month curriculum were easily swayed to the 16-month curriculum after they learned about the field rotations and the opportunity for placement at more than one site. More difficult was the decision for the three Fellows who could have entered the M.S.W. program as Advanced Standing students (students with B.S.W.s), because switching to the 16-month curriculum would necessitate an extra semester of school. Each of these Fellows explained that the benefits of the Fellowship outweighed the extra semester and tuition.

CONCLUSION:
FUTURE DIRECTIONS
FOR GERIATRIC SOCIAL WORK RECRUITMENT

Recruitment of students into geriatric social work will continue to be a high-priority issue as the population of older Americans continues to swell. Recruitment efforts should take several directions, as suggested by these data. First, whether or not funding exists for widespread full-fledged Fellowship programs, the creation of more supportive environments for gerontological education is essential. Group learning formats–in which students can share knowledge and experiences and establish ties that "anchor" them to the field–seem to be one promising method for attracting students to geriatric social work and ensuring their long-term involvement.

Second, because the development of interest in social work with older adults occurs as an evolving process, it is important that recruitment efforts begin early in a student's career. Through field assignments that take undergraduate students (who may not already be interested in gerontology) into diverse older adult environments and classroom assignments that expose students to aging issues, the fears, stigma, and lack of awareness that Fellows described as being barriers to choosing gerontological social work can be eradicated. It is equally important to demonstrate the variety of settings in which social workers can engage in geriatric work, and the variety of groups encompassed within the population of older adults–that is, to encourage individuals to think about what Liza termed the "really creative and interesting ways that you can work with the elderly." Nursing home work as the only opportunity available to geriatric social workers is a stereotype that needs to be put to rest. Furthermore, as suggested by focus group participants, flexibility in selecting concentration areas at the M.S.W. level should be provided, to ensure that students who might grow interested in Adults and Elderly topics after beginning their M.S.W. education are not penalized for changing their concentrations.

It is well-documented that the population of older adults of color is rapidly expanding in the U. S., and this trend will have significant implications for recruitment of students into geriatric social work. Field placement sites should offer multiple opportunities to work with minority populations, as suggested by one Fellow whose interest in gerontology grew directly out of her interest in minority issues. The opportunity to "pioneer" in the field of services to minority elders may be attractive to students such as Mona, who explained that she sees "all of us as pioneers in the sense that the Asian population is really growing and for those of us who are starting out now, 12 or 13 years from now we'll be the people who have broken some ground. . . . I see another benefit from this, being some sort of pioneer." Recruitment into geriatric social work programs of students of color should also be a high priority for educators.

It is also important to recognize the ways in which formal Fellowship opportunities may legitimate the field of geriatric social work and create pride in social work itself. As one Fellow noted, "I think people feel kind of alien toward geriatric care . . . but [they will come to see it] as legitimate because . . . there is a Fellowship program [akin to the many children and youth-oriented fellowship programs]." Another Fellow who is getting a dual degree in Public Health explained that she felt renewed pride in social work as she described the Fellowship program to her peers and advisors in the School of Public Health: "Being able to say, 'this is something special that the social work school is doing, and this is how they're getting involved in things other than the average social work experience,' that's really rewarding."

As the six Hartford-funded Geriatric Fellowship programs nation-wide evolve, it is important to continue to monitor outcomes in terms of sustained interest and commitment to geriatric social work post-graduation. Getting students to choose geriatric social work as a field is only the first step in ensuring that the needs of our growing elderly population are met.

NOTE

1. All names and identifying features have been changed to protect the identity of respondents.

REFERENCES

Kane, M. N. (1999). Factors affecting social work student's willingness to work with elders with Alzheimer's disease. *Journal of Social Work Education*, 35 (1), 71-85.

Lubben, J., Damron-Rodriguez, J., & Beck, J. (1992). A National Survey of Aging Curriculum in Schools of Social Work, *Geriatric Social Work Education,* 18 (3/4),157-174.

National Institute on Aging (1987). *Personnel for Health Needs of the Elderly Through the Year 2020.* Bethesda, MD. National Institutes of health, Public Health Service, Dept. of Health and Human Services, DHHS publication No. 87-2950.

Rohan, E. A., Berkman, B., Walker, S. & Holmes, W. (1994). The Geriatric Oncology Patient: Ageism in Social Work Practice. *Journal of Gerontological Social Work,* 23 (1/2), 201-221.

Chapter 7

Strengthening Geriatric Social Work Training: Perspectives from the University at Albany

Regina M. Bures, PhD
Ronald W. Toseland, PhD
Anne E. Fortune, PhD

SUMMARY. This paper presents an overview of the relationship between population aging in the United States, the growing demand for geriatric social workers, and how that need can be met through graduate-level social work training. We describe the basic components of graduate level social work training and discuss two key elements in the training of geriatric social workers. Focussing on a recent initiative by

Regina M. Bures is a Research Fellow affiliated with the Institute of Gerontology at the University at Albany, State University of New York, and the New York State Office for the Aging. Ronald W. Toseland is Professor of Social Work and Director, Institute of Gerontology, University of Albany, State University of New York, 135 Western Avenue, Albany, NY 12222. Anne E. (Ricky) Fortune is Professor of Social Work, University at Albany, State University of New York, Albany, NY 12222.

The authors would like to thank Judy Postmus and Linda Mertz for their assistance in the preparation of this paper.

[Haworth co-indexing entry note]: "Strengthening Geriatric Social Work Training: Perspectives from the University at Albany." Bures, Regina M., Ronald W. Toseland, and Anne E. Fortune. Co-published simultaneously in *Journal of Gerontological Social Work* (The Haworth Social Work Practice Press, an imprint of The Haworth Press, Inc.) Vol. 39, No. 1/2, 2002, pp. 111-127; and: *Advancing Gerontological Social Work Education* (ed: M. Joanna Mellor, and Joann Ivry) The Haworth Social Work Practice Press, an imprint of The Haworth Press, Inc., 2002, pp. 111-127. Single or multiple copies of this article are available for a fee from The Haworth Document Delivery Service [1-800-HAWORTH, 9:00 a.m. - 5:00 p.m. (EST). E-mail address: docdelivery@haworthpress.com].

10.1300/J083v39n01_10

the John A. Hartford Foundation, we discuss the program in geriatric social work training recently implemented at the University at Albany School of Social Welfare and the consequences of improved training and awareness in geriatric social work for the social work community. *[Article copies available for a fee from The Haworth Document Delivery Service: 1-800-HAWORTH. E-mail address: <docdelivery@haworthpress.com> Website: <http://www.HaworthPress.com> © 2002 by The Haworth Press, Inc. All rights reserved.]*

KEYWORDS. Geriatric social work, social work education, Albany-HIAP

BACKGROUND: THE AGING OF AMERICA

Increases in longevity and improvements in health mean that Americans are living longer and healthier lives. The 2000 Census indicates that the population of the United States is aging and that the proportion of the population over age 85 is increasing. The median age of Americans has increased to an all-time high of 35.3 years and the population aged 85+ increased 41% between 1990 and 2000. While the total population over 65 increased only slightly between 1990 and 2000, the aging of the large Baby Boom cohorts portends a sharp increase in the elderly population in coming decades. The aging of the Baby Boomers led to an increase of 49% in the population 45-54 (U.S. Census Bureau, 2001).

For social workers, these changes in demographic structure translate into changing demands for services and service delivery. As the population of the United States ages, health and human service professionals are facing growing demands to formulate policies and to provide services that will enhance the physical, mental, and social well being of older adults. Geriatric health promotion is a necessary component of policies that will ensure successful aging, and thus keep older persons independent longer. Yet the increasing size and diversity of the older population will present many new challenges for health and social service agencies. These include negotiating and addressing cultural differences, variations in family support, transportation needs, and psychological impairments among aging clients. An important aspect of practice with the elderly is that social work practitioners sensitize themselves to the experience of aging and avoid stereotypes and negative images that interfere with effective helping.

The needs of the aging are inseparable from the need to develop and enhance aging expertise and awareness among health care and service providers.

Faced with growing numbers of older persons with changing needs, service providers will be forced to reevaluate ongoing programs and to develop new ones. More geriatric social workers are needed to provide and promote effective services and policy.

NEED VS. DEMAND FOR GERIATRIC SOCIAL WORKERS

The changing living arrangements and family patterns of elders also affect service needs and delivery (Toseland, Smith & McCallion, 2001). There are several reasons for this. Older persons are more likely to live independently, either alone or with a spouse. Mobility is greater than in past generations so that fewer adult children live near their parents thereby reducing their ability to provide care on a daily basis. More women work outside the home than in past generations, limiting their availability to serve in the caregiving role. These changes mean that social workers are likely to be called upon more frequently to help frail older persons and distant caregivers coordinate home and health services, and to serve in care management roles that will enable older adults to remain living independently in their homes later in life.

Another factor affecting the need for social work services is the aging of the population. Chronic disabilities increase rapidly with advanced age. For example, the prevalence of Alzheimer's Disease doubles for every decade people live beyond the age of 65 (Khachaturian & Radebaugh, 1996). Thus, while the prevalence of Alzheimer's Disease in those who are 65 to 74 year is less than 5%, the prevalence for those over age 85 is over 45% (Evans, 1996).

Despite recent reports of improved health and reduced disabilities among the aging population (Manton, Corder, & Stallard, 1997; Spillman & Pezzin, 2000), the rapid growth of oldest segments of the population limits the impact of these gains: There are many more older persons with chronic disabilities now than in the past who need social work services (Toseland & Smith, 2001).

Despite a growing need for social work services, the factors that shape the demand for social workers have changed little in the past 50 years. Hollis and Taylor (1951) identified a number of factors that shape the demand for social workers. These factors include demographic trends, expanding government functions, and changing social patterns (Hollis and Taylor, 1951). Demographic trends shape social work needs by contributing to changes in population composition. Increases and decreases in government services to meet the well-being needs of population members change the demand for services provided by social workers. Changes in social patterns, due to immigration, economic changes or changes in family structure, also increase the demand for social workers.

These factors are particularly relevant to the growing demand for geriatric social workers. Increases in government supported services for elders at both local and national levels are associated with increased service coordination demand, for example, the coordination of health care and supportive services. While population aging in the United States may increase the number of older persons and families who have service needs, Barth (2001, 35) points out that "a distinct difference exists between need and effective demand for social work services." For example, shifts in the financing of health care may restrict payment of services so that need exists, but out-of-pocket costs are high. With funding limited or unavailable, service demand may decline. Because the demand for social workers depends on the demand for social work services, public policy can have a powerful impact on it.

SOCIAL WORK EDUCATION

Although the demand for social workers is still driven by the traditional factors identified by Hollis and Taylor (1951) half a century ago, the structure of social work education has changed substantially in the past 50 years. The most important change has been an increasing standardization of programs in social work education offered by colleges and universities. In the United States, social workers are trained professionals who have completed degree requirements at accredited colleges or universities. The accreditation body, CSWE, sets minimal standards of education and required content. Furthermore, most states license or certify social workers based on their degree and experience levels. For example, in New York, social workers may apply for licensing if they have an MSW from a CSWE accredited school and meet the appropriate licensing examination requirements. Initial licensing usually occurs at the intermediate, or generalist, level. New York State also allows Certified Social Workers with at least three years of experience providing supervised psychotherapy services to apply for privileges that qualify them as reimbursable providers of psychotherapy services (for insurance purposes).

Currently there are three levels of social work education in the United States: undergraduate, master's, and doctoral. The purpose of the undergraduate degree in social work is to prepare students for professional practice as generalists. Undergraduates generally take two years of liberal arts courses and then major in social work, spending a minimum of 400 hours in field practica (Council for Social Work Education, 2001a). At the master's level, students are prepared for advanced practice in an area of concentration. The first year of the master's program focuses on the foundations of social work curriculum and the field practicum. In the second year of the master's program, students take advanced courses in their chosen concentration and field practica (Council for Social Work Education, 2001b). Doctoral study in social work prepares students for research and teaching.

The quality of social work education is maintained through standards established by the Council of Social Work Education (CSWE). At the undergraduate and master's levels, social work training is accredited. These standards include structural factors such as number of faculty, required content, and student outcome measures that programs must attain. Doctoral programs are not accredited by CSWE; they are reviewed by the individual institutions (Frumkin and Lloyd, 1995).

GERIATRIC SOCIAL WORK TRAINING NEEDS

Social workers fill a variety of roles in service agencies: including caseworker, supervisor, and administrator. While many social workers acknowledge the necessity of incorporating geriatric knowledge into their service provision roles, few identify as aging specialists or geriatric social workers. The majority of social workers employed in health care settings serve older persons, and more than 60% of the National Association of Social Worker's (NASW) members report the need for aging knowledge (Damron-Rodriguez & Lubben, 1997; Peterson & Wendt, 1990). Yet, less than 5% of NASW members identify "aging" as the primary focus of their practice (Gibelman & Schervish, 1997).

The disparity between the lack of aging training for social workers and the increasing need for aging knowledge in practice settings has made the infusion of gerontological content into the general social work curriculum an important priority. Most practicing social workers received little or no prior training in gerontology (Klein, 1996). This training deficit reflects an historical lack of institutional and departmental support for aging curricula in the United States (Dawson & Santos, 1996). Three-fourths of all MSW programs have no faculty identified with aging and only 10% of all social work students take a gerontology course (Damron-Rodriquez & Lubben, 1997). For social work schools, the demand to turn out more aging-competent social workers has increased faster than either the level of student interest or the field's training capacity. Berkman and colleagues (2000) recognize this deficit and argue for the development of geriatric social work faculty through a number of means including fellowship and training programs.

KEY ELEMENTS OF GERONTOLOGY-COMPETENT
SOCIAL WORK TRAINING

To prepare social work students to work effectively with the older persons, it is essential that MSW programs increase awareness of and sensitivity to the experience of aging among their students. A clear understanding of the challenges and frustration faced by older adults can help students to develop the skills they will need to be empathic, realistic, and effective practitioners. When working with younger individuals, social workers generally have the advantage of having experienced similar developmental issues. In contrast, few social work practitioners have experienced the developmental issues faced by older persons. To minimize the effect of a lack of personal experience, it is essential that social work programs train students to be aware of their perceptions of and attitudes toward aging and older people. Students should also be sensitized to the issues with which older persons may struggle.

Two key elements in the effective training of geriatric social workers are: (1) emphasizing human development over the life course and infusing gerontological material into the generalist MSW curriculum, and (2) working with local service agencies to give students hand-on training in aging programs and services. By incorporating these elements into the MSW curriculum, schools of social work will ultimately increase the number of MSW-level social workers educated in geriatric social work practice and create new roles and opportunities for social workers in the aging field.

GERONTOLOGY IN THE SOCIAL WORK CURRICULUM

The most direct way to raise awareness of stereotypes and negative images of aging and the tremendous variability among older persons is by incorporating material and courses in gerontology and human development in the general social work curriculum. Stereotypes and negative images of aging can interfere with effective helping, whereas an awareness of one's own stereotypes about older adults promotes effective helping. Often negative images and stereotypes are subtle. For example, social work practitioners may be more likely to underestimate the capabilities of older clients than lay helpers (Wills, 1978). This may happen because social workers frequently work with older adults who do not function at optimal levels. Stereotypes and negative images can be modified by reading and studying about what it is like to be older and by talking with older adults about their experiences. Recent research (Ragan and Bowen, 2001) suggests that to effectively improve attitudes about aging both education and reinforcement should be used.

Students should also be taught that chronological age may not be very help-ful in understanding the experience of a particular individual. Experienced so-cial work practitioners have come to recognize that knowledge about stages of adult development is often more helpful than chronological age in understand-ing older adults (see, for example, Knight, 1986). Health status varies tremen-dously from person to person: Many individuals remain in excellent health in their seventies; others may experience poor health in their sixties.

Other sources of variability in the aging experience include both historical context and individual characteristics (gender, race, and ethnicity). The unique experiences of different historical cohorts, women, and racial groups are likely to have a profound impact on the lives of older persons and the way they react to social workers. It is also important for students to become aware of the ways that cultural factors may effect the process of engagement and relationship building, as well as an individual's overall receptivity to receiving health and social services. Some cultures may have negative attitudes toward the use of mental health and social services, and older adults from these cultures may be reluctant to seek out needed services.

STUDENT INTERACTION WITH LOCAL PROGRAMS AND SERVICES

As part of the MSW training, students should experience working with lo-cal service agencies to get hands-on training in aging programs and services. The expected increase in frail older people living in the community, along with changes in care systems, suggests that there is likely to be an even greater demand for social workers to act as case managers, and supervisors of paraprofessional case managers, in future years. To live in the community, frail older persons of-ten require a number of services that are frequently provided by professional and paraprofessional helpers under the auspices of a number of different orga-nizations. Social workers are often called upon to develop service plans and to set-up, coordinate, and monitor the delivery of a set of health and social ser-vices. Since chronic conditions can change over time, social workers have to review plans periodically, reassessing the situations of their elderly clients and making changes in service plans as needed.

As information and referral sources, geriatric social workers have to be fa-miliar with the wide range of community resources and services available to older persons and their families. At a basic level, social work students need to be aware of the local, state and federal programs that are designed to ensure the standard of living for older persons. These include programs that provide for the financial, nutritional, health, and housing needs of the older population.

Social workers are also often called upon to help frail older persons access health programs and services that can help them to live independently in the community. Thus, familiarity with how to access home care programs, day treatment programs, and outpatient and inpatient services are essential components of geriatric social work training.

When training social work students to assess the frail elderly, it is essential that they learn to view the elder as a part of a larger family system. Assessment of older persons also requires an intensive evaluation of support networks. It is a necessary step to determine the availability of both primary and secondary caregivers. As older adults become frail, they may rely on their spouse, their adult children, and other family members for support. If family members are unavailable, frail older persons often rely on friends, neighbors, or members of the clergy for assistance. The service needs of family and informal caregivers may themselves be substantial and providing effective services involves addressing the needs of the caregiver(s) as well as the individual.

While the family may seek assistance for the older person, family caregivers seeking assistance may themselves be in need of services or assistance. Geriatric social workers should be prepared to suggest services for both the older person and their caregiver(s). To do so requires knowledge about respite services, adult day care programs, counseling programs, support groups, and other services available in the local community that can ease the burdens experienced by the family members who care for the older person. Helping caregivers to reduce the burden of caregiving and to work through issues and problems that are interfering with their ability to provide care can often be as useful as intervening directly with frail elderly clients.

Geriatric social work students should be prepared to make use of a team approach, and the use of specialists and consultants, when working with aging clients. Because some older individuals experience complicated interactions between their physical, psychological and social functioning, a team approach to assessment and intervention is often warranted (for reviews, see Applegate, Deyo, Kramer, & Meehan, 1991; Schmitt, Farrell, & Heinemann, 1988; Rubenstein, Stuck, Sui, & Weiland, 1991).

THE HARTFORD INITIATIVE

A recent initiative by the John A. Hartford Foundation focuses on addressing this increasing demand for geriatric social workers and the changing work environments that require geriatric social work skills and expertise. The John A. Hartford Foundation has a long-standing commitment to educating professionals for geriatric practice. The Hartford Foundation has funded programs in health and aging for more than twenty years. In the past, their focus had been on the medical and nursing fields, supporting the training of geriatric physicians and nurses. In the mid-1990s, the Hartford Foundation expanded their focus, launching a major new initiative, "Strengthening Geriatric Social Work." This initiative seeks to improve the well being of older adults by strengthening the field of geriatric social work. Consisting of three inter-related programs, this initiative seeks to facilitate the expansion of America's social work education programs to meet the needs of its aging population. These programs aim to establish standards for geriatric social work practice, support the development of junior faculty, and train future geriatric social workers. The Hartford Foundation has provided funding to three organizations to implement these programs. These organizations are the Council on Social Work Education (CSWE), The Gerontological Society of America (GSA), and The New York Academy of Medicine (NYAM).

In response to the Hartford aim of establishing standards for social work practice, CSWE has launched Strengthening Aging and Gerontology Education for Social Work (SAGE-SW). The goal of SAGE-SW is to help social work schools train gerontology-competent social workers. To help meet the needs of the aging population in the United States, SAGE-SW combines education and outreach: Educating *all* social workers and reaching out to a variety of health and social service organizations to assess needs, develop strategies for cooperation, and develop social work curriculum.

To support the development of junior faculty, the Hartford Foundation has provided funding through the GSA for two programs designed to mentor the next generation of geriatric social workers: the Hartford Geriatric Social Work Faculty Scholars Program and the Hartford Geriatric Social Work Doctoral Fellows Program. These programs will help to improve the research capacity for building better services for older persons in the United States. Over a two-year period, Faculty Scholars undertake geriatric research projects and participate in a series of faculty development institutes. Hartford Doctoral Fellows are selected from advanced doctoral students whose dissertations address issues germane to improving the well being of older persons and their families. As Doctoral Fellows, students receive two years of stipend support and participate in professional development activities. These two programs are designed to attract outstanding talent to geriatric social work with the goal of addressing the current lack of social workers who can meet the diverse and special health care needs of America's increasing older population.

The third arm of the Hartford's educational initiative, the Geriatric Social Work Practicum Development Program (GSWPDP), seeks to develop field practica in aging by increasing the number of sites training social work professionals to meet the needs of older adults. In addition to training more geriatric social workers, a goal of this initiative is to develop new roles for social workers, by influencing the field agencies that are involved in the MSW training. This increase in training sites will lead to improved services and service delivery capacity. NYAM serves as the coordinating center for GSWPDP by providing technical assistance and support to the six schools funded to develop and implement geriatric social work training programs, fostering cross-site communication, building a database of resources, developing evaluation criteria, and facilitating dissemination to social work educators and professionals.

The School of Social Welfare at the University at Albany was one of six schools selected to implement their models of geriatric social work training by the Hartford Foundation. The Albany Hartford Internships in Aging Program (Albany-HIAP) combines academic coursework and field practica in their training program. Albany-HIAP has chosen to emphasize the development of new roles for geriatric social workers as part of a larger project that will bring together local social service agencies to develop new services for older people.

GERIATRIC SOCIAL WORK AT THE UNIVERSITY AT ALBANY

New York State has the second largest elderly population in the United States. In the coming decades, the aging of the Baby Boom and longer life expectancies mean that the population of New York State will age rapidly. New York's population aged 60 and older will grow from 3.2 million individuals in 1995 to 4.4 million by 2025, with significant increases in the oldest-old and minority populations (Sutton, 1999). The Capital Region, in which the University at Albany is located, has a slightly larger proportion of older persons than New York State and one of the rural counties participating in the Albany program has the largest proportion of older persons in the state.

The Institute of Gerontology was established in the late 1960s as a center for teaching, research, and service at the University at Albany School for Social Welfare. The Albany Hartford Internships in Aging Program (Albany-HIAP) is housed within the Institute of Gerontology's Center for Excellence in Aging Services (CEAS). The purpose of CEAS is to increase opportunities for service and education in the Albany, New York region by developing resources to provide continuing education and consultation to community agencies.

The Albany-HIAP training program seeks to increase the number of MSW-level geriatric social workers by: encouraging the infusion of gerontology content into the generalist MSW curriculum; creating new roles and opportunities for social workers in the aging field; working with agencies to develop and expand aging programs and services; and developing empirically based guidelines and exemplars for practice with older adults, their families, and their caregivers. The Albany-HIAP Consortium represents a collaboration among the School of Social Welfare, University at Albany, and 9 agencies that provide services to older adults in the Capital District and rural Northeastern Region of New York State. The agencies include not-for-profit health care systems, a health insurer, a sectarian family service agency, a voluntary organization serving those with Alzheimer's disease, a grass-roots not-for-profit organization serving Hispanic persons, and the state agency coordinating services for older persons. They provide a range of services to older persons on a continuum from well to end-of-life. They reach diverse constituencies, including persons of color and urban and rural populations. The Consortium agencies serve as sites for field placements for Albany-HIAP interns.

To increase the number of MSW students educated in geriatric social work practice, Albany-HIAP actively recruits MSW students to participate in the program. In the first year of the two-year Albany-HIAP MSW curriculum, students complete the generalist MSW curriculum. In addition to the regular MSW curriculum, the Albany-HIAP students attend a non-credit Seminar on Aging, which includes content on aging process, practice skills for work with older persons, and related services and policies. First year Albany-HIAP students are placed in agencies that serve persons of varying ages, but all the sites provide opportunities to work with older adults and families as well as younger persons. The field instruction for the first year student is two days a week.

In the second year, Albany-HIAP students take a special curriculum with in-depth content on aging and services for older persons. Second year Albany-HIAP students are assigned to one or more of the Consortium sites. The second year internship consists of a rotation among programs (within a site or between sites) to allow students to work with older adults and their families on a continuum from well to end of life. For example, at a hospital, students spent 9 weeks in an outpatient care management clinic, then 9 weeks in an intensive care unit, 9 weeks on a medical floor, and 9 weeks in a hospice for dying persons and their families. Another student rotated among agencies, educating persons with dementia at a voluntary Alzheimer's association, working with physicians to improve their diagnoses of dementia, and leading reminiscence groups in a nursing home. In most sites, students also carry a few cases throughout the year and through multiple services. For example, students who began in the outpatient clinic followed elderly patients from that service to in-patient units or assisted living facilities.

Students specialize in either clinical practice (service to individuals, families, and groups) or management of human service agencies. However, to further develop their leadership skills students complete a Leadership Development Project in which they learn skills from the other specialization. Thus, all students have the opportunity to apply both clinical and management skills in working with their field agency to develop new programs and services. Some examples of Leadership Development Projects for the clinical students include: planning and marketing a new counseling program for home-bound elderly, educating physicians about dementia assessment tools, and working with a community-based case management program to provide transportation services to older persons in a rural area. The management students participated in referral and information services for rural elderly and in crisis management teams.

While maintaining and expanding the MSW specialization in geriatric social work is the centerpiece of the University at Albany's commitment to training geriatric social workers, the School of Social Welfare also offers training for Doctoral students with a specialization in geriatric social work. Students combine coursework and research training. Financial support for these advanced students is available from a variety of sources including research assistantships associated with applied gerontological research projects and the independent Doctoral Fellowships offered through the Hartford Foundation. Examples of recent and ongoing dissertation research topics include social worker involvement in end-of-life decision making, adult protective services, and supportive services for caregivers.

Although the doctoral and MSW programs are educationally separate, the Hartford initiatives have created a synergy that enhances the educational experience of students in both programs. For example, doctoral students work as Coordinator and Evaluator for the HIAP program. They learn career-enhancing skills in education and curriculum for geriatric social work, in program evaluation, and in development of empirically based models of practice and education. Some of the Albany-HIAP students work on faculty or doctoral student projects as their Leadership Development Project. For example, the initiative to educate physicians about dementia was a collaboration between a faculty member and a HIAP agency and dementia-education groups run by another student were part of an intervention research project.

Beyond the curriculum, the goals of Albany-HIAP are to create new roles and opportunities for social workers in the aging field and to help agencies develop and expand programs for the aging population. These goals are addressed by working to keep Consortium members involved in Albany-HIAP and encouraging agencies to work collaboratively on new projects. This is a significant accomplishment given that service providers had often competed for resources and clients and many consortium members had not previously worked together. The full Consortium, with agency, faculty, and student representatives, meets quarterly to provide guidance to the overall project. Consortium members also participate in three working committees (Curriculum and Field, Community Relations and Recruitment, and Long-Range Planning) on a monthly basis. These committees guide the project and do some of the work, for example, screening potential students.

Although members lament the large number of meetings, the frequent interaction around the educational project has had positive consequences beyond the curriculum. By meeting around a common goal that benefits all, agency representatives engage each other and begin to establish trust in a noncompetitive environment. In one community, agency representatives were surprised at the variety of services available to older persons through their agencies. They assigned one student a Leadership Development Project to prepare a comprehensive resource guide in English and Spanish. Eventually, beginning collaboration around resources developed. Several agencies shared their benefactor lists for fund-raising for the educational project. Several agencies collaborated to submit small requests to foundations to extend services to older persons in remote rural areas. Others began discussion about new culturally sensitive hospice services for Jewish and Hispanic older persons. The Consortium agencies also joined under the leadership of a faculty member with other agencies, state and county legislators, and government officials to propose an Aging Friendly Community initiative, to improve coordination among health services for older persons in the region. Such collaboration is historically rare in the region.

The Consortium committees had a serendipitous effect on student development as well. Student representatives were invited as regular members of all committees. For those who participated, it was a mind-boggling opportunity to see interorganizational politics and collaboration on a level they had not envisioned. Upon graduation, they cited the Consortium committees as making a major contribution to their education and expanding their horizons to see service delivery in its regional context.

Another approach to creating social work roles and expanding programs for older persons is through the services provided by students. The Leadership Development Projects were intended to develop, implement or evaluate new services. While that goal was too ambitious to be implemented across the board, new services and services that would not otherwise have been available were offered, and several involved social workers in new roles. For example, the project to educate physicians about dementia involved social workers in entirely new roles as medical educators doing outreach to local physician's offices. At one hospital, staff saw the emergency room as exclusively medical territory, and acknowledged no role for the social work student placed there. The student created a social work role-systematizing and coordinating post-ER medical and social services–and was able to convince medical and business personnel that social work service was efficient. Other students worked in a managed care organization, in traditional roles of quality assurance but also in non-traditional roles including grant development and developing protocols for effective service. These efforts to change roles and services through student projects are undoubtedly the most difficult and ephemeral of the Albany-HIAP efforts, because the student's educational experiences must be paramount when the various project goals are balanced.

A final thrust for new roles and services is the effort to create empirically based guidelines and exemplars for practice with older adults and their families. The project itself is part of development of a new model of field education for social work students. In addition, students help develop protocols for coordination of service for families of persons with dementia, and several faculty have developed guidelines for informational groups for such families.

CONCLUSION

According to the 2001 Educational Policy and Accreditation Standards of the Council for Social Work Education (2001d): "The profession of social work is based on the values of service, social and economic justice, dignity and worth of the person, importance of human relationships, and integrity and competence in practice. With these values as defining principles, the purposes of social work are:

- To enhance human well-being and alleviate poverty, oppression, and other forms of social injustice.
- To enhance the social functioning and interactions of individuals, families, groups, organizations, communities, and society by involving them in accomplishing goals, developing resources, and preventing and alleviating distress.
- To formulate and implement social policies, services, and programs that meet basic human needs and support the development of human capacities.
- To pursue policies, services, and resources through advocacy and social or political actions that promote social and economic justice.
- To develop and use research, knowledge, and skills that advance social work practice.
- To develop and apply practice in the context of diverse cultures."

These standards reflect the importance of independence and the democratic context of American life. To meet the needs of our aging population, the field of social work must work together with community and health service agencies to apply these principles to the distinct service needs of the elderly.

Addressing the needs of an older population that is increasing both in size and diversity requires strong community ties and creative approaches to service delivery. We have outlined an approach to geriatric social work training that has two main components: (1) incorporating training specializing in service to older persons in Master of Social Work (MSW) degree programs, and (2) developing community alliances that will lead to the creation of new roles for social workers and new programs for older persons. At the University at Albany, training specializing in service to older persons has been incorporated into the MSW program in a number of innovative ways. Students are placed in a variety of fieldwork settings, working with aging persons from wellness to end of life. Practitioners and leaders in aging services work with social work students to serve as community-based mentors. The development of community alliances enables us to serve as a catalyst in bringing agencies to work together to develop new services for older persons. Some outcomes of these alliances include: the development of social work positions in agencies that did not previously employ social workers; an emphasis on understanding the interactions aging persons have with a variety of agencies; and efforts to improve the coordination of planning and service delivery.

The practice environment is rapidly becoming more home- and community-based while field practica training is more institutionally based (Greene, 1997; Berkman et al., 1998). For social workers the changing service delivery environment includes: the impact of managed care on aging services, increasing recognition of the needs of adult caregivers, development of new residential and community-based services such as assisted living, the growing use of geriatric case managers, and an upsurge in interdisciplinary services. The ultimate goal of social work training is to prepare students with the skills and experiences to effectively meet the health and social needs of the populations that they serve. As the population of the United States continues to age, the demand for gerontology-competent social workers will continue to increase. With the support of programs such as the Hartford Initiative, graduate schools of social work will be prepared to meet that demand.

REFERENCES

Applegate, W., Deyo, R., Kramer, A., & Meehan, S. (1991). "Geriatric evaluation and management: Current status and future research directions." *Journal of the American Geriatric Society* 39: 2S-7S.

Barth, M. C. (2001). *The Labor Market for Social Workers: A First Look*. Report prepared for the John A. Hartford Foundation.

Berkman, B., Silverstone, B., Simmons, W. J., Valland, P. J., & Judith L. Howe. (2000). "Social Work Geriatric Practice: The Need for Faculty Development in the New Millennium." *Journal of Geriatric Social Work* 349 (1): 5-23.

Berkman, B., Silverstone, B., & Simmons, W. J. (1998). *Social work gerontological practice: The need and strategic proposals for professional development.* Paper prepared for the John A. Hartford Foundation.

Council on Social Work Education. (2001a). *Curriculum Policy Statement for Baccalaureate Degree Programs.* Alexandria, VA: CSWE Online. <http://www.cswe.org/> (5/1/01).

Council on Social Work Education. (2001b). *Curriculum Policy Statement for Master's Degree Programs.* Alexandria, VA: CSWE Online. <http://www.cswe.org/> (5/1/01).

Council on Social Work Education. (2001c). *A Blueprint for the New Millennium.* Alexandria, VA: Council for Social Work Education/SAGE-SW.

Council on Social Work Education. (2001d). *Proposed Educational Policy and Accreditation Standards (Draft for Public Comment April 2001).* Alexandria, VA: CSWE Online. <http://www.cswe.org/> (5/1/01).

Damron-Rodriquez, J., and Lubben, J. (1997). The 1995 WHCoA: An agenda for social work education and training. In, Saltz, C, (Ed.), *Social work response to the 1995 White House Conference on Aging: From issues to actions.* New York: The Haworth Press, Inc., 65-77.

Dawson, G. D., & Santos, J. F. (1996). *National survey: Funding for geriatric health and mental health care trainers.* Presentation at the Annual Meeting, Association for Gerontology in Higher Education, Philadelphia, PA.

Evans, D. (1996). Descriptive epidemiology of Alzheimer's disease. in Khachaturian, Z. & Radebaugh, T. (Eds.) Alzheimer's disease: Cause(s), diagnosis, treatment, and care. Boca Raton: CRC Press.

Frumkin, M., and G. A. Lloyd. (1995). "Social Work Education," in *Encyclopedia of Social Work 19th Edition.* Washington, DC: NASW Press, pp. 2238-2247.

Gibelman, M., & Schervish, P. (1997). *Who we are: A second look.* Washington, DC: NASW Press.

Greene, R. R., Barusch, A., and Connelly, R. (1990). *Social work and gerontology: An update.* Washington, DC: Administration on Aging and the Association of Gerontology in Higher Education.

Greene, R. R. (1997). "Social work in the 21st century: Will educators be ready?" *Progress Notes Indiana University School of Social Work* 1 (2): 1.

Hollis, E. V., and A. L. Taylor. (1951). *Social Work Education in the United States.* Westport, CT: Greenwood Press.

Khachaturian, Z., & Radebaugh, T. (Eds.) (1996). Alzheimer's disease: Cause(s), diagnosis, treatment, and care. Boca Raton: CRC Press.

Klein, S. (Ed.). (1996). *A national agenda for geriatric education: White Papers.* Rockville, MD: Health Resources and Services Administration.

Knight, B. (1986). *Psychotherapy with older adults.* Beverly Hills: Sage.

Manton, K. G., Corder, L. S., & Stallard. E. (1997). "Chronic disability trends in elderly United States populations: 1982-1994." *Proceedings of the National Academy of Sciences of the United States of America* 94 (6): 2593-8.

New York State Office on Aging and The State Society on Aging of New York. (2000). *Project 2015: The Future of Aging in New York State*. Albany: NYSOFA.

Peterson, D. A., & Wendt, P. F. (1990). Employment in the field of aging: A survey of professionals in four fields. *The Gerontologist*, 30 (5): 679-85.

Ragan, A. M., & A. M. Bowen. 2001. "Improving Attitudes Regarding the Elderly Population." *The Gerontologist* 41: 511-515.

Rubenstein, L., Stuck, A., Sui, A., & Weiland, D. (1991). "Impacts of geriatric evaluation and management programs on defined outcomes: Overview of the evidence." *Journal of the American Geriatrics Society* 39, 98-104.

Schmitt, M. H., Farrell, M. P., & Heinemann, G. D. (1988). "Conceptual and methodological problems in studying the effects of interdisciplinary geriatric teams." *The Gerontologist* 28 (6), 753-764.

Spillman, B. C., & Pezzin, L. E., (2000). "Potential and active family caregivers: Changing networks and the "sandwich generation." *Milbank Quarterly* 78 (3): 347-74, 339.

Sutton, D. L. (1999). *Demographic Projections to 2025*. Report prepared by the New York State Office for the Aging.

Toseland, R., & Smith, T. (2001). *Supporting Caregivers Through Education and Training*. A technical assistance monograph prepared for the National Family Caregiver Support Program Initiative of the U. S. Administration on Aging.

Toseland, R., Smith, G., & McCallion, P. (2001). "Helping Family Caregivers." In A. Gitterman (Ed.), *Handbook of social work practice with vulnerable and resilient populations* (2nd ed.). NY: Columbia University Press, pp. 548-581.

U. S. Census Bureau. (2001). "Nation's Median Age Highest Ever, But 65-and-Over Population's Growth Lags, Census 2000 Shows." *United States Department of Commerce News*. Washington, DC: U. S. Bureau of the Census. Accessed online 5/24/01 (http://www.census.gov/Press-Release/www/2001/cb01cn67.html).

Wills, T. (1978). "Perceptions of clients by professional helpers." *Psychological Bulletin* 85: 968-1000.

Chapter 8

The Hunter Experience:
Innovations in the Field Practicum

Joann Ivry, PhD
Bernadette R. Hadden, PhD

SUMMARY. Rotation in field education is a new phenomena with potential for increasing student's knowledge of increasingly complex social work practice environments. With support from The John A. Hartford Foundation, the Hunter College School of Social Work/Brookdale Center on Aging Geriatric Field Practicum Partnership Program developed and implemented a field rotation model. The goal of Hunter's rotation model is to maximize student exposure to the continuum of care in geriatric social work services. This paper describes the process of developing a field rotation model, and presents early results on exposure to the continuum of care and the impact of rotation on students and field instructors. Pre-

Joann Ivry is Associate Professor and Assistant Dean at the Hunter College School of Social Work, 129 East 79th Street, New York, NY 10021. Bernadette R. Hadden is Assistant Professor at the Hunter College School of Social Work.

The authors wish to acknowledge the contributions of Ms. Maria Hodges, MSW, Project Faculty Advisor/Field Liaison and Ms. Glynn Rudich, MSW, Director of Field Education at the Hunter College School of Social Work, for the development and implementation of the Hartford/Hunter field rotation model.

[Haworth co-indexing entry note]: "The Hunter Experience: Innovations in the Field Practicum." Ivry, Joann, and Bernadette R. Hadden. Co-published simultaneously in *Journal of Gerontological Social Work* (The Haworth Social Work Practice Press, an imprint of The Haworth Press, Inc.) Vol. 39, No. 1/2, 2002, pp. 129-144; and: *Advancing Gerontological Social Work Education* (ed: M. Joanna Mellor, and Joann Ivry) The Haworth Social Work Practice Press, an imprint of The Haworth Press, Inc., 2002, pp. 129-144. Single or multiple copies of this article are available for a fee from The Haworth Document Delivery Service [1-800-HAWORTH, 9:00 a.m. - 5:00 p.m. (EST). E-mail address: docdelivery@haworthpress.com].

liminary results suggest that students and field instructors responded positively to field rotation. With improved skill at administering rotations in field education, field instructors and social work educators may be more responsive to its greater utilization. *[Article copies available for a fee from The Haworth Document Delivery Service: 1-800-HAWORTH. E-mail address: <docdelivery@haworthpress.com> Website: <http://www.HaworthPress.com> © 2002 by The Haworth Press, Inc. All rights reserved.]*

KEYWORDS. Field rotation model, geriatric social work education, practicum partnership

FIELD EDUCATION IN SOCIAL WORK

The field practicum is an indispensable component of social work education (CSWE, 1992; Cuzzi, Holden, Chernack, Rutter & Rosenberg, 1997). The field education experience provides students the opportunity to expand their understanding of social problems, human behavior, and social welfare programs and policies through the application and integration of academic knowledge and practice skills. Approximately 40% of student's time in their overall social work educational experience takes place in field practica (Lindeman & Mellor, 1999).

Since the founding of the first professional school of social work, field education has been characterized by an intensive one-to-one professional teaching relationship developed and maintained during a "a year long assignment under the mentorship of an individual field instructor" (Cuzzi, Holden, Rutter, Rosenberg, & Chernack, 1996, p. 74). This field educational model has had a tenacious hold on social work education. Surprisingly, alternative or nontraditional field education arrangements have not been sufficiently explored (Cuzzi et al., 1996; Long & Heydt, 2000). While a rotation model is used in other health care professional educational programs such as medicine, nursing and psychology, it has not been incorporated into social work routinely. This has occurred, despite appeals to better educate and prepare social work students for social work practice in a changing service environment.

External forces, such as the dramatic changes in the health care field and the need to train social work students in rapid assessments and crisis interventions, have led to some modifications in the standard social work field education model. Additionally, the rapid growth of the aged population and the concomitant demand for health care professionals trained to provide health and social services to older adults and their families is another external force prompting the need for changes in social work education. The profession has been exhorted to increase the number of aging-competent social work practitioners to serve this emergent population (Scharlach, Damron-Rodriguez, Robinson & Feldman, 2000). As a critical element in social work education, the field practicum experience becomes a central arena for training future cadres of needed professional gerontological social workers. Rotation in field education may be a way to ensure that students receive maximum exposure to the range and varieties of gerontological social work practice in today's world.

A review of the literature identified two studies which reported the use of rotation in the social work field practicum. The social work faculty and staff at the University of Utah Medical Center implemented rotation to expose students to a "wide range of concepts and skills necessary for social work to make an impact on health, or more modestly, even to survive as a profession within the complex organization of health services and personnel" (Dalgleish, Kane & McNamara, 1976, p. 167). Rotation there consisted of three successive service assignments and a change of field instructor per assignment, thereby replacing the typical year-long field practicum and the one-to-one assignment of student to supervisor. More recently a field rotation model, consisting of three successive ten-weeklong field placements with three different supervisors, was implemented in a large urban hospital (Cuzzi, Holden, Rutter, Rosenberg & Chernack, 1996; Cuzzi, Holden, Chernack, Rutter, & Rosenberg, 1997). These authors contend that rotation in social work field education can ensure that students are exposed to the "characteristics and demands of contemporary practice" (Spitzer, Holden, Cuzzi, Rutter, Chernack, & Rosenberg, 2001, p. 79). Moreover, they suggest that the concept of field rotation need not be limited to the structure defined in their study, but can be extended to include different types of rotating field assignments. As they write, "[T]he number and progression of rotations will ultimately be determined by the combination of expressed need and learning capacity of the individual student" (Spitzer et al., 2001, p. 88). So too, will the needs and capacities of participating field placement sites influence the nature of the field rotation model developed and implemented as was the experience of the Hartford/Hunter Field Practicum Partnership Program.

THE EVOLUTION OF A MODIFIED FIELD ROTATION MODEL

The Hunter School of Social Work/Brookdale Center on Aging Field Practicum Partnership Program, sponsored by The John A. Hartford Foundation, conceptualized, developed and implemented a modified field rotation model. The practicum partnership field sites represent a diverse group of agencies serving an heterogenous aging population in New York City. The program's advisory committee approved modifying the field rotation as an expeditious way to ensure that students in Hunter's program receive maximum exposure to the aging-rich experiences available in the partnership field practicum sites. The committee concluded that through some type of field rotation, students would enhance their knowledge of the aging process, be exposed to a range of aging related problem areas and the concomitant continuum of care, and expand their repertoire of social work intervention skills in geriatric services.

Field rotation, however, is not only a radical departure from the conventional social work field education paradigm, it is also a major variation on how field education at Hunter usually operates. Typically, Hunter social work student interns spend three days in a field practicum per academic year, and are assigned one field instructor for the entire academic year. In some health care settings, students receive a primary and secondary field assignment, and thus, have additional supervision from a second field instructor who is differentiated from the primary one by the designation of task supervisor (Marshack, 1986).

The specific aspects of Hunter's field rotation model evolved during the planning and implementation phases of the program through the thoughtful deliberations of an active and committed advisory committee. Considerable discussion ensued about the nature of an acceptable field rotation model, one which would achieve the goal of maximum exposure to contemporary gerontological practice but would not compromise the fundamental educational values inherent in the traditional field education model. In the first conception of the Hunter field education rotation model, students were to spend two days in a primary field site and a third day in an associate site. Primary and associate field sites would alternate each semester. As such, each agency would have a student for two days per week in the first semester, and for one day in the subsequent semester. This arrangement would have resulted in agencies having students in field placement for much less time per year than in the traditional model. Additional reservations raised about the field rotation model were that it might:

1. compromise the quality of students' field education experiences by depriving them of continuity of learning in service provision and client care;
2. deprive students of the benefits of the one-to-one student-supervisor relationship over an academic year;
3. be too disruptive, due to changing primary and associate agency assignments each semester;

4. require too much field time in learning agency policies and programs thereby, detracting from time needed to acquire practical skills.

The practical difficulties of implementing a traditional field rotation led to a compromise plan in which Hunter student interns would be assigned to a modified field rotation. They would be placed for one year in two agencies paired to ensure complementary and contrasting field experiences, and receive supervision from a field instructor in the primary site and from a task supervisor in the associate site. The following principles were formulated to protect valued aspects of the traditional field education model and to mitigate potential hazards of a field rotation model,

1. the project's field liaison would work closely with students and field practicum sites to arrange field rotations to meet students' educational needs (e.g., major method concentration) and agency requirements (e.g., supervisor availability);
2. consortium field practicum sites would be paired to ensure student exposure to a wide range of complementary and contrasting service experiences;
3. field placement sites would be either in two separate agencies or in two departments within one large institution;
4. students would be assigned to a primary field placement for two days per week and to an associate site for one day per week for the entire academic year;
5. at the primary field practicum site, students would be assigned a field instructor who would have major responsibility for supervision and evaluation;
6. at the associate field practicum site, students would also be assigned a field instructor, known as the task supervisor, to provide on-site supervision and contribute to the evaluation of the student's field performance;
7. field instructors and task supervisors would meet with the program's field liaison prior and during the rotation year to clarify supervisory roles and responsibilities, develop appropriate student assignments, and coordinate student activities;
8. students would participate in a summer internship at one of the agencies to which they were assigned in preparation for the rotation year.

The successful implementation of the project's field rotation model is due to the strength of the school-field partnership. In addition, the above-stated principles guided the implementation of the modified field rotation model and the work of the program's field liaison who, in close collaboration with educational coordinators from field practicum sites, carefully customized each student's field rotation educational experience. Innovations in field education are relatively rare, and we have just completed the first year of an experimental process. The remainder of this paper will present our preliminary results and describe the viewpoints of student interns, field instructors and task supervisors on the summer internship and the modified field rotation experience.

FACILITATING ADJUSTMENT TO A MODIFIED ROTATION MODEL THROUGH A SUMMER INTERNSHIP

The Student Experience

Since both students and field instructors are less familiar with a rotation model, the Hunter Program provided paid summer internships for the first and second cohort of Hartford students to orient them to their future field placement sites and familiarize them with the continuum of services provided to the elderly. This arrangement will continue with the third cohort of students. At the end of their internship experience, two students from the first cohort (summer 1999/2000) and ten from the second cohort (2000/2001) completed a self-administered standardized questionnaire with both closed and open-ended questions to evaluate their experience in the summer internship program.

All twelve students (100%) indicated that their assignment increased their appreciation of the agency's services and client population. Eight students rated their internship experience as good, and four rated their experience as excellent. Students performed a variety of tasks during their internship as presented in Table 1. All students reported that they obtained in service training, seven performed administrative tasks, five provided group work services to clients, four were involved in research related activities, assessment, supportive services, and information and referral services, and three provided case management/concrete services, supportive counseling and community organizing, advocacy, policy and program planning.

The Field Instructor Experience with the Summer Internship

Students were assigned field instructors to supervise their summer internships. Four field instructors completed a Social Work Intern Evaluation at the end of the summer 2000/2001 internship. The self-administered standardized evaluation completed by the field instructors also contained both closed and open-ended questions to evaluate their and the student's experience in the summer internship program. The length of the summer internship was flexible, based on agency need and student availability, and ranged from 15 days to 24 days through the summer. Two field instructors reported that their student

TABLE 1. Activities/tasks performed by student interns during summer 1990/2000 and 2000/2001 (N = 12)

Activities/tasks performed by student interns	# Students engaged in task
1. In-service training	12
2. Research related activities	4
3. Administrative tasks	7
4. Assessment	4
5. Case management/concrete services	3
6. Supportive counseling	3
7. Supportive services	4
8. Group work	5
9. Community organizing, advocacy, policy and program planning	3
10. Intake and assessment	4
11. Information and referral	4

completed 15 days in the summer internship, one student completed 20 days and a fourth completed 24 days. Workday arrangements differed as well, with some students working a 2-3 days a week and/or a full week over a period of 3 to 10 weeks.

Two of the field instructors reported that the length of the internship was sufficient (Table 2), whereas one reported that the length was insufficient, indicating that "we would have loved to have the student with us for a longer period, she was extremely helpful." One field instructor at an agency where the student was placed for 10 weeks indicated that the internship was "too long" and did not elaborate on the reason for the response. Three field instructors reported that they would host summer social work interns in the future. One field instructor reported that they would "possibly" host another social work intern in the summer, elaborating with regard to the whole year rotation model that "[H]aving a full-time 2nd year student only 2 days a week is somewhat problematic. The student's schedule, including team rounds, staff meeting and supervision does not leave that much time for home visits which are quite timely."

Students and field instructors clearly valued the summer internship which increased students' appreciation of the agency's services and client population. None of the students had a negative experience with their summer internship and overall ratings of the internships were extremely positive. Field instructors valued the experience of working with social work interns prior to

TABLE 2. Field instructor's opinions regarding the length of the internship period and attitudes about hosting summer social work interns in the future

Variable	% Responses		
	Yes	No	Possibly
1. Length of the internship was sufficient	50%	25%	0%
2. Would host social work interns in the future	75%	0%	25%

their field placement. Field instructors responses indicated that they gained as much as the students.

EVALUATION OF THE MODIFIED FIELD ROTATION MODEL

Methodology

The Hunter Program obtained information regarding the students' clients, the case situations to which they were exposed, exposure to practice methods and services provided by the field practicum site, potential areas of confusion/conflict with the modified rotation model, and opinions about exposure to such a model. In the spring of 2001, the first cohort of Hartford students completed a survey evaluating the rotation model they were exposed to during the fall 2000 and spring 2001 semesters.

Data were simultaneously collected from field instructors and task supervisors to obtain descriptive information regarding their experience with the modified rotation model for Hartford students. The aim of the assessment was to obtain information regarding changes made in student caseload assignment, accommodations made between field instructors and task supervisors at different sites and overall opinions regarding the rotation model.

Ten students and eight field instructors/task supervisors completed separate self-administered assessment instruments at the end of the spring 2001 semester. The instruments contained closed and open-ended questions with a section on their opinions regarding the rotation model rated on a 5-point Likert scale. Data were processed using a standard statistical package, SPSS for Windows, Version 9.0. Frequency distributions were produced for the questions on the instruments. Tables that represent results of the data analysis have been organized by topic area. The report first presents findings regarding the students and thereafter for the field instructors and task supervisors.

For ease of interpretation, most response categories have been converted to percentages. Any instances in which a column falls short of, or exceeds 100% may be attributed to the rounding of data and overlap.

RESULTS

The Student Experience with Modified Rotation

Client Groups and Case Situations

All ten students (100%) were exposed to client groups that included well older adults, low-income elderly, cognitively impaired and physically challenged elderly. Exposure to nursing home residents was the lowest (30%) and perhaps reflected the fact that only one nursing home is currently involved in the consortium partnership (see Table 3).

Practice Methods

The majority (80%) of students were exposed to casework with individuals and families, with more than half (60%) exposed to group work and less than a third (30%) exposed to community organizing, advocacy, policy and program planning. This distribution is consistent with the practice method selections of the general student population at the Hunter College School of Social Work (see Table 4).

Exposure to Range of Services

The majority (90%) of students were exposed to information and referral services in keeping with the type of services students are often exposed to in standard field practicum placements. Half (50%) were exposed to home health aide services while only one student (10%) in each case was exposed to adult day health care, outpatient mental health, foster care, residential care, home repair, emergency services, and dialysis service provision (see Table 5).

Student Responses to Areas of Confusion and Conflict

Two fifths (40%) of the students reported that there was a lack of communication between the field instructor and task supervisor about the field practicum evaluation. Fewer students (30%) reported confusion regarding the primacy of the field instructor and only two reported that having a task supervisor from the associate agency hampered their field work experience (see Table 6).

TABLE 3. Client groups students worked with and/or case situations exposed to during field practicum

Population served by agency	% Students exposed to type of population
1. Well older adults	100%
2. Low income elderly	100%
3. Cognitively impaired elderly	100%
4. Physically challenged elderly	100%
5. Mentally ill elderly	70%
6. Ethnic specific elderly	70%
7. Abused neglected elderly	60%
8. Nursing home resident	30%

TABLE 4. Students' field practicum experiences by practice method

Practice method utilized in agency	% Students exposed to practice method
1. Casework with individuals and families	80%
2. Group work	60%
3. Community organizing, advocacy, policy and program planning	30%

TABLE 5. Students' exposure to range of services provided by field practicum site

Students' exposure to range of services	% Students exposed to services
1. Information and referral services	90%
2. Home health aide services	50%
3. Exercise programs, recreation, continuing care retirement community, home health care, acute care	40%
4. Adult day care, congregate meals, legal and protection services, nursing home services, homemaker services, home delivered services	30%
5. Respite care, assisted living, E.R.S. systems, palliative/hospice care, chronic care	20%
6. Adult day health care, outpatient mental health, foster care, residential care (board and care), home repair services, emergency services, dialysis services	10%

TABLE 6. Students' reported areas of confusion/conflict with a rotation model

Areas of confusion/conflict with a rotation model field practicum	Responses		
	Yes	No	Missing
1. Lack of communication between the student and field instructor/task supervisor about the practicum evaluation	40%	60%	0%
2. Confusion regarding primacy of field instructor	30%	70%	0%
3. Provision of a task supervisor from the associate agency hampered the student's experience in gerontology/aging	20%	70%	10%

Student Opinions of the Modified Rotation Model

Students were very positive about the rotation model despite the existence of some problems. Responses on a five point Likert scale indicated that the majority (78%-89%) of students was positive about the rotation model. Eighty nine percent (n = 8) reported that their personal objectives had been achieved, that the time devoted to the rotation model was well spent and worthwhile, that the model added to their knowledge of geriatrics, and that as a result of the rotation model experience, they felt more confident working with the elderly. Seventy eight percent (n = 7) of the students reported that they would recommend a rotation model of field practicum training in gerontology to other students. None strongly disagreed with any of the statements (see Table 7).

THE FIELD INSTRUCTOR AND TASK SUPERVISOR EXPERIENCE WITH A MODIFIED ROTATION

The modified rotation model generally did not result in an alteration of the tasks assigned to students in both semesters. Five field instructors (63%) reported that they did not have to alter the tasks assigned in both semesters because of the rotation model. Three field instructors (38%) however, did construct assignment of cases differently. For example, one field instructor "tried to assign the most educational cases," while another "did not assign clients who needed more intensive case management due to the one-day placement" and a third did not assign elder abuse cases "because of the complexity of these situations, the lack of clarity and the need for daily availability of the worker."

Impact on Quality of a Modified Field Rotation

The quality of the field supervision was more often affected positively than negatively by the rotation model. Fifty percent (n = 4) of the field instructors

TABLE 7. Student opinions regarding exposure to rotation in the field practicum*

Students Opinions Regarding the Rotation Model	Strongly Disagree N (%)	Disagree N (%)	Agree N (%)	Strongly Agree N (%)	No Opinion N (%)
My personal objectives for exposure to a rotation model of field practicum training have been achieved	0	1 (11)	6 (67)	2 (22)	0
I would recommend a rotation model of field practicum training in gerontology to other students	0	1 (11)	2 (22)	5 (56)	1 (11)
The time devoted to this rotation model experience in gerontology was well spent and worthwhile	0	1 (11)	3 (33)	5 (56)	0
The rotation model of field practicum with the elderly added to my knowledge of geriatrics	0	1 (11)	3 (33)	5 (56)	0
As a result of this experience, I feel more confident working with the elderly	0	0	3 (33)	5 (56)	1 (11)

*Only 9 students completed this section

and task supervisors reported that they were able to spend as much time with the student as they would have in the standard model. Additionally, two instructors (25%) reported that supervision was more focused because of less time spent with the student, and only one (13%) instructor reported that too much time in supervision was spent on coordinating tasks between the two sites. None reported that supervision was stressful or that too much had to be covered in too little time (see Table 8).

Communication Between Field Instructor and Task Supervisor

Overall, communication between field instructors and task supervisors at the different sites was good (see Table 9). Most (88%) communicated with each other through the two semesters of the field placement and 75% (n = 6) reported that having two field instructors as provided through the rotation model enhanced their student's experience in gerontology.

Impact on Student Learning

Field instructors and task supervisors were divided regarding the amount of learning students obtained in the rotation model as compared with students in the standard model. Fifty percent (n = 4) reported that students exposed to a ro-

TABLE 8. Impact of the use of a rotation model in field practicum on the quality of field supervision

Quality of field supervision	% Responses
1. Not able to spend as much time with student as would in a regular model	50%
2. Supervision was more focused	25%
3. Too much time in supervision spent on coordinating tasks between the 2 sites	13%

TABLE 9. Communication between field instructors and task supervisors and ramifications of "multiple" field instructors

Variable	% Responses	
	Yes	No
1. There was communication between field instructors and task supervisors about field practicum evaluation	88%	13%
2. Having a second field instructor/task supervisor enhanced the student's experience in gerontology/aging	75%	13%

tation model learned more than students in the standard model. However, almost all the instructors (88%) reported that the exposure of students to a greater variety and array of tasks and clients, as provided by the rotation model, enhanced their overall knowledge and practice skills regarding the elderly (see Table 10).

More than half (63%) of the field instructors reported that the completion of the Field Practicum Evaluation differed for students in a rotation model as compared with students in the standard model. The rotation model required that field instructors and task supervisors meet to evaluate their students' performance in the field practicum. Some field instructors reported that the input of the task supervisor was valuable in that it validated their perceptions of the student.

Overall Evaluation of the Modified Rotation Model

Field instructors and task supervisors were generally in agreement that the rotation model is valuable. Seventy-five percent (n = 6) of the field instructors and task supervisors reported that they would recommend a rotation model to other field instructors and task supervisors, and 50% (n = 4) reported that the rotation model added to their student's knowledge of geriatrics/gerontology. Finally, 63% reported that their students felt more confident working with the elderly as a result of being exposed to a rotation model in their field practicum (see Table 11).

TABLE 10. Field instructor and task supervisor perceptions of rotation model impact on student learning, and knowledge and practice skills

Variable	% Responses
1. Students exposed to the rotation model learned *more* than other students in a regular/standard model	50%
2. Students' exposure to a greater variety and array of tasks and patients in the rotation model *enhanced* their overall knowledge and practice skills with the elderly	88%

TABLE 11. Field instructor and task supervisor's opinions regarding the modified rotation model*

Field instructor and task supervisor's opinions regarding the rotation model	Strongly Disagree N (%)	Disagree N (%)	Agree N (%)	Strongly agree N (%)	No opinion N (%)
1. I would recommend a rotation model of field practicum instruction in geriatrics/gerontology to other supervisors	0	1(13)	6 (75)	0	0
2. The rotation model of field practicum with the elderly added to my student's knowledge of geriatrics/gerontology	0	1 (13)	3 (38)	1 (13)	2 (25)
3. As a result of this experience, my student feels more confident working with the elderly	0	1 (13)	4 (50)	1 (13)	1 (13)

*Only 7 field instructors and task supervisors completed this section

CONCLUSIONS

The successful implementation and positive evaluation of the modified rotation model by students and their field instructors and task supervisors revealed that a modified rotation model for a geriatric field practicum is feasible. The findings indicated that the Hunter Geriatric Field Practicum modified rotation model achieved the goal of exposing students to a continuum of care in the provision of services to the elderly. Students were primarily positive about the rotation model and were exposed to a diversity of client groups and case situations as provided by the consortium field practice sites. The few problem areas expressed regarding supervision such as communication between field instructor and task supervisor, their respective responsibilities, and questions about appropriate student field assignments will be remedied with ongoing in-

put and review by the Hunter program staff in collaboration with agency partners.

Field instructors and task supervisors also responded positively to the modified rotation model. Communication between field instructors and task supervisors at both the primary and secondary placements occurred and having the
input of more than one field instructor or task supervisor enhanced the quality
of the field practicum evaluation. Some modifications may need to be made in
the construction of the assignment of cases due to the nature of the rotation
model. While some problems exist with the time distribution effects of a modified rotation model in field practicum training, supervision was more focused,
communication between instructors necessitated by the model was positive
and having an additional field instructor and task supervisor was regarded as
beneficial. Although field instructors and task supervisors were divided regarding the amount of learning students in the modified rotation model obtained compared with students in the standard model, there was general
agreement that students exposed to a modified rotation model enhanced their
overall knowledge and practice skills regarding the elderly.

Preliminary results strongly indicate that the modified rotation model
clearly achieved its objectives that is, to increase the knowledge and practice
skills of social work students in social work geriatric services. The accomplishment of this objective is further supported by the field instructor and task
supervisor's agreement that their students were more confident working with
the elderly as a result of being exposed to a rotation model. As the program advances and program and agency staff become more familiar with and skilled at
administering a modified rotation model in geriatric field practicum training,
the years ahead may show increased support for its continued use.

REFERENCES

Council on Social Work Education (1992). *Educational Policy and Accreditation
Standards.* Alexandria, VA, p. 142.

Cuzzi, L., Holden, G., Chernack, P., Rutter, S., & Rosenberg, G. (1997). Evaluating social work field instruction: Rotations versus year-long placements. *Research on Social Work Practice, 7* (3), 402-414.

Cuzzi, L., Holden, G., Rutter, S., Rosenberg, G., & Chernack, P. (1996). A pilot study
of fieldwork rotations vs. year long placements for social work students in a public
hospital. *Social Work in Health Care, 24* (2), 73-91.

Dalgleish, K. B., Kane, R. A., & McNamara, J. J. (1976). Rotating social work students
within a medical center. *Health and Social Work, 1* (2) 166-171.

Lindeman, D., & Mellor, J. (1999). The distinctive role of gerontological social work:
An editorial. *Continuum, 19* (1), 1-6.

Long, D. D., Heydt, & Margo, J. (2000). Qualitative analysis of a BSW field placement with a hospital-owned physician practice in a skilled nursing facility. *Social Work, 25* (3), 210-218.

Scharlach, A., Damron-Rodriguez, J., Robinson, B., & Feldman, R. (2000). Educating social workers for an aging society: A vision for the 21st century. *Journal of Social Work Education, 36* (3), 521-540.

Spitzer, W., Holden, G., Cuzzi, L., Rutter, S., Chernack, P., & Rosenberg, G. (2001). Edith Abbott was right: Designing fieldwork experiences for contemporary health care practice. *Journal of Social Work Education, 37* (1), 79-90.

Chapter 9

Strengthening Geriatric Social Work Through a Doctoral Fellowship Program

James Lubben, DSW, MPH
Linda Krogh Harootyan, MSW

SUMMARY. Doctoral training is a key juncture for addressing the severe shortage of aging-savvy social workers. Today's doctoral students in social work are tomorrow's faculty who, in turn, will train the next generation of practitioners and who will undertake research critical to improving practice. Increasing the number of geriatric social work doctoral students entering the pipeline can solve the shortage of properly trained social workers. The Hartford Doctoral Fellows program provides dissertation support, mentorship and leadership development to attract and cultivate the next generation of geriatric social work faculty who will become teachers, role models, and mentors for future generations of

James Lubben is National Director of the Hartford Doctoral Fellows Program & Professor of Social Welfare and Urban Planning at UCLA. Linda Krogh Harootyan is Program Officer of the Hartford Doctoral Fellows Program and Deputy Director of The Gerontological Society of America.

The authors wish to acknowledge Laura Robbins and Stuart Kirk who offered sage advice and counsel on earlier versions of this manuscript.

[Haworth co-indexing entry note]: "Strengthening Geriatric Social Work Through a Doctoral Fellowship Program." Lubben, James, and Linda Krogh Harootyan. Co-published simultaneously in *Journal of Gerontological Social Work* (The Haworth Social Work Practice Press, an imprint of The Haworth Press, Inc.) Vol. 39, No. 1/2, 2002, pp. 145-156; and: *Advancing Gerontological Social Work Education* (ed: M. Joanna Mellor, and Joann Ivry) The Haworth Social Work Practice Press, an imprint of The Haworth Press, Inc., 2002, pp. 145-156. Single or multiple copies of this article are available for a fee from The Haworth Document Delivery Service [1-800-HAWORTH, 9:00 a.m. - 5:00 p.m. (EST). E-mail address: docdelivery@haworthpress.com].

10.1300/J083v39n01_12

social workers caring for older persons and their families. *[Article copies available for a fee from The Haworth Document Delivery Service: 1-800-HAWORTH. E-mail address: <docdelivery@haworthpress.com> Website: <http://www.HaworthPress.com>* © 2002 by The Haworth Press, Inc. All rights reserved.]*

KEYWORDS. Geriatric social work, doctoral training, fellowship program, faculty development

INTRODUCTION

The number of older people, particularly the oldest old (85+), is growing, and they need assistance to remain active and self-sufficient. Social workers play a critical role in supporting the well being and vitality of older persons. Unfortunately, there is a well-documented critical shortage of properly trained social work practitioners and the faculty needed to train them (Berkman et al., 2000; Scharlach et al., 2000; Damron-Rodriguez & Lubben, 1997). Today's doctoral students in social work are tomorrow's faculty who will train the next generation of practitioners and undertake research necessary to develop the empirical basis for defining best practice. The dearth of properly trained social workers cannot be solved unless the current shortage of geriatric social work doctoral students entering the pipeline can be overcome.

Over the last five years, very few graduates from social work doctoral programs produced a dissertation related to aging. Limited funding, insufficient mentors and lack of peer support are among the reasons students are not choosing geriatrics and are being pulled into other areas of study. Accordingly, the Hartford Doctoral Fellows program was established to recruit, sustain, and train a cadre of talented doctoral students in geriatric social work.

The Hartford Doctoral Fellows Program is a component of the multi-faceted Geriatric Social Work Initiative (GSWI) supported by the John A. Hartford Foundation. More information on the GSWI can be found at *<www.gswi.org>*. Among the various programs supported by the initiative, the Hartford Faculty Scholars program is most closely aligned to the goals and objectives of the Doctoral Fellows program. Both programs cultivate faculty leaders in gerontological education and research. The Faculty Scholars Program supports the career development and research of talented faculty whereas the Doctoral Fellows provides dissertation support, mentorship and leadership development for promising students. The ultimate goal of all GSWI programs is to form partnerships with a wide array of social work education programs to address the shortage of aging-savvy social workers, who will improve the care, health and well being of older adults and their families.

Founded in 1929, The John A. Hartford Foundation has long promoted health care, training, research and service system innovations to enhance the well being and vitality of older adults. Many of these efforts seek to improve the practice skills of current and future health professionals. Accordingly, *geriatrics* is more commonly used than *gerontological* to describe appropriate practice expertise regardless of specific profession (e.g., medicine, nursing or social work). Geriatric social work is defined as the expert practice of social work with older adults and their families within a variety of settings. Further, gerontology, particularly social gerontology, could be thought of as a core social science discipline that under girds geriatric social work practice. Accordingly, Hartford Doctoral Fellows are expected to become expert in both some aspect of the social science of aging (gerontology) and some form of social work practice with older adults and their families.

THE URGENT NEED FOR A QUALIFIED WORKFORCE IN GERIATRIC SOCIAL WORK

Longevity should be celebrated as one of the greatest achievements of the 20th century. It will profoundly transform our society and health care systems in the 21st century, requiring an increased cadre of community health care professionals trained to meet the special needs of older adults. In planning for that future system of community health care, it is especially important to consider the family of older persons, in part because families are, and will continue to be, the source of most care. When it comes to working with families and delivering health care within a community setting, social work has long been recognized as a central component of the interdisciplinary team of community health care professionals.

Although there are over 600,000 practicing social workers in the United States, few are specifically trained for geriatric practice. The National Institute on Aging projects a current need for 40,000-50,000 geriatric social workers, while less than 10% of that number are currently available (USPHHS-NIA, 1987; Gilbeman & Schervish, 1993). Similar to other health care professions, less than 5% of all masters in social work (MSW) students presently specialize in aging (Lubben, J. et al., 1992; Damron-Rodriguez et al., 1997). These findings are particularly striking given a survey by the National Association of Social Workers (NASW) that found 62% of its responding members believe aging knowledge is essential to their practice (Peterson & Wendt, 1990).

Although the proportion of students at the doctoral level is more encouraging, it is still grossly inadequate. Only 7% of the 1,350 social work doctoral dissertations completed during the five-year period of 1995-1999 considered a gerontological topic (see Table 1). On the other hand, 41 of the 67 doctoral programs produced at least one dissertation, suggesting a foundation for future growth in geriatric social work education.

TABLE 1. Geriatric Social Work Doctoral Dissertations 1995-1999

6 dissertations in geriatric social work:	**1 dissertation in geriatric social work:**
☐ UCLA	☐ Arizona State University
☐ University of Pennsylvania	☐ Barry University
	☐ Boston University
5 dissertations in geriatric social work:	☐ Bryn Mawr College
☐ Columbia University	☐ Florida State University
☐ Fordham University	☐ New York University
☐ SUNY-Albany	☐ Simmons College
	☐ Smith College
4 dissertations in geriatric social work:	☐ Tulane University
☐ University of Michigan	☐ UC Berkeley
☐ University of Texas-Austin	☐ University of Chicago
	☐ University of North Carolina
3 dissertations in geriatric social work	☐ University of Tennessee
☐ University of Minnesota	☐ University Wisconsin-Madison
☐ University of Southern California	
☐ University of Utah	**No dissertations in geriatric social work:**
☐ Virginia Commonwealth University	
☐ Washington University at St Louis	☐ (26 programs)
☐ Yeshiva University	
2 dissertations in geriatric social work:	Note: Data for this table were drawn from multiple sources. The Group to Advance Doctoral Education in Social Work (GADE) maintains a website that contains a listing of all of its member programs along with program descriptions. The number of geriatric social work dissertations by university was drawn from the UMI database using Proquest. With more than 1.6 million entries, this database ranges from the very first dissertation awarded in the U.S. in 1861 on up to the present. For further details, see the following website: <*www.lib.umi.com/dissertations*>
☐ Adelphi University	
☐ Boston College	
☐ Brandeis University	
☐ Case Western Reserve University	
☐ Catholic University of America	
☐ University of Alabama	
☐ University of Denver	
☐ University of Georgia	
☐ University of Illinois-Chicago	
☐ University of Maryland at Baltimore	
☐ University of Pittsburgh	
☐ University of Texas-Arlington	
☐ University of Washington	
☐ Virginia Commonwealth University	

DOCTORAL DISSERTATIONS IN GERIATRIC SOCIAL WORK
1995-1999

Given the critical shortage of faculty trained in geriatrics and gerontology, it is not surprising that talented social work students at both the masters and doctoral levels are not being encouraged to develop an interest in aging. Instead, these students are being recruited into other fields of practice and scholarship. A key to understanding this problem and designing a solution resides in the training of the next generation of social work faculty.

THE JOB MARKET FOR SOCIAL WORK FACULTY

In 1999 there were over 250 openings for junior faculty appointments in social work programs throughout the country. There was approximately an equal number of social work doctorates awarded that year (CSWE, 2000). The equivalent number of new doctorates awarded in social work might suggest market equilibrium. However, only about half of all of the social work doctorates awarded went to individuals seeking a faculty appointment. The other graduates chose a practice-based career path or one specializing in research without teaching. Thus, many faculty searches ended in failure. Virtually all of the advertised faculty positions in social work were listed as "open," suggesting that a geriatric social work applicant would have been able to compete for those positions.

BARRIERS TO DOCTORAL STUDY IN GERIATRIC SOCIAL WORK

Given the current and projected shortage of geriatric social workers, it would be most strategic to fill as many open positions with faculty properly trained in geriatrics and gerontology. Such a strategy requires overcoming at least five major obstacles that impede the recruitment, sustaining and training of doctoral students in geriatric social work: (1) limited financial support; (2) limited number of social work faculty mentors trained in geriatrics; (3) limited teacher training and career guidance; (4) limited peer support and learning; and (5) limited status of geriatric social work as a field of study and practice.

Limited financial support is particularly crucial. Dawson and Santos (1997) found that social work ranks near the bottom in funding for geriatric-care training among seven disciplines studied. Compared to other disciplines, doctoral students in social work, regardless of field of study, receive only a modest amount of financial support. The Council on Social Work Education (CSWE) reports that only 52% of full-time doctoral students receive any financial support (CSWE, 1999). Of these, only a small portion receives financial support for geriatrics. Given the paucity of support to social work doctoral students in general, it is understandable that financial assistance is extremely powerful in either reinforcing a student's interest or deflecting them into new areas.

The limited number of social work faculty presently identified with geriatrics or gerontology is also problematic. For example, without faculty mentorship, a student is often handicapped in locating appropriate repositories of research on aging including specialized databases. Further, this can impede the student's gaining access to other important campus resources on aging including lectures and colloquia, and can limit their entry into a community of geriatric and gerontological scholars and the growing number of geriatric social work professional organizations. In addition, lack of faculty mentorship presents another barrier to doctoral students transitioning into a teaching career. There is a lack of training on teaching, curriculum building or basic skills (e.g., resume writing, "job talks" and interviewing) for a successful academic career. Although not part of their regular job descriptions, many faculty members, of their own accord, offer such guidance to students in whose careers the faculty member has an especially strong interest. Thus, until enough geriatric social work faculty members are on staff, doctoral students with an interest in aging are at a competitive disadvantage.

Peer support and cohort building are important to career trajectories. The small number of geriatric social work doctoral students in most programs and their lack of organizational support limits cohort building and peer-support. Much of doctoral education involves learning how to share one's work in progress, as well as how to learn from others working on related topics. The collegiality fostered by shared learning at the doctoral level enhances the development of skills essential for successful faculty careers.

Until the introduction of the Hartford Doctoral Fellows and other GSWI programs, geriatric social work endured a relatively low status among social work doctoral level faculty and students, hindering recruitment of talented doctoral students to this field. Indeed, geriatrics and gerontology had a hard time competing for intellectual turf with the prestigious NIMH social work research centers, the ubiquitous Child Welfare training centers, and the groundbreaking opportunities funded by various sources for research among HIV populations.

THE KEY COMPONENTS
OF THE HARTFORD DOCTORAL FELLOWS PROGRAM

The Hartford Doctoral Fellows program focuses on students in full-time doctoral programs from whence social work faculty is recruited. In 1998, the Council on Social Work Education (CSWE) reported that there were 1,127 students in full-time doctoral programs (CSWE, 1999). These full-time programs are the most likely source of teachers for future generations of social work practitioners because their mission is to train scholars to advance the field of social welfare and the practice of social work through research and knowledge development. Full-time tenure track faculty are seldom drawn from the ranks of part-time doctoral programs because of the career preferences of the student and because these doctoral programs de-emphasize the acquisition of scholarly skills so essential for a faculty appointment.

The program intervenes at a critical juncture in a social work doctoral student's career decision-making, the selection of the dissertation area. This is the point where students demonstrate their capacity for independent scholarship. The selection of one's specific dissertation topic is momentous to career trajectories, establishing the initial research agenda for junior faculty. Indeed, a scholar's first cluster of publications tends to be drawn from his or her dissertation research and these in turn open up additional research grant opportunities. It is also often at the moment of choosing a dissertation topic, that many students encounter an assortment of challenges and opportunities that can deflect them away from pursuing a career in geriatric social work.

The Hartford Doctoral Fellows program consists of four key components:

1. *Supplemental academic career counseling*
2. *Professional development*
3. *Cohort building and peer networking*
4. *Dissertation grants*

Supplemental Academic Career Guidance. Addressing the shortage of geriatric social work faculty mentors, the Hartford Doctoral Fellows Program faculty and staff provide counsel and guidance regarding strategic career planning and decision making designed to augment support offered by the Fellow's own home institution. Hartford Doctoral Fellows are assisted through professional mentoring and networking to take full advantage of an extensive network of gerontologists and social work scholars, including members of the Geriatric Social Work Listserv maintained with support from the Hartford Faculty Scholars Program, as well as Internet-based resources available through The

Gerontological Society of America (GSA), CSWE, and the other Hartford sponsored projects.

Professional Development. The Fellow's professional development is strengthened through two institutes each year that focus on enhancing scholarly and teaching skills, peer support and cohort identification. Institutes emphasizing scholarly development are held in conjunction with the GSA Annual Scientific Meeting. Institutes emphasizing academic career planning and development are held in conjunction with the Annual Program Meeting of the CSWE.

Cohort Building and Network Development. Fellows are well integrated into their cohort, as well as that of the Hartford Faculty Scholars. Additionally, the Fellows are introduced to leading gerontologists and social work educators. This cohort building and peer networking are accomplished through collaborative and interactive in-person meetings, multimedia virtual conferences, skill building institutes and social events. A special "Retreat" Institute is planned for 2004 when all current and previous Hartford Doctoral Fellows and Faculty Scholars will convene to activate and facilitate their collective power and skills for heightening awareness and effecting positive change. These cohort building and peer networking strategies are designed to build a solid foundation and structure for continued combined efforts to improve and expand the field of geriatric social work. Indeed, it is anticipated that many interesting career opportunities will be first made known to Fellows through some type of informal social exchanges among the Hartford Faculty Scholars and Fellows. Already, some of the Faculty Scholars and Doctoral Fellows have identified common research interests and exchanged intellectual and professional support.

Doctoral Dissertation Grants. The dissertation grants address other barriers that impede the training of geriatric social workers at all levels of education. The size, competitiveness and prestige of this dissertation grant will also increase the status of geriatric social work not only in the fellow's university but also in other social work doctoral programs wishing for future success for their students. This funding is designed to increase the visibility of geriatric social work doctoral training and in turn attract more doctoral students to geriatrics.

The dissertation grants are worth $20,000 per year for up to two years. They are designed to protect 50% of a Fellow's time for concentrated effort on the dissertation research project and are to be paid as a stipend. A maximum of $5,000 per year of the dissertation grant may be used for expenses directly related to the Fellow's research project including travel to professional meetings to present findings. Hartford Doctoral Fellows who complete all dissertation requirements prior to the start of the second year are not eligible for the second year dissertation grant. However, they continue to receive support to attend professional development institutes during the second year of their fellowship and maintain their involvement in their cohort of Fellows.

For each year the Fellow receives the $20,000 dissertation grant, his or her university is required to provide additional financial support equal to $10,000 per year in the form of tuition waivers, research assistantships, teaching assistantships, grants-in-aid, or scholarships. The brightest and most talented doctoral students often get hired as teaching assistants for undergraduate and master level courses. A talented geriatric social work student hired as a teaching assistant in one of these courses will undoubtedly encourage more students to consider a career in geriatric social work. The $10,000 match requirement is intended to increase the likelihood of the Hartford Fellow being selected as a teaching assistant. The experience and skills acquired by being a teaching assistant will be important when the Fellow applies for a faculty position.

SELECTION PROCESS FOR HARTFORD DOCTORAL FELLOWS

Through a national Request for Proposals (RFP) and rigorous selection process, at least twenty-four advanced doctoral students in social work will be selected over three waves of recruitment. There were seven Fellows selected in 2001 and up to nine more are to be selected in July 2002. The final wave will take place in 2003. The overall quality and focus of the dissertation proposal, as well as the scholarship training capacity of the degree granting institution and faculty, is central to the selection process. Further, the dissertation must examine a set of research questions that search for ways to improve the health and well being of older persons, their families and caregivers. At least one member of the Doctoral Fellow's dissertation committee must possess expertise in gerontology or geriatrics.

A most important criterion considered in the selection of Hartford Doctoral Fellows is that the dissertation research contributes to improving the health and well being of older persons, their families and caregivers. This obviously allows for a wide array of topics, but those that link health care with more traditional aspects of social care are especially favored. A second criterion is the scholarly rigor of the proposed doctoral dissertation. It has to be good science. Further, the selection committee considers the qualifications of the applicant to carry out proposed research. Appropriate and substantial preparatory work is essential to meet this criterion. The applicant must also demonstrate a commitment to geriatrics and gerontology, as well as to seeking a full-time faculty position in an accredited social work program. Two other criteria concern the applicant's university. One evaluates the capacity of the applicant's doctoral program for training gerontological scholars and social work faculty and the other evaluates the nature and extent of the university's support for the applicant. Finally, the proposed dissertation must be able to be completed within the two-year timeframe of the fellowship.

THE FIRST COHORT OF DOCTORAL FELLOWS

Twenty-one applications were received in the first wave of recruitment in 2001. All applicants received independent evaluations from three members of the National Advisory Committee. Based upon average scores obtained from this first phase of the selection process, semi-finalists were identified who were in turn reviewed by all members of the National Advisory Committee. Seven Doctoral Fellows were selected in 2001. One university (Kansas) produced two Fellows in this round. Many of the dissertations considered issues associated with end-of-life care, perhaps a reflection of the large Soros Foundation Project on Death in America (*www.soros.org/death/*) that includes a special initiative aimed at social workers. Overall, the research interests of applicants were quite varied. For example, topics ranged from spirituality among terminally ill to access to Medicare home health care in the wake of the Balanced Budget Act.

EXPECTED OUTCOMES

The ultimate goal of the Hartford Doctoral Fellows program is to develop new knowledge of social work's contributions to health outcomes and ways to improve the lives of older persons and their families. The program is expected to increase the desirability of geriatric social work as a field of practice, teaching and research. It will help cultivate the next generation of geriatric social work faculty who will become teachers, role models and mentors for future generations of social workers caring for older persons and their families. The Fellows program fosters an intellectually stimulating, mutually supportive network of faculty and students involved in geriatric social work doctoral research and training. It capitalizes on the excitement and momentum generated by the other Hartford programs and infuses the same excitement into social work doctoral education.

CONCLUSION

A remedy to the insufficiency of both geriatric social work faculty and practitioners resides in the current cohort of doctoral students. Doctoral students are especially vulnerable as they near the dissertation stage of their program, having drained their financial resources during the prior years to develop basic skills of scholarship. Just when doctoral students are finally prepared to commence dissertation research projects, many are diverted to different topical areas where financial support is available. The students are often enticed to pursue topics whose study is subsidized by faculty in research areas with more robust history and support than is enjoyed by geriatrics. At this pivotal point of development, such diversion results in permanent loss to the field of geriatrics. A scholar's first cluster of publications tends to be drawn from his or her dissertation research and provides the launch pad for additional research grant opportunities in that area. Thus, once diverted, these future faculty members are all too often lost to geriatrics. Accordingly, The Gerontological Society of America, with close to $2.5 million of funding from the John A. Hartford Foundation, established the Hartford Doctoral Fellows program to attract, train and retain future geriatric social work faculty members, through a doctoral dissertation fellowship program. The Hartford Doctoral Fellows eventually will directly serve as educators, researchers and mentors, and will also influence the culture of leadership at schools of social work nationally, with geriatric strength. This new cadre of geriatric social work faculty will teach the next generation of aging-savvy social workers, who will improve the care, health and well being of America's rapidly growing population of older adults.

REFERENCES

Berkman, B., Silverstone, B., Simmons, W. J., Volland, P. J. & Howe, J. L. (2000). Social work gerontological practice: The need for faculty development in the new millennium. *Journal of Gerontological Social Work, 34* (1), 5-23.

Council on Social Work Education (CSWE). (1999). Statistics on social work education in the United States. Washington, DC: CSWE.

Council on Social Work Education (CSWE). (1999). Statistics on social work education in the United States. Washington, DC: CSWE.

Damron-Rodriguez, J., & Lubben, J. (1994). Multidisciplinary factors in gerontological curriculum adoption in schools of social work. *Gerontology and Geriatrics Education, 14* (4), 39-52.

Damron-Rodriguez, J., & Lubben, J. (1997). The 1995 White House Conference on Aging: An agenda for social work education and training. In C. Saltz (Ed.), *Social work response to the 1995 White House Conference on Aging: From issues to actions* (pp. 65-77). New York: The Haworth Press, Inc.

Damron-Rodriguez, J., Villa, V., Tseng, H., & Lubben, J. (1997). Demographic and organizational influences on the development of gerontological social work curriculum. *Gerontology and Geriatrics Education, 17* (3), 3-18.

Dawson, G. D., & Santos, J. F. (1997). Investigation of funding for geriatric-care training in seven disciplines. *Gerontology & Geriatrics Education, 17* (3), 39-74.

Gibelman, M. & Schervish, P. H. (1993). Who we are: The social work labor force as reflected in the NASW membership. Washington, DC: NASW Press.

Lubben, J., Damron-Rodriguez, J., & Beck, J. (1992). National survey of aging curriculum in schools of social work. *Journal of Gerontological Social Work, 18* (3-4), 157-171.

Peterson, D. A., & Wendt, P. F. (1990). Employment in the field of aging: A survey of professionals in four fields. *The Gerontologist, 30,* 679-684.

Scharlach, A., Damron-Rodriguez, J., Robinson, B., & Feldman, R. (2000). Educating social workers for an aging society: A vision for the 21st century. *Journal of Social Work Education, 36* (3), 521-538.

U. S. Department of Health and Human Services (1987). Personnel for health needs of the elderly through the year 2020. USDHHS-NIA Pub. #87-2950.

SECTION III.
MODELS FOR PRACTICE:
CLASS AND FIELD CURRICULUM
PROGRAMS

Introduction to Section III

M. Joanna Mellor, DSW
Joann Ivry, PhD

The subsequent chapters focus on educational practice. Basing their programmatic endeavors on the rationale and principles discussed in the introductory section, the authors in this last section of the volume offer educational practice solutions, sharing their experiences and evaluating their outcomes. Integration of classroom and fieldwork practice is emphasized. Some of the authors approach integration from the classroom perspective with knowledge learned in class being extended to the practicum site while others view it from the opposite direction with skills acquired through practice being incorporated into the classroom learning.

The settings and circumstances of the described models are diverse, encompassing the education of undergraduate and graduate students, rural and urban environments, a handful of student participants or several hundred over a period of years. Some of the projects require the vision and enthusiasm of one dedicated ed-

[Haworth co-indexing entry note]: "Introduction to Section III." Mellor, M. Joanna, and Joann Ivry. Co-published simultaneously in *Journal of Gerontological Social Work* (The Haworth Social Work Practice Press, an imprint of The Haworth Press, Inc.) Vol. 39, No. 1/2, 2002, pp. 157-158; and: *Advancing Gerontological Social Work Education* (ed: M. Joanna Mellor, and Joann Ivry) The Haworth Social Work Practice Press, an imprint of The Haworth Press, Inc., 2002, pp. 157-158. Single or multiple copies of this article are available for a fee from The Haworth Document Delivery Service [1-800-HAWORTH, 9:00 a.m. - 5:00 p.m. (EST). E-mail address: docdelivery@haworthpress.com].

10.1300/J083v39n01_13

ucator and others demand a collaborative approach but all offer models of gerontological education undertaken to develop practitioners with the knowledge, beliefs and skills necessary to meet the challenges of our aging society.

Olson's chapter reports on the evaluation of a curriculum module designed to enhance gerontological knowledge and interest of undergraduate and graduate students. Outcomes were not always as anticipated and readers will find the discussion of the findings of interest and pertinent to their own educational expectations. As counterpoint to Olson, Hegeman provides an overview of the history and impact of service learning in eldercare for undergraduates, elders and agency staff. These two chapters (curriculum and practice) provide a basis for the remaining chapters in this section.

Gleason-Wynn and Liley both focus on the integration of classroom learning with the hands-on experience in the field, albeit with very different models. Gleason-Wynn describes an experiential exercise aimed at assisting social work students to utilize geriatric knowledge learned in the classroom to prepare for social work practice, and Liley reports on the degree to which a group of students felt that their classroom learning prepared them for field placements within medical settings. Dorfman views integration of class and practice from the standpoint of the practice world and describes the value of involving students and seniors together in friendly visiting and oral history with its impact on growth of knowledge and attitudes taught via an interdisciplinary, undergraduate course. Finally Eldemire-Shearer shares the Family Study, a skills based program which involves students with older persons and their families on an individual basis. The Family Study is an integral part of an academic course that is built around the hands-on experience.

These chapters and those that preceded them in the School Based Initiatives section offer programs and models of some diversity. They all, however, exemplify the principles of integration of class and practice and interdisciplinary learning for interdisciplinary gerontological care that are identified in the opening chapters. How we, as educators and practitioners, choose to follow these precepts will be individual and idiosyncratic to our circumstances but these articles provide us with a roadmap for our endeavors.

Chapter 10

A Curriculum Module Enhances Students' Gerontological Practice-Related Knowledge and Attitudes

Carole J. Olson, MSW

SUMMARY. The incorporation of greater gerontological content in social work curricula has been recognized as a pressing educational need
for many years. Many social work students are not exposed to the specialized knowledge and skills needed to effectively serve older adults. A
frequently reported barrier to curricular development in aging is the perception that the curriculum is too full to accommodate significant additions. This empirical study explored the potential for a limited
curriculum module to enhance MSW and BSW students' gerontological
practice-related knowledge, attitudes, and interest. Findings suggest that
a brief, concentrated educational intervention is a promising avenue for
increasing knowledge about assessment and intervention with older

---

Carole J. Olson is a doctoral candidate in the College of Social Work, University of
Kentucky, 673 Patterson Office Tower, Lexington, KY 40506-0027 (E-mail: colson@
mis.net).

The author expresses her gratitude to Surjit Dhooper, PhD, for his valuable guidance in this research and the preparation of the manuscript.

[Haworth co-indexing entry note]: "A Curriculum Module Enhances Students' Gerontological Practice-Related Knowledge and Attitudes." Olson, Carole J. Co-published simultaneously in *Journal of Gerontological Social Work* (The Haworth Social Work Practice Press, an imprint of The Haworth Press, Inc.) Vol. 39, No. 1/2,
2002, pp. 159-175; and: *Advancing Gerontological Social Work Education* (ed: M. Joanna Mellor, and Joann
Ivry) The Haworth Social Work Practice Press, an imprint of The Haworth Press, Inc., 2002, pp. 159-175. Single
or multiple copies of this article are available for a fee from The Haworth Document Delivery Service
[1-800-HAWORTH, 9:00 a.m. - 5:00 p.m. (EST). E-mail address: docdelivery@haworthpress.com].

10.1300/J083v39n01_14 *159*

adults, and for enhancing positive attitudes toward them, especially among undergraduate students. *[Article copies available for a fee from The Haworth Document Delivery Service: 1-800-HAWORTH. E-mail address: <docdelivery@haworthpress.com> Website: <http://www.HaworthPress.com> © 2002 by The Haworth Press, Inc. All rights reserved.]*

KEYWORDS. Attitudes toward elderly, practice interests, teaching methods, social work education

INTRODUCTION

The incorporation of greater gerontological content in curricula of social work programs has been recognized as a pressing educational need for many years (Berkman, Dobrof, Harry, & Damron-Rodriguez, 1995; Damron-Rodriguez & Lubben, 1997; Greene, Barusch & Connelly, 1990; Nelson, 1988). Many social workers have not acquired the specialized knowledge and skills needed to work with elders and their families as part of their formal education (Greene, Vourlekis, Gelfand & Lewis, 1992; Quam & Whitford, 1992). Nonetheless, the majority of social workers report that they require knowledge of aging in their practice (Peterson, 1990), and the demand for social workers with knowledge of aging is only expected to grow.

Incorporation of gerontology into the required, rather than elective, curricula at both the MSW and BSW levels deserves attention for several reasons. First, elective courses and specialized concentrations in aging, when available, are predominantly a graduate school phenomenon (Lubben, Damron-Rodriguez & Beck, 1992). Consequently, the majority of BSW students do not have access to social work courses that deal primarily with aging. However, a higher proportion of baccalaureate social workers than of masters-level social workers report aging as their primary practice area (Gibelman & Schervish, 1997), and jobs for BSW graduates often are in public social services and residential facilities where the most vulnerable elders are served. Secondly, among MSW students who can and do declare an area of concentration, only four percent choose aging (Council on Social Work Education, 1999), and only five percent of all MSW students take an aging course (Berkman et al., 1995). This is partly due to the breadth of social work practice and the variety of electives available. But a result is that the number of social workers who pursue educational preparation to work with elders is far smaller than the number who report they need knowledge of aging in their practices. Finally, older adults will be increasingly pervasive among the clientele of social workers, regardless of the field of practice (e.g., health care, mental health, protective social services).

Student recruitment into gerontological social work also is identified as a significant challenge (Damron-Rodriguez & Lubben, 1997). In terms of practice interests, social work students tend to rate geriatric social work low in comparison with other fields of practice (Abell & McDowell, 1990; Butler, 1990; Rubin, Johnson & DeWeaver, 1986).

Attitudes among social work students toward the elderly population have received limited attention. In Palmore's (1982) review of the literature on attitudes toward elders, negative and ambivalent attitudes were found to be widespread among various societies. While attitudes were found to vary widely among different cultures, ratings of older age groups tended to be more negative than ratings of other age groups, and there tended to be more stereotypes associated with old age than younger ages. Concern in higher education that ageism may prevail among college students has stimulated a good deal of empirical examination, but results have been mixed. Schwalb and Sedlacek (1990) found generally negative attitudes among college students in 1979 and again in 1988. But other studies have suggested that college students' attitudes toward elders may be more neutral than negative (Mosher-Ashley & Ball, 1999; Reed, Beall & Baumhover, 1992; Shoemake & Rowland, 1993), or even slightly positive (Murphy-Russell, Die & Walker, 1986).

Particularly in the health professions, attitudes toward older people have been shown to affect work preferences or career choices. In their review of the gerontological nursing education literature, Philipose, Tate, and Jacobs (1991) determined that the majority of nursing students held negative attitudes toward older adults. This was reflected in nurses' career choices, with geriatric nursing the least preferred specialty and elders the least preferred age group for which to provide care. Positive attitudes among nursing students toward elders appear to correlate with positive views about working with elders (Gomez, Young & Gomez, 1991). In a survey of 663 entering medical students over the course of six consecutive years, Wilderom et al. (1990) discovered that attitudes toward elders were essentially neutral, and that only a small percentage (3%) of the sample were willing to consider a geriatrics specialization. Kane (1999) surveyed 333 MSW and BSW students and found generally neutral attitudes toward older people and a moderate willingness to work with them. Out of 15 preferred areas of practice, 14.8 percent of the sample indicated a preference to work in geriatrics.

Educators in a variety of disciplines and professions have attempted to assess the impact of educational programs in gerontology and geriatrics on students' attitudes and interests in working with older adults. Palmore (1982) offers a basic theoretical model in which knowledge about aging and elderly adults is hypothesized to positively affect both attitudes and behavior. Several studies representing various disciplines lend support to Palmore's hypothesis.

Angiullo, Whitborn, and Powers (1996) found that positive shifts in attitudes toward older adults occurred among students who completed a psychology of aging course. In an introductory psychology course, Murphy-Russell et al. (1986) found that attitudes changed positively following a special workshop series on aging. Course work in gerontological nursing enhanced attitudes toward elders among baccalaureate nursing students (Aday & Campbell, 1995; Dellasega & Curriero, 1991; Fox & Wold, 1996). Haulotte and McNeil (1998) observed attitudes to shift toward greater understanding and appreciation of elderly people among a small sample of students from various majors who completed a course in nursing home social work.

Even in the absence of educational interventions, knowledge or perceived knowledge about aging and older adults may play a positive role. In a study of factors affecting social work students' willingness to work with elders with Alzheimer's Disease, both knowledge of the disease and perceived sufficiency of geriatric knowledge were significantly correlated with willingness to work with elders with Alzheimer's Disease (Kane, 1999).

Educational programs in aging do not consistently produce a positive effect on preferences to work with older adults, however. In a study of over 200 medical, nursing and social work students in Israel by Carmel, Cwikel, and Galinsky (1992), no significant changes in attitudes or work preferences occurred among any of the studied groups following courses in gerontology. While Dellasega and Curriero (1991) found positive attitude change among baccalaureate nursing students following clinical work with elders, students' intentions to work with geriatric patients remained low. A study by Davis-Berman and Robinson (1989) suggested that course work in aging may even lessen preferences to work with older adults. Twelve undergraduate social work students enrolled in an aging course developed a significantly lessened preference to work with elderly persons at posttest, even though the course and instructor were evaluated favorably by students. As Davis-Berman and Robinson state, this demonstrates that increased knowledge of aging not only may fail to effect more positive attitudes, but may even mediate against intentions to work with elderly adults. Given the study's limited sample size, however, this may not be representative of social work students generally.

Social work students' knowledge about aging and intervention with older adults, and their attitudes toward older adults and practice with this age group, are of consequence to social work education. First, the accuracy and completeness of students' knowledge has implications for their abilities to provide effective services to older clients. And their perceptions of aging and older adults have significant ramifications for the degree and quality of intervention that will be provided. Thus, the attitudes of social work students toward elders and gerontological social work, and the question of whether or not positive atti-

tudes and interest in social work with elders can be fostered through the required social work curricula, deserve further examination.

National surveys (as cited in Greene et al., 1990), designed to gain further
understanding about the gerontological education needs of social workers, reveal a consensus about needed content. Strong needs are identified for assessment techniques and methods of intervention for elderly clients, especially
those with mental impairment. The social work practice courses are a logical
place to infuse this content.

While schools of social work overwhelmingly recognize the importance of
knowledge in aging, a frequently reported barrier to curricular development in
aging is the perception that the curriculum is too full to accommodate significant additions (Lubben et al., 1992). This study thus was implemented to explore the potential for a limited curriculum module in gerontological social
work to positively impact students' practice-related knowledge concerning
older adults, as well as their attitudes toward elderly persons and interests in
working with them. Instruction on elder-specific assessment and intervention
was provided to MSW and BSW practice students with the use of a brief module that could be easily incorporated into the regular course curriculum.

METHOD

Sample and Design

Study participants consisted of 96 MSW and BSW students enrolled in social work practice courses at a large public university in a southeastern state
during one semester. Four sections of a graduate course (Advanced Generalist
Social Work Practice I[1]) and two sections of an undergraduate course (Social
Work Practice I[2]) were utilized. At the MSW level, two of four course sections
served as the experimental group, with the other two serving as the control. At
the BSW level, one section served as the experimental group, and the other as
the control. Demographic characteristics of study participants are displayed in
Table 1.

Procedure

Data were collected by means of a 50-item questionnaire administered during class periods approximately five weeks into the semester, and again five to
six weeks later. Students were advised that participation was voluntary and responses anonymous. Between administration of the pretest and posttest, the

TABLE 1. Demographic Characteristics of Study Participants (N = 96)

	MSW Students		BSW Students	
	Experimental	Control	Experimental	Control
	n = 33	*n* = 33	*n* = 13	*n* = 17
Age				
Range	22-51	22-54	20-26	19-50
Mean	31.52	33.12	21.38	24.18
Gender				
Female	27 (82%)	25 (76%)	10 (77%)	16 (94%)
Male	6 (18%)	8 (24%)	3 (23%)	1 (6%)

experimental groups each received a brief curriculum module in gerontological social work, described under "Intervention" below.

Intervention

A curriculum module providing an overview of social work practice with older adults and their families was developed and delivered by the author to the experimental groups. It was two and one half hours in length and was delivered in its entirety within two or three class sessions. The module's design and content were reflective of its primary purpose, which was to educate students about salient aspects of social work practice with older adults. The content was informed by numerous sources that fell into two primary categories: (1) the empirical literature identifying gerontology social work education needs, and (2) social work and mental health practice literature specific to psychosocial and psychotherapeutic intervention with older adults. The module was largely didactic in delivery, with the use of a corresponding slide presentation and one educational video (Hollander, 1998).

The introductory component of the module addressed myths and realities concerning normative and non-normative aging that are especially pertinent to social work practice. For instance, the facts that most elders live independently without assistance, and enjoy levels of life satisfaction as high as that of any other age groups, were highlighted. Students also were advised of some of the empirical data that has been gained from longitudinal studies of aging, such as that dementia is not an inevitable part of aging, and that personality remains fairly stable through older adulthood. It was explained that some of the physiological changes that were once thought of as normal aging, such as cognitive decline and mobility deficits, are now understood as frequently being the result of disease or disuse. The myth of family abandonment of elders was discounted with evidence that 90 percent of elder care is provided by families.

The second part of the module focused on assessment of older adults and their families. Some common impediments to good assessments were discussed, such as biases about aging held by social workers and by older people themselves, and fears common to elders concerning incompetence, helplessness, and loss of autonomy. Physical, cognitive and emotional ramifications of sensory and other important losses were emphasized. The presenter also described and demonstrated some of the skills that enhance rapport-building and communication with elderly clients.

Social work interventions that are especially appropriate for elderly clients, especially elders with chronic impairment, were described in the third portion of the module. Included were clinical case management, and reminiscence and life review therapies. It was emphasized that elderly adults without significant cognitive impairment benefit from various modalities of psychotherapy and other social work interventions as much as other age persons.

Discussions of two specific psychosocial difficulties commonly encountered in working with older adults, depression and dementia, made up the final part of the module. Included for both types of illnesses were prevalence rates, risk factors, assessment, and treatments. Risk and motivations for suicide among older adults were discussed. Common communication and behavior problems encountered with persons with dementia (e.g., agitation, wandering), and interventions that are appropriate, received brief attention, as well as the judicious manner in which use of chemical and physical restraints must be approached.

MSW and BSW students received the same basic content, although some modifications appropriate to course level were made. The primary difference was that MSW students received greater and more specific psychotherapeutic content, and there was greater use of clinical language and concepts.

Instrument

Three dependent variables were measured on pretest and posttest: (1) knowledge of gerontological social work practice concepts, (2) attitudes toward elderly adults, and (3) interest in working with elderly clients. Knowledge of gerontological practice concepts was measured by a true-false quiz consisting of 20 items composed by the author and addressing some of the salient knowledge that social workers should possess in working with elderly adults. A few items dealt with certain myths of aging, such as *Families generally are too quick to place their elderly relatives in nursing homes,* and *Most people develop senile dementia if they live long enough.* Other items addressed practice concepts, such as *Memory problems may respond to medical or psychosocial intervention,* and *Depressed older adults benefit from psychotherapy as much as younger adults do.* The knowledge portion of the questionnaire reflected content delivered to both MSW and BSW students. The 20-item quiz appears in the Appendix.

Attitudes toward elderly adults were assessed with the use of 22 paired positive and negative descriptors (adopted from Shoemake & Rowland, 1993). Rather than having participants check *yes* or *no* to each descriptor as Shoemake and Rowland did, however, the items were arranged in a seven-point Likert scale format in order to broaden the choices. The more positive adjectives (e.g., progressive, independent, generous) appeared on the left-hand side of each scale, and the more negative ones (e.g., old-fashioned, dependent, selfish) on the right. Attitude scores ranged from 22 to 154. The lower the participants' scores, the more positive their attitudes were considered to be. This modified scale revealed high reliability with a Cronbach's alpha of .91.

Interest in working with elderly clients was measured on a scale of one to three. Possible responses were (1) *I doubt that I would like it,* (2) *It would be okay,* and (3) *I think I would really like it* (adopted from Shoemake & Rowland, 1993).

In addition to basic demographic information (age and sex), five items on the pretest questionnaire asked participants about their relationships and experiences with elderly persons. This included current and previous paid or volunteer work experience with elders, the existence of meaningful relationships in their lives with elderly adults, and the general quality of their previous experience with elderly people. Some studies have demonstrated close contact with elders to be a potent variable positively influencing students' attitudes toward elders (e.g., Haulotte & McNeil, 1998; Murphy-Russell et al., 1986; Rosencranz & McNevin, 1969), while others have not established such a relationship (e.g., Angiullo et al., 1996; Carmel et al., 1992; Johnson & Wilson, 1990).

Additional pretest items asked participants for their perceptions concerning the attitudes of their professional role models (i.e., social work educators and practitioners) toward gerontological social work. Perceived negative attitudes of physicians have been found to reduce positive attitudes of medical students toward elderly patients (Wilderom et al., 1990).

RESULTS

Sample

Mean ages between the experimental and control groups, at both the MSW and BSW levels, were equivalent. There was a considerable gender ratio difference between the BSW experimental and control groups, but this difference was not statistically significant due to the small numbers of men in both groups. Demographic characteristics of study participants ($N = 96$) are displayed in Table 1.

Background Variables

(1) *Current experience with elders in a practicum or service learning setting.* Only a few of the MSW students were in an educational practicum during the semester in which data were gathered. However, as a curricular requirement of the undergraduate practice course, all BSW students were involved in service learning (four hours per week of volunteer work in a social service agency). Students were asked to estimate the percentage of the clients in their current practicum or service-learning setting who were elderly. Only six respondents reported working with a client population that was 20 percent or greater elder persons. Among the 37 total respondents that were involved in a practicum or service learning experience, this variable was found to be positively correlated with only one dependent variable, students' pretest interest in working with elderly clients ($r = .478$, $p < .05$).

(2) *Previous volunteer or paid work experience with elders.* Asked whether or not they had worked with "a lot of elderly people" in their past paid or volunteer work, approximately 40 percent of the MSW students and 20 percent of the BSW students responded that they had. The t-test comparisons suggested that students who previously had worked with a lot of elderly people had significantly more interest in working with elderly clients at the time of pretest, $t(91) = 2.74$, $p < .05$.

(3) *Current or previous meaningful relationship with an elderly person.* A large majority of participants (88.5%) reported having a current or previous meaningful relationship with at least one elder. Subjects who responded affirmatively to this item were asked to check all the relationships that applied from a list of five. The most frequently reported relationship (reported by 65.6% of the sample), was with *grandparent(s)*. This was followed by: *other relative or friend* (48%), *someone encountered in a practicum or work experience* (26%), *parents* (17.7%), and *someone encountered in a volunteer experience* (9.4%). Using t-test comparisons, students who reported having a meaningful relationship with an elder had significantly greater interest in working with elderly clients, $t(94) = 2.37$, $p < .05$, and significantly more positive attitudes toward elderly adults, $t(94) = -3.71$, $p < .001$, on pretest.

(4) *Quality of previous experiences with elderly people.* Participants were asked to rate the general quality of their previous experiences with elderly people. Possible responses on a scale of one to five were *negative, somewhat neg-*

ative, neutral, somewhat positive, or *positive.* A robust 90.6 percent reported their previous experience with elders to be generally *positive* or *somewhat positive,* with *positive* the most frequent response given (65.6%). This variable was positively correlated on pretest with both positive attitudes toward elders ($r = .332, p < .001$) and interest in working with elderly clients ($r = .455, p < .001$).

(5) *Perceptions of social work role models' attitudes toward social work with elderly clients.* The distributions of responses for the two categories of professional role models, social work educators and social work practitioners, were very similar and are averaged here for purposes of simplification. The majority of subjects (65%) perceived their social work role models' attitudes toward gerontological social work as positive or somewhat positive. Only three percent perceived such attitudes to be negative. The remainder either perceived attitudes to be neutral (13%), or they did not know (18.3%). No significant correlation was found between this variable and any of the dependent measures.

Posttest Results

(1) *Knowledge of gerontological social work practice concepts.* Posttest knowledge scores were significantly higher for the MSW group exposed to the module than for the MSW control group. Knowledge scores also were significantly higher for the BSW group exposed to the module than the BSW control group. The BSW experimental group demonstrated greater knowledge gain than the MSW experimental group, perhaps because of their lower initial level of knowledge. Knowledge scores for MSW and BSW students are displayed in Table 2.

(2) *Attitudes toward elderly people.* The MSW experimental group was marginally but significantly more positive in their attitudes than the MSW control group prior to intervention; thus, change scores were used for analysis. However, both groups exhibited positive shifts in attitudes, and change scores were not found to be significantly different. Pretest and posttest attitude scores for the MSW students are displayed in Table 3.

The BSW experimental and control groups were equivalent on this measure at pretest. As with the MSW students, both groups demonstrated positive shifts in attitudes regardless of exposure to the module. Nevertheless, the BSW group exposed to the module demonstrated significantly more positive attitudes on posttest than their control counterparts. Pretest and posttest attitude scores for the BSW students are displayed in Table 3.

(3) *Interest in working with elderly clients.* On pretest, the MSW experimental students demonstrated more interest in working with elderly clients

TABLE 2. Scores on Knowledge of Gerontological Practice Concepts (N = 96)

	No Module		Module		
	M	SD	M	SD	t
MSW Students					
Pretest	15.39	2.36	14.97	1.74	−0.83
Posttest	14.60	2.28	17.04	1.48	4.78***
BSW Students					
Pretest	13.41	2.74	13.31	2.46	−0.11
Posttest	13.36	1.74	17.00	1.96	5.12***

Note. Theoretical range of scores is 0-20.
***$p < .001$.

TABLE 3. Scores on Attitudes Toward Elderly People (N = 96)

	No Module		Module		
	M	SD	M	SD	t
MSW Students					
Pretest	73.03	14.71	66.03	4.56	−1.94*[a]
Posttest	77.43	14.23	58.43	15.85	−2.89
BSW Students					
Pretest	74.18	19.30	65.15	16.97	−1.34
Posttest	69.21	13.49	49.08	11.14	−4.21***

Note. Theoretical range of scores is 22-154, with lower scores representing more positive attitudes. Thus, negative change in scores represents positive shift in attitudes.
[a]Due to statistically significant difference in MSW students' pretest scores, change scores used for analysis; however, difference in change scores was not statistically significant.
*$p < .05$. ** $p < .01$ ***$p < .001$.

than their counterparts in the MSW control group, a difference that was statistically significant. Consequently, change scores were used for analysis in the MSW student population. There were slight declines in interest levels in both the experimental group and the control group, but the difference in change between groups was not statistically significant. Pretest and posttest interest scores for MSW students are displayed in Table 4.

No change occurred in the interest level of the BSW group exposed to the module, while interest in the BSW control group declined. Consequently, posttest interest scores were significantly higher for the BSW experimental group than the BSW control group. Interest scores for the BSW students are displayed in Table 4.

TABLE 4. Scores on Interest in Working with Elderly Clients (N = 96)

| | No Module | | Module | | |
	M	SD	M	SD	t
MSW Students					
Pretest	2.12	0.70	2.48	0.76	2.03* [a]
Posttest	1.71	0.76	2.39	0.74	2.17
BSW Students					
Pretest	2.06	0.56	2.38	0.51	1.65
Posttest	1.86	0.53	2.38	0.51	2.63*

Note. Theoretical range of scores is 1-3.

[a]Due to statistically significant difference in MSW students' pretest scores, change scores were used for analysis; however, difference in change scores was not statistically significant.

* $p < .05$.

DISCUSSION

Findings indicate that the delivery of a brief curriculum module in gerontological social work practice was successful in achieving its primary objective, which was to increase knowledge. Students at both the MSW and BSW levels who were exposed to the module demonstrated significantly greater knowledge of salient practice concepts in gerontological social work than their counterparts who did not receive the module.

A pleasant initial finding was that both MSW and BSW students demonstrated favorable baseline attitudes toward elderly people. Nonetheless, the BSW students who received the module demonstrated significantly more positive attitudes on posttest than the BSW control group.

Attitudinal differences between the MSW experimental and control groups were not significant following intervention. This may be a reflection of the greater maturity and experience graduate students generally bring to educational programs, a consequence of which may be more crystallized attitudes. BSW students' attitudes generally may be more malleable.

Both MSW and BSW students indicated their interest in working with elderly clients to be somewhat positive on pretest. Interest in working with elderly clients did not change among students exposed to the module, except for a slight decline in the MSW group. This may be due to a moderately high initial interest level. Nonetheless, an implication of this finding is that increased knowledge about aging and enhanced attitudes toward elders do not necessarily correlate with increased desire to work with older adults. Preferences for certain client groups most likely are the culmination of many influences over time, and more extensive or varied interventions probably are needed if such a change is the primary goal. Ideally, didactic learning should be reinforced with experiential learning, such as through exposure to elderly people with a wide range of functional abilities. Another possible reason for the finding that interest did not change in a positive direction may be the content of the module itself. Elderly adults who are most likely to need social services are those who have physical frailty and/or cognitive impairments, and as such, the author felt it would be negligent to restrict content to positive aspects of aging or confine discussion to the well elderly. The findings of Rubin et al. (1986) suggest it is not unusual for social work students' interests in a variety of client groups to dissipate as they are exposed to the realities of practice over the course of their professional education.

Both the presence of a current or previous meaningful relationship with an elderly person, and the general quality of participants' previous experiences with elders, were positively correlated with positive attitudes toward elderly people and interest in working with elderly clients. However, meaningful comparisons are limited by the fact that large majorities of the participants reported a meaningful relationship with an elder and rated the quality of their previous experiences as positive or somewhat positive.

MSW and BSW students demonstrated considerable similarity in their generally favorable attitudes toward elderly people and interest in working with elderly clients. They mainly differed from one another in the greater familiarity with gerontological social work practice concepts (or enhanced ability to guess correct answers) demonstrated by MSW students prior to intervention. However, BSW students exposed to the module demonstrated more knowledge gain than did MSW students, and equal levels of knowledge between MSW and BSW students were demonstrated at posttest.

This study is limited in its generalizability to other MSW and BSW student populations by the fact that it was carried out within the social work program of one university. For instance, participants' rural versus urban orientations were not included in the demographic information gathered. While the university draws students from urban, suburban, and rural populations, the region is largely rural and partially Appalachian, with strong extended family networks an integral part of the culture.

Pretest sensitization is a limitation of pretest-posttest designs. Following the pretest, participants may have become more sensitive to issues involving aging and older adults, and this may have accounted for the positive shifts in attitudes toward elders that occurred in all groups, regardless of exposure to the curriculum module. Exposure to the social work practice and other curricula during the period in which the study took place also might have influenced positive attitude change toward vulnerable client populations in general.

Last, there is always the risk in studies such as this one that responses will be influenced by social desirability. That is, participants might have tried to present themselves in the best possible way or the politically correct way that they thought they should, such as on items concerning attitudes toward elders, despite the fact that the questionnaires were confidential. A future such study may be enhanced by the additional assessment of socially desirable response styles among participants.

NOTES

1. Advanced Generalist Social Work Practice I familiarizes MSW students with multidimensional and in-depth approaches for work with individuals, couples, families, and group systems, using the advanced generalist model of practice within a systems framework.
2. Social Work Practice I introduces BSW students to social work practice theory, provides instruction in professional social work practice skills with individuals and families, and examines the functions of the social worker in direct delivery of social services.

REFERENCES

Abell, N., & McDowell, J. R. (1990). Preparing for practice: Motivations, expectations & aspirations of the MSW class of 1990. *Journal of Social Work Education, 26* (1), 57-64.

Aday, R. H., & Campbell, M. J. (1995). Changes in nursing students' attitudes and work preferences after a gerontology curriculum. *Educational Gerontology, 21,* 247-260.

Angiullo, L, Whitborne, S. K. & Powers, C. (1996). The effects of instruction and experience on college students' attitudes toward the elderly. *Educational Gerontology, 22,* 483-495.

Berkman, B., Dobrof, R., Harry, L., & Damron-Rodriguez, J. (1995). Social Work. In S. M. Klein (Ed.), *A national agenda for geriatric education: White papers.* Rockville, MD: U.S. Bureau of Health Professions, Health Resources & Services Administration.

Butler, A. C. (1990). A reevaluation of social work students' career interests. *Journal of Social Work Education, 26* (1), 45-56.

Carmel, S., Cwikel, J., & Galinsky, D. (1992). Changes in knowledge, attitudes, and work preferences following courses in gerontology among medical, nursing, and social work students, *Educational Gerontology, 18,* 329-342.

Council on Social Work Education. (1999). *Statistics on social work education: 1998.* Alexandria, VA: Author.

Damron-Rodriguez, J., & Lubben, J. E. (1997). The 1995 WHCoA: An agenda for social work education and training, *Journal of Gerontological Social Work, 27* (3), 65-77.

Davis-Berman, J., & Robinson, J. D. (1989). Knowledge on aging and preferences to work with the elderly: The impact of a course on aging. *Gerontology and Geriatrics Education, 10* (1), 23-36.

Dellasega, C., & Curriero, F. C. (1991). The effects of institutional and community experiences on nursing students' intentions toward work with the elderly. *Journal of Nursing Education, 30* (9), 405-410.

Fox, S. D., & Wold, J. E. (1996). Baccalaureate student gerontological nursing experiences: Raising consciousness levels and affecting attitudes. *Journal of Nursing Education, 35* (8), 348-355.

Gibelman, M., & Schervish, P. H. (1997). What we do: Areas of practice, practice focus, and functions performed. In *Who we are: A second look.* (pp. 100-127). Washington, DC: National Association of Social Workers.

Gomez, G. E., Young, E. A., & Gomez, E. A. (1991). Attitude toward the elderly, fear of death, and work preference of baccalaureate nursing students. *Gerontology and Geriatrics Education, 11* (4), 45-56.

Greene, R. R., Barusch, A. S., & Connelly, J. R. (1990). *Social work and gerontology: Status report.* Washington, DC: Association for Gerontology in Higher Education.

Greene, R. R., Vourlekis, B. S., Gelfand, D. E., & Lewis, J. S. (1992). Current realities: Practice & education needs of social workers in nursing homes. *Journal of Gerontological Social Work, 18* (3/4), 39-54.

Haulotte, S., & McNeil, J. (1998). Integrating didactic and experiential aging curricula. *Journal of Gerontological Social Work, 30* (3/4), 43-57.

Hollander, F. (Producer & Director). (1998). *The Aging Mind* [videotape]. (Available from Aquarius Health Care Videos, P. O. Box 1159, Sherborn, MA 01770).

Johnson, M. S., & Wilson, J. F. (1990). Influencing attitudes toward the elderly early in a physician assistant training program. *Gerontology and Geriatrics Education, 10* (3), 11-21.

Kane, M. N. (1999). Factors affecting social work students' willingness to work with elders with Alzheimer's disease. *Journal of Social Work Education, 35* (1), 71-85.

Lubben, J. E., Damron-Rodriguez, J. A., & Beck, J. (1992). A national survey of aging curriculum in schools of social work, *Journal of Gerontological Social Work, 18* (3/4), 157-175.

Mosher-Ashley, P. M., & Ball, P. (1999). Attitudes of college students toward elderly persons and their perceptions of themselves at age 75. *Educational Gerontology, 25,* 89-102.

Murphy-Russell, S., Die, A. H., & Walker, J. L. (1986). Changing attitudes toward the elderly: The impact of three methods of attitude change. *Educational Gerontology, 12* (3), 241-251.

Nelson, G. M. (1988). Personnel and training needs in geriatric social work. *Educational Gerontology, 14,* 95-106.

Palmore, E. (1982). Attitudes toward the aged: What we know and need to know. *Research on Aging, 4* (3), 333-348.

Peterson, D. A. (1990). Personnel to serve the aging in the field of social work: Implications for educating professionals, *Social Work, 35* (5), 412-415.

Philipose, V., Tate, J., & Jacobs, S. (1991). Review of nursing literature: Evolution of gerontological education in nursing. *Nursing and Health Care, 12* (10), 524-530.

Quam, J. K., & Whitford, G. S. (1992). Educational needs of nursing home social workers at the baccalaureate level. *Journal of Gerontological Social Work, 18* (3/4), 143-156.

Reed, C. C., Beall, S. C., & Baumhover, L. A. (1992). Gerontological education for students in nursing and social work: Knowledge, attitudes, and perceived barriers. *Educational Gerontology, 18,* 625-636.

Rosencranz, H. A., & McNevin, T. E. (1969). A factor analysis of attitudes toward the aged. *Gerontologist, 9,* 55-59.

Rubin, A., Johnson, P. J., & DeWeaver, K. L. (1986). Direct practice interests of MSW students: Changes from entry to graduation. *Journal of Social Work Education, 22* (2), 98-108.

Schwalb, S. J., & Sedlacek, W. E. (1990). Have college students' attitudes toward older people changed? *Journal of College Student Development, 31,* 127-132.

Shoemake, A. F., & Rowland, V. T. (1993). Do laboratory experiences change college student's attitudes toward the elderly? *Educational Gerontology, 19,* 295-309.

Wilderom, C. P. M., Press, E. G., Perkins, D. V., Tebes, J. A., Nichols, L., Calkins, E., Cryns, A. G., & Schimpfhauser, F. (1990). Correlates of entering medical students' attitudes toward geriatrics. *Educational Gerontology, 16,* 429-446.

APPENDIX

Instrument Used to Measure Knowledge
of Gerontological Social Work Practice Concepts

The following items are True/False. Decide whether each statement is "true" or "false," and circle the appropriate letter.

T F   1. The majority of elderly people live independently without assistance with activities of daily living.

T F   2. Families generally are too quick to place their elderly relatives in nursing homes.

T F   3. The percentage of elderly people who live in nursing homes has been decreasing over the past decade.

T F   4. Most people develop senile dementia if they live long enough.

T F   5. Elderly people who are admitted to nursing homes are older and sicker than they used to be.

T F   6. People become more resistant to change as they age.

T F   7. Memory problems in elderly persons may respond to medical or psychosocial interventions.

T F   8. The rates of major depression are higher in the elderly than in younger adults.

T F   9. Life satisfaction is as high among elderly adults as it is among younger adults.

T F 10. Tactile communication, or touch, is less appropriate with elderly clients than with younger ones.

T F 11. Memory problems may be a symptom of depression in elderly adults.

T F 12. Elderly adults who are depressed are less likely to commit suicide than younger adults who are depressed.

T F 13. Depressed elderly adults benefit from psychotherapy as much as younger adults do.

T F 14. The process of life review with elderly clients may do more harm than good by focusing their attention too much on the past.

T F 15. Alzheimer's Disease usually has a sudden and severe onset.

T F 16. The risk for developing dementia increases with advancing age.

T   F   17. Elderly clients are less likely to need concrete services and case management than younger clients.
T   F   18. The behavior problems of elderly adults with advanced dementia are treatable with medical or environmental interventions.
T   F   19. When elderly clients have cognitive impairment, it is unnecessary to obtain their involvement in decision-making or problem-solving.
T   F   20. Hearing loss may cause elderly people to be more suspicious of others.

Chapter 11

Service Learning in Elder Care: Ten Years of Growth and Assessment

Carol R. Hegeman, MS
Beverly Horowitz, PhD, OTR/L
Lynn Tepper, EdD
Karl Pillemer, PhD
Leslie Schultz, BS

SUMMARY. This article includes an overview of the history and rationale of service learning in elder care, a description of the varied service learning in elder care programs initiated by the Foundation for Long Term Care and other entities, the empirical and qualitative impacts of service learning in elder care projects on students, elders and the host agency staff. It concludes with recommendations and resource materials for implementation, expansion and incorporation into effec-

Carol R. Hegeman is Director of Research, Foundation for LTC, Albany, NY. Beverly Horowitz is Clinical Associate Professor, the School of Health Technology and Management, Stony Brook University, Stony Brook, NY. Lynn Tepper is Associate Clinical Professor of Public Health, Columbia University. Karl Pillemer is Professor, Department of of Human Development and Director of Cornell Gerontology Research Institute, Cornell University, Ithaca, NY. Leslie Schultz is Research Support Specialist, Cornell Gerontology Research Institute, Cornell University, Ithaca, NY.

[Haworth co-indexing entry note]: "Service Learning in Elder Care: Ten Years of Growth and Assessment." Hegeman et al. Co-published simultaneously in *Journal of Gerontological Social Work* (The Haworth Social Work Practice Press, an imprint of The Haworth Press, Inc.) Vol. 39, No. 1/2, 2002, pp. 177-194; and: *Advancing Gerontological Social Work Education* (ed: M. Joanna Mellor, and Joann Ivry) The Haworth Social Work Practice Press, an imprint of The Haworth Press, Inc., 2002, pp. 177-194. Single or multiple copies of this article are available for a fee from The Haworth Document Delivery Service [1-800-HAWORTH, 9:00 a.m. - 5:00 p.m. (EST). E-mail address: docdelivery@haworthpress.com].

10.1300/J083v39n01_15

tive collegiate pedagogy and gerontological social work practice, with an emphasis on how social work faculty can collaborate with other disciplines in service learning. *[Article copies available for a fee from The Haworth Document Delivery Service: 1-800-HAWORTH. E-mail address: <docdelivery@haworthpress.com> Website: <http://www.HaworthPress.com> © 2002 by The Haworth Press, Inc. All rights reserved.]*

KEYWORDS. Service learning, community service, education, elder care, informal support

INTRODUCTION

The Foundation for Long Term Care (FLTC) has nurtured the concept of service learning in elder care for over 10 years. In service learning in elder care programs, colleges, students, and community agencies join forces to enhance care for the elderly and student learning about aging. Although there are certainly similarities, service-learning programs are not necessarily the same as the practica, preceptorships and internships that are so well established in social work and nursing education. While the program described here has been overwhelmingly used in undergraduate education, there is nothing which precludes graduate programs focused in this area.

A service learning in elder care project is specifically designed to (a) include a seminar requiring a high amount of both student-to-student and student-to-faculty interactions so that all the different service experiences of students are placed in appropriate and wide-ranging academic, political and psychosocial contexts, and (b) assure that the service is developed and requested by the agency to meet real needs of the elderly. What is most unique about service learning in elder care is its ability to blossom in almost *any discipline* within a college as long as there is articulation with disciplines such as social work, nursing, gerontology, psychology or sociology. This ability adds to the scope of services that can be provided and the number of students able to participate.

There is a particular relevance to social work education. While the majority of students come from gerontologocially-oriented and/or health-oriented disciplines, service learning in elder care now includes other majors such as architecture and business management. The inclusion of the social work perspective (from both faculty and students) in such a mixed academic setting can help to assure that a holistic view of the individual aged and the social milieu surrounding them is understood.

Conversely, the social work educational experience itself is enriched by service learning. While formal internships are well established, the great variety of informal placements social work students can experience in a service learning setting can be enriching for students. Lastly, pedagogy is enriched: Almost all faculty feel that student participation in seminars which explore and put into context the wide array of experiences students have in service learning is exceptional. Social work principles and concepts can be explored from a greatly wider perspective.

PROJECT GOALS

The short-term goals of the FLTC's varied service learning in elder care programs are:

> 1. to enhance the quality of academic learning about elder care issues and policy in various disciplines by integrating meaningful community service into coursework; and,
> 2. through these service-learning courses, to address immediate societal needs in the community surrounding the participating college.

The long-term project goal is to create a citizenry prepared for the challenges an aging society will bring. Since the attitude of today's college students will shape eldercare policy in the future, programs that educate as many college students as possible about the aging experience have a great societal value. A service-learning experience in which students debate the costs of care, equity, the "no care" zone and other health care and social issues is the best way–perhaps the only way–to prepare students for the elder-care challenges of today and tomorrow.

PROGRAM RATIONALE

Service learning in the health professions is an emerging concept. The Surgeon General's deputy recommends that some form of service learning be a required component of health professional education (Lurie, 2000). Similarly, the Pew Health Professions Commission concludes "the nation and its health professionals will be best served when public service is a significant part of the typical path to professional practice (UCSF Center for the Health Professions, cited in Seifer, 2001).

FLTC's service learning in elder care programs are an important component of this service learning movement. They were developed as a reaction to demographic challenges: an increasing number of aging Americans and a decreasing number of the pool of professional and volunteer caregivers. In 1900, one in 25 Americans was over 65, but by 1990, one in eight Americans was elderly (Goldstein, A. and Damon, B., 1993). Of these, nearly 40 percent of the elderly not living in institutions were limited by chronic care conditions (Freudenheim, 1996). The future needs are even more significant: The elderly population will *double* between 1995 and 2050, with most of this growth occurring in the years from 2010-2030 (the years the "baby boom" becomes elderly and today's college students will be decision makers). The "oldest-old" (those 85+) are the most rapidly growing group of the elderly. This group is most likely to need help with the activities of daily living, with a 50 percent chance of needing such help (U.S. Census Statistical Brief, *Sixty Five Plus in the United States*, 1995).

By contrast, there is a decreasing number of people able or willing to care for the aging population. The number of aides needed is expected to grow by 76 percent from 1996 to 2006, yet ombudsmen in 41 states report that nursing homes already cannot recruit or retain the aides they need (Editorial, *New York Times*, February 4, 2000). In 2000, 92 percent of nursing homes, 82 percent of home health agencies and 70 percent of adult care facilities in New York state were experiencing shortages (Heim and Tucker, 2000).

In response to these challenges, the Foundation for Long Term Care, in concert with 27 diverse colleges and elder-care providers, has systematically developed and studied service learning in elder care programs for over ten years as a way of both adding informal supports to the elder care system and to educating students about aging.

PROJECT DEFINITION

According to the Federal Corporation for National Service, "service-learning combines service to the community with student learning in a way that improves both the student and the community" (www.cns.gov). In the FLTC programs, of course, we focused on the service learning that is associated with service to the aged and/or the chronically ill.

Distinction from Other Forms of Experiential Education

Service learning is distinguished from other approaches to experiential education by its "intention to equally benefit the provider and the recipient of service as well as to ensure equal focus on both the service being provided and the learning that is occurring (Furco, 1996). Figure 1 provides a useful framework

FIGURE 1. Distinctions Among Service Programs

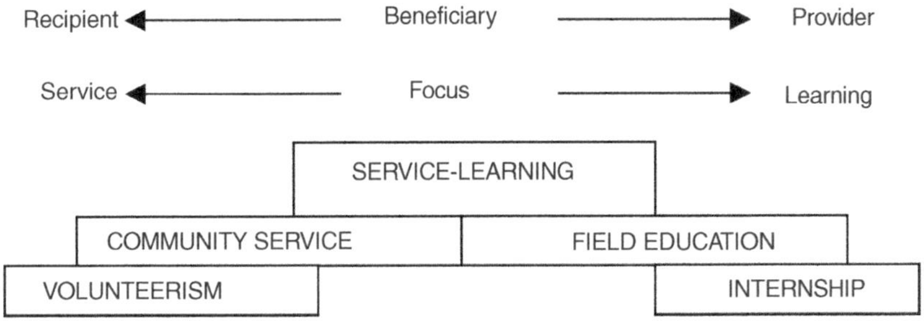

Recipient ◄───────────── Beneficiary ─────────────► Provider

Service ◄───────────── Focus ─────────────► Learning

SERVICE-LEARNING	
COMMUNITY SERVICE	FIELD EDUCATION
VOLUNTEERISM	INTERNSHIP

for placing service learning in the array of experiential activities offered by colleges. Seifer (2001) clarifies this further:

> Traditionally, experiential learning in the health professions is primarily concerned with its impact on student development and learning. Service learning can impact and benefit at least five important stakeholders: students, faculty, educational programs, community organizations and community members.

When a service-learning class is operating at its potential, what students are learning in their classrooms makes them more effective in their service and conversely, what students are experiencing in their service are making them better, more engaged students. One might imagine the hyphen in service-learning to be an equal sign (Hegeman, C. in Seperson and Hegeman, 2001).

All of the FLTC service learning in elder care projects, which involved over 1200 students from 28 colleges, share these commonalties:

- the colleges develop, and students participate in, one or more credit-bearing courses in service learning in elder care, either in a discipline in which elder care studies naturally fits (such as social work, nursing, human services, psychology, sociology or any of the allied health fields) or one which is interdisciplinary in nature and includes one of these disciplines;
- as part of the course work, students provide meaningful service in elder care as defined by elders themselves, by elder-care providers or by advocates (usually from 30-50 hours per semester, but there are variations by colleges based on credit-hours and other college requirements); and,
- the seminar has rigorous academic components that place the service in meaningful political, social and academic context and uses techniques

appropriate for eliciting reflection and debate about how their experiences reflect policy and practice challenges inherent in elder care. Typically, a case study and a policy paper are required. In other words, the service and the class work must intertwine and enrich each other.

Within this structure, there is an almost infinite variety in services and course content and emphasis. For example, courses run from BSW programs might look like either of these hypothetical models (with many more possible):

- students visit the isolated elderly in their homes while their academic seminar focuses on the policies and politics of home care entitlements and how the experiences of the students show strength and weaknesses in the policies;
- students conduct a variety of small group activities in senior centers, adult day programs and nursing homes while their seminar focuses on innovations in elder care service delivery and how students perceive the nature of care in these agencies.

Courses from schools of nursing in previous FLTC models included a program in which students run wellness clinics for elders living indepedently while learning the policy issues of health care for the aging and discussing how their service has made them view the health care system for the aged (Saladino, S. in Westacott and Hegeman, 1996).

A service learning in elder care program sponsored by a non-traditional program included an architecture technology program in which students developed designs for senior adult day care programs (Sprayregan and Sperling in Seperson and Hegeman, 2001).

An example of an interdisciplinary service learning in elder care program included a program run which offered an interdisciplinary program entitled "Communicating with the Linguistically Impaired Elderly Clients." This course is being team taught by faculty from the department of nursing, psychology and communication sciences and disorders. Students are taught how to communicate with people with dementia and then in turn put what they have learned in practice in educating staff in area nursing homes (Van Derveer, C., Riquelme, L. and Gomberg, D. 2000). Clearly, no two models will be alike and the potential variety is vast.

History of Service Learning in Elder Care

While service learning itself has a long history, the needs of the elderly had not been a primary focus of service learning programs until the FLTC pioneered it. The FLTC service learning programs were developed over time in different waves and with different external funders including the US Department of Education's Fund for the Improvement of Post Secondary Education (FIPSE), the Federal Corporation on National and Community Service and a private foundation which wishes to remain anonymous. From 1980-2000, over 1200 students from 27 participating colleges worked with over 6000 elders.

However, after the FLTC initiation, the Association for Gerontology in Higher Education (AGHE) and the University of Pittsburgh jointly developed an intergenerational service-learning program. (McCrea, 1998) and the Stephen F. Austin State University, Texas developed a program similar to that developed by the FLTC (Watson et al., 1997).

Findings from Related Studies

A faculty member in one of the FLTC's early service learning in elder care projects reports that her service learning experience in a service learning in elder care program based in a sociology department resulted in positive impacts in "three focused themes: inspiration and respect, education and learning, and interest and enjoyment" (Pine 1996.) McCrea (1998) noted that, in the AGHE/University of Pittsburgh's Intergenerational Service Learning Program, 64 percent of faculty who participated believed that service learning components increased student interest in course content, and all faculty reported that volunteer experiences complemented course work; 78 percent of 230 participating students reported that their service-learning experience contributed a great deal to what would have been learned in a traditional course; 92 percent of participating agencies reported these programs contributed to their organization; and, 88 percent said it was beneficial to individual clients. A structured intergenerational visitation program for nursing home residents within a school of nursing found substantial improvement in resident's psychosocial and physical condition while positively impacting nursing students views on aging (Newman, Lyons, & Onawola, 1985).

In an unpublished study, Watson (2001) found no measurable short-term (one semester, four months) improvement in atttitudes/commitment to community service or improved perceptions of the elderly. Watson hypothesized that the lack of change resulted from the short time period and a selection effect: Participating students were juniors and seniors with prior experience with the elderly who were already predisposed to view the elderly positively. As will be seen, the FLTC's larger study was more positive, although the same selection effect is suspected.

Faculty members running programs in service learning in health and allied health care disciplines report that it enhances professionalism, provides opportunities to develop inter-personal skills, critical thinking, and social responsibility while also responding to diverse unmet community health needs. Agencies participating in these kinds of service learning programs report the students enabled them to provide services to increased numbers of undeserved clients to better serve their communities (Bayne, Barker, Higgs, Jenkin, Murphy & Symnoground, 1994; Callister & Hobbins-Garbett, 2000; Seifer, 1998; Simoni & McKinney, 1998).

Interdisciplinary service-learning projects with students from medical technology, medical dietetics, respiratory therapy, nursing, speech and language pathology, pharmacy, social work, and optometry and medicine have been implemented to provide health screenings, and counseling to address unmet health needs in community settings, including rural areas (Rudmann, Ward & Varekojis, 1999.) Other models have sought to augment clinical services in rural undeserved areas utilizing senior-level students in medicine, nursing and pharmacy (Wiese, Howard & Stephens, 1979).

Allied health, occupational and physical therapy programs service-learning projects also show positive impacts. Such programs focused on fall prevention, health screenings, home assessments for "at risk" community living elders, recreation and fitness, and friendly visitation. In all programs students gained knowledge and skills and agencies reported benefits for clients (Greene, 1997; Horowitz, 2000; Thomas, Reigart, & Trickey, 1998). One project spearheaded by physical therapy developed a multidisciplinary fall prevention program for undeserved elders, including educational brochures in multiple languages, a video and web site, for older adults and health professionals (Newton, 2000).

Service learning out of the health care arena is more common than any of the models discussed so far. Research on service learning from all disciplines and activities (most commonly education and community building) shows that it too is an effective way to expand classroom education to provide hands on learning and build leadership while reconnecting students with communities to promote volunteerism (Cleary, Kaiser-Drobney, Ubbes, Stuhldreher & Birch, 1998; Stanton, 1990). Learn and Service America, a component of the Corporation for National Service (CNS) one of the FLTC's funders, found: (1) strong relationships between service experiences and course content when students performed 20 + hours per semester and had opportunities for class discussion and (2) a strong correlation between participation in a service-learning course and increased civic responsibility (Gray, Ondaatje & Zakaras, 1999).

Evaluation of the FLTC's Service Learning in Elder Care Programs

The five main objectives of the evaluation of the FLTC's service learning programs were: (1) to detail the characteristics of participating students; (2) to assess student views regarding the success of the program; (3) to explore changes in student attitudes on several dimensions over their involvement in the project; (4) obtain assessments from selected participating elder service agencies of the success of the program; and, (5) obtain assessments from individuals who received services from the program.

Methods

In the initial seminar for each semester, students completed a pretest questionnaire. A posttest questionnaire was completed in the last seminar session of each semester. Although well over 1,000 students from twenty-five educational institutions at twenty-eight diverse campuses completed these forms, the following results are based only on the 912 students who completed both pre- and post-tests.

Characteristics of Participating Students

Students who participated:

- ranged in age from 18 to 67 years. Sixty-four percent of the students fell within the traditional college ages of 18-23, leaving 36 percent of students older than 23, signifying a large number of older returning students in the group. This is also reflected by the mean age for the group: 27 years of age.
- tended to be upper classmen. Fifty-eight percent were in their senior year, 22 percent were in their junior year, and 11 percent were in their sophomore year. Only five percent were freshman and only three percent were graduate students.
- were predominantly female. Seventy-eight of students were female and 22 percent were male.
- were divided almost equally into students who were part of a formal gerontology minor or concentration within their major (48 percent) and those whose major had no formal gerontological concentration. (52 percent)
- had a variety of majors: 44 percent in social sciences, including social work and human services; 27 percent in nursing; 17 percent in allied health; and, in keeping with the FLTC efforts to diversify service learning, six percent were majoring in architectural technology, and five percent in management/communication.
- had a variety of career plans: 30 percent social work/counseling; 28 percent allied health; 26 percent nursing; 13 percent architecture and design; 3.3 percent management and communications.

The students' services were friendly visiting (40 percent), recreation/activities work (25 percent), health promotion (10 percent), and social services (9 percent). The remaining services were varied.

Assessment of Students' Views Regarding the Success of the Program

Students' assessments of the service learning experiences were overwhelmingly positive. Specifically:

- almost all (97 percent) of the students reported that they would recommend the program to other students;
- almost all (96 percent) felt that they learned a lot in this program;
- most students (86 percent) felt this program was one of the best experiences they had in college.

Open-ended statements from the students give a context for these numbers:

> *"It was enjoyable to learn about a group of people that my age group forgot existed."*

> *"This experience will help me to be more politically conscious to the needs of the elderly."*

> *"You can make a difference in an elder's life by just being there with them."*

> *"I learned not to treat the elderly as children . . . they are capable of doing for themselves."*

> *"Being old does not mean that you are any less than a younger person . . . the elderly are just like us . . . they have good days and bad days."*

> *"I learned that with the frustrations of working with the elderly also comes a lot of fulfillment."*

> *"I learned a lot about history . . . peoples' personal stories made it come alive."*

> *"I got some good advice and I made some new friends."*

> *"Many of the folks I worked with were open to new ideas and enjoyed talking about their lives . . . this surprised me a little."*

Students were asked to respond to open-ended questions about their work experience and the coursework. Seventy-eight percent of the students offered at least one suggestion for improving the work experience. Seventeen percent of the students indicated a desire for more hours at their placements, reflecting a desire to make the experience more intense. Other suggestions for improvement included a desire for more variety in the work; less role ambiguity; identification of more activities that are stimulating for the older people and more orientation to the placement. Student responses also indicated that more attention should be paid to expediting student interactions with workers in their service setting

One interesting question is whether students who had prior experience with aging-related issues would have a different response to the program from students without such experience. To address this issue, we examined whether satisfaction was lower or higher for students (1) who were part of an organized gerontology program; (2) who had previously worked with the aged for pay; and (3) who had done volunteer work with the elderly in the past. Although satisfaction was slightly less for those students who had previously worked with the aged for pay, there were, however, no significant differences between the experienced and inexperienced students on any of the relevant satisfaction variables.

Assessment of Student Attitudes

A number of Likert-like scales were included in the pre-test and the post-test to measure such changes in attitudes toward the aged, attitudes toward community service work, and attitudes toward working with the elderly and chronically ill or disabled. These items were repeated on the posttest to allow for an assessment of changes over the semester. In sum, there were statistically significant changes in attitudes towards the elderly, but no statistically significant changes in attitudes toward community service or towards careers in aging services.

Attitudes Toward the Elderly

Participants were asked to rate nine statements about the elderly on a 1-4 scale, with 4 representing the most positive answer. Therefore, the highest possible score was 36. Scores ranged from 16 to 35 at the pretest, indicating that student's attitudes to the elderly were generally very positive to begin with. The mean of this scale increased from 24.7 to 25.69, a change that is significant at the level of $p < .000$ (t-test), representing a positive change in attitudes toward the elderly over the course.

Particularly significant changes ($p < .01$) were observed on several of the individual items. While 61 percent of the students at the pretest agreed with the statement "Most people are set in their ways and unable to change," only 44 percent did so at the posttest. In the pretest, 84 percent agreed with the statement "Older people become wiser with old age" compared to 90 percent at the posttest.

Attitudes Toward Community Service

Participants were asked to rate a series of statements about attitudes toward community service (strongly agree, agree, disagree, strongly disagree), with a higher score indicating a more positive attitude. The scale ranged from 16 to 28 at the pretest. These scores show, as with the attitudes toward the elderly scales, that the students' attitudes toward community service prior to entering the course were generally very positive to begin with. None of the changes observed on individual items were found to be significant. Although 97.5 percent of the students agreed that "It is important to help people in general, whether you know them or not" on the pretest and on the posttest, all the scores for all of the other items in this scale decreased very slightly. For example, in response to the statement "It is the community's responsibility to take care of people who can't take care of themselves," 89 percent of the students agreed at the pretest while 88 percent agreed at the posttest. While 99 percent of the students agreed with the statement "I am good at helping people" at the pretest, 96 percent agreed at the posttest. Ninety-five percent of the students agreed at the pretest that "Careers in service to others can be more rewarding than other careers," 93 percent agreed at the posttest. It is possible that as Watson (2001) hypothesized, a selection effect was present as these responses were very positive to begin with. It is also possible findings reflect a more realistic view of community service as well as their own abilities regarding elder care.

Attitudes Toward Work with the Elderly

Students were asked the extent to which they agreed with a series of statements regarding their attitudes toward working with elderly persons. Statements included, for example, "People who work with older people have interesting jobs." The scale ranged from 10 to 28 at the pre-test. The mean of this scale decreased slightly from 21.6 at the pretest to 21.49 at the posttest. Although this change was not statistically significant for the total scale, several individual items demonstrated significant changes in student attitudes toward work with the elderly. For example, while 35 percent of the students at the pretest agreed with the statement "It would be very stressful to work with older people or people with chronic conditions," 44 percent of the students at the posttest agree to this statement. Ninety two percent of the students at the pretest agreed with the statement "I don't have the ability to work with older people" decreasing to 85 percent agreement at the posttest. As before, we suggest that this change is a reflection of a more realistic view on the part of some students regarding this type of work rather than an increased negative attitude.

In contrast to the previous examples, 91 percent of the students agreed with the statement "Working with older people is an interesting job" in the pre-test, while 95 percent agreed in the posttest. The student's experience in the service learning program seems to have supported a more realistic understanding of work with the elderly while simultaneously reinforcing the students' generally positive feelings regarding how interesting it is to work with the elderly.

While these findings indicate that, in the aggregate, we have not changed the desire of students to work with the aged, it is evident that they may view support for the aging and aging services in general more positively.

AGENCY PERSPECTIVES

There was a modest one-semester evaluation of the impact of service learning on 21 different elder care providers. On the average, each of these agencies hosted two students, with a range from one to eight students. Based on findings from a self-administered mail survey, almost all agency staff (96 percent) felt that the students were very responsible; and 74 percent felt students were well-prepared for the work experience.

In terms of perceived impact on clients, 96 percent said their client's lives had been enhanced and 91 percent said that the quality of their client's lives had improved as a result of the student activities. Overall, all facility respondents thought it was successful with 87 percent saying the program was "very successful," and the remainder that it was "somewhat successful." Lastly, all agency respondents said they would recommend the program to another agency/facility.

When asked about the benefits to the recipients, the most frequent response to this question could be summarized in the term "companionship." The positive results of this interaction fell into two categories–personal one-on-one time and greater community/social interaction. Respondents often noted that their agency was unable to give enough personal attention to their clients, and that the students gave clients much needed individual attention.

IMPACT ON THE RECIPIENTS OF THE SERVICE

There was also a one-semester study of the impact of the students' service on recipients. Thirty-three recipients were surveyed from rural and urban areas of New York state. Seventy-five percent of the recipients completed the survey themselves with the remainder having someone assisting or acting as a proxy. Fifty-five percent received service from students at an adult-day care program, 30 percent at a senior center, nine percent in their own home, with the remainder at a group home, independent housing or some other location. In terms of specific activities, recipients reported receiving help in two major areas: (1) exercise and massage (reflecting that one of the communities surveyed has service learning emanating from a physical therapy department) and (2) friendly visitation and conversation. Several respondents stated that the student assisted the client in learning basic computing skills, showing the individual nature of the service learning experiences.

Recipients were overwhelmingly positive about the experience. Of the 50 percent that reported having a regular caregiver, 85 percent felt that having a student working with them reduced the strain on their caregiver, with 41 percent saying that it was reduced significantly. When asked "How enjoyable were these activities?" 98 percent said they found them enjoyable, with 60 percent answering "very enjoyable." Eighty-three percent reported that the student made it easier for them to remain living at home. An overwhelming majority (98 percent) reported that working with the student made their life better or more pleasant with 51 percent reporting that it "improved a lot." Finally, all of the respondents said they would recommend the service-learning program to someone else.

When asked what they liked most about their involvement with the student, nearly all respondents commented on the benefits of companionship and social interaction and responses such as "she was able to relate to me," "gave me incentive to try something new," and "a friend" typified the results.

Most recipients did not have any suggestions for improving the program. Several respondents, however, suggested that the program was too short or that they wanted more visits or longer visits.

A common debate among the project director and faculty has been the issue of attachment: What happens to the elder when the student leaves? What happens to the student when a resident dies? Students receive a service-learning handbook (Westacott and Hegeman, 1996) which discusses this issue and FLTC faculty orientation discusses them in detail. From these evaluations, it seems as if the issues are managed well although they remain an ongoing challenge.

IMPLICATIONS FOR FACULTY

While a consistent faculty concern is the extra time such a program takes in terms of additional student placements, student queries and relationships with elder care agencies, faculty has been extremely supportive of the project, both because it is professionally rewarding and energizing (Roodin, 2000) and because faculty enjoys "the degree of dedication" shown by students (Harter, Ladrigan and Machemer in Westacott and Hegeman, 1996). Further options and innovations in service learning in elder care are virtually unlimited, making available and creative efforts in developing them an exciting option.

IMPLICATIONS FOR SOCIAL WORK EDUCATION

As for the impact of social work education, it certainly seems the further development of service learning in elder care by social work faculty will have several compelling benefits: increased community-college interactions; more services for the aged members in the communities surrounding the colleges; an effective and invigorating pedagogy; the potential for a practical way to assure interdisciplinary collaboration; and an effective way to prepare society for the changes an aging society will bring to all.

In addition, the emerging emphasis on service learning in generic health care seems to demand that social work also participate. In particular, the development of multi-disciplinary service learning in elder care programs will allow students from other disciplines to have an enriched view of the psycho-social needs of the aging.

REFERENCES

Bayne, T., Barker, J., Jenkin, S., Murphy, D. & Synoground, G. (1994). Student experiential learning: A collaborative community practice project. *Journal of Public Health Nursing, 11* (6), 426-430.

Callister, L. & Hobbins-Garbett, D. (2000). Enter to learn, go forth to serve: Service learning in nursing education. *Journal of Professional Nursing, 16* (3), 177-183.

Cleary, M., Kaiser-Drobney, A., Ubbes, V., Stuhldreher, W. & Birch, D. (1998). Service-learning in the "third sector": Implications for professional preparation. *Journal of Health Education, 29* (5), 304-311.

Corporation for National Service (1996). *The Internet Guide to National Service Networking.* Washington, DC.

Couch, Larry (1992). *Let Us Serve Them All Their Days: Younger Volunteers Serving Homebound Elderly Persons.* Washington, DC: The National Council on the Aging.

Driscoll, Amy, Sherril B. Gelmon, Barbara A. Holland, Seanna Kerrigan, Amy Spring, Kari Grosvold, and M.J. Longley (1998). *Assessing the Impact of Service Learning: A Workbook for Strategies and Methods.* Portland, OR: Portland University, Center for Academic Excellence.

Droge, David. (compiled and edited). (1996). *Disciplinary Pathways to Service-Learning.* Mesa, AZ: Campus Compact National Center for Community Colleges.

Eyler, Janet, Dwight E. Giles Jr. and Angela Schmiede (1996). *A Practitioner's Guide to Reflection in Service-Learning: Student Voices Reflections.* Nasville, TN: Vanderbilt University.

Freudenheim, E. (Ed.), (1996). *Chronic Care in America: A 21st Century Challenge.* Princeton, NJ: Robert Wood Johnson Foundation.

Furco, A. (1996). Service-learning: a balanced approach to experiential education. *Expanding Boundaries: Serving and Learning, 1,* 2-Maryland: Cooperative Educations Association for the Corporation for National Service.

Goldstein, A. and Damon, B. (1993). *We the American Elderly.* U.S. Department of Commerce. Economics and Statistics Administration. Bureau of Census.

Gray, M., Ondaatje, E. & Zakaras, L. (1999). Combining service and learning in higher education: Summary report for the Corporation for National Service. Santa Monica: RAND Education.

Greenberg, J. (1997). Service-learning in health education. *Journal of Health Education, 28* (6), 345-349.

Greene, D. (1997). The use of service learning in client environments to enhance ethical reasoning in students. *AJOT, 51* (10), 844-852.

Hegeman, C. "Definitions and Rationale," *Service Learning in Elder Care: Making Connections.* (tentative title, in press). Westport, CT: Greenwood Publishing.

Heim, D. and Tucker, N. (2000) "The Staffing Crisis in New York's Continuing Care System." Albany New York: The New York Association of Homes and Services for the Aging.

Horowitz, B. (2000). Service learning and occupational therapy. Paper presented at the Annual Scientific Meeting of The Gerontological Society of America, Washington, DC.

Kendall, Jane C. and Associates (1990) *Combining Service and Learning a Resource Book for Community and Public Service.* Vol. I, Raleigh, NC: National Society for Internships and Experiential Education.

Kendall, Jane C. and Associates (1990). *Combining Service and Learning a Resource Book for Community and Public Service.* Vol. II, Raleigh, NC: National Society for Internships and Experiential Education.

Kendall, Jane C, John S. Duley, Thomas C. Little, Jane S. Permaul and Sharon Rubin (1986). *Strengthening Experiential Education Within Your Institution.* Raleigh, NC: National Society for Internships and Experiential Education.

Luce, Janet (ed.) (1988). *Service Learning: An Annotated Bibliography Linking Public Service with the Curriculum.* Volume III of Combining Service and Learning: A Resource Book for Community and Public Service. Raleigh, NC: National Society for Internships and Experiential Education.

Lurie N. Healthy people 2010: setting the nation's public health agenda. Academic Medicine. 2000 Jan; 75 (1): 12-3.

McCrea, J. (1998, Nov.). First year service-learning programs flourish. *AGHE Exchange, 22* (2), 1; 3.

National Service-Learning Clearinghouse (2000). Status of Service Learning in the US. (on-line) (www.nicsl.coled.umn.edu/res/mono/status2.htm).

Newman, S., Lyons, C. & Onawola, R. (1985). The development of an intergenerational service-learning program at a nursing home. *The Gerontologist, 25* (2), 130-133.

Newton, R. (2000, November). Fall prevention project. Poster presented at the Annual Scientific Meeting of The Gerontological Society of America, Washington, DC.

New York Times. Editorial. February 4, 2000.

Pillemer, K. "An Evaluation of Service Learning in Elder Care." Unpublished report prepared for the Foundation for Long Term Care, Albany, NY.

Pine, P. (1997). Learning by sharing: An intergenerational college course. *Journal of Gerontological Social Work, 28* (1/2), 93-102.

Renner, Tanya and Michele Bush (1997). *Evaluation and Assessment in Service-Learning.* Mesa, AZ: Campus Compact National Center for Community Colleges.

Roodin, P (2000). Symposium discussant, "Not for Gerontologists Only: The Impact of Service Learning in Elder Care." Scientific Meeting of the Gerontological Society of America.

Rudmann, S.V., Ward, K., & Varekojis, S. (1999). University-community partnerships for health: A model interdisciplinary service-learning project. *Journal of Allied Health, 28* (2), 109-112.

Saladino, S. (1996) "Case Study: School of Nursing CCNY," In Westacott, B. and Hegeman, C. (Ed.). *Service Learning in Elder Care.* Albany, NY: Foundation for Long Term Care.

Scannell, Tess and Angela Roberts (1994). *Young and Old Serving Together: Meeting Community Needs Through Intergenerational Partnerships.* Washington, DC: Generations United.

Seifer, S. (1998). Service-learning: Community-campus partnerships for health professions education. *Academic Medicine, 73* (3), 273-277.

Seifer, S. (2001.) <www.futurehealthg.uscf.edu/from_the_director.html>.

Seperson, S. and Hegeman, C. (Eds.) (2001). *Service Learning and Elder Care: Making Connections* (in press) Westport, CT: Greenwood Publishing Group.

Simoni, P. & McKinney, J. (1998). Evaluation of service learning in a school of nursing: Primary care in a community setting, *Journal of Nursing Education, 37* (3), 1228-128.

Sprayregan, A. and Sperling, P. "Service Learning with the Elderly and Chronically Ill for Architectural Students in Urban College." Seperson, S. and Hegeman, C. (Eds.) (2001). *Service Learning and Elder Care: Making Connections* (in press) Westport, CT: Greenwood Publishing Group.

Stanton, T. (1990). Liberal arts, experiential learning and public service: Necessary ingredients for socially responsible undergraduate education. In J. Kendall et al. (Eds.). *Combining service and learning: A resource book for community and public service (Vol. 1)* (pp. 175-188). Raleigh: National Society for Internships and Experiential Education.

Stanton, T. (1990). Service learning and leadership development. In J. Kendall et al. (Eds.). *Combining service and learning: A resource book for community and public service (Vol. 1)* (pp. 337-352). Raleigh: National Society for Internships and Experiential Education.

Stone, Louise (1997). *A Handbook For Understanding and Implementation Service Learning.* Kentucky: University of Kentucky.

Thomas, K., Reigart, E. & Trickey, B. (1998). An interdisciplinary service learning experience in geriatrics for occupation and physical therapy students. *Gerontology and Geriatrics Education, 19* (2), 81-9.

UCSF Center for the Health Professions <http://futurehealth.uscf.edu/from the director.html>.

Van Derveer, C., Riquelme, L. and Gomberg, D. 2000 Symposium "Not for Gerontologists Only: The Impact of Service Learning in Elder Care," Scientific Meeting of the Gerontological Society of America.

Watson, J. B. Jr., Carol Church, Ray Darville, and Sandy Darville. (1997). "University-Community College Partnership Development for Eldercare Service-learning: A Model for Rural Community Impact." Expanding Boundaries: Building Civic Reponsibility in Higher Education, Volume II: 59-64.

Watson, J. B. personal communication with C. Hegeman.

Westacott, B. and Hegeman, C. (1996). *Service Learning in Elder Care: A Resource Manual.* Albany, New York: The Foundation for Long Term Care.

Wiese, W. & Stephens, J. (1970). Augmentation of clinical services in rural areas by health sciences students. *Journal of Medical Education, 54*, 917-925.

Wiese, W., Howard, C. & Stephens, J. (1979). Augmentation of clinical services in rural areas by health sciences students. *Journal of Medical Ethics.* 54 (12), 917-924.

CNS Web Pages, <www.cns.gov>.

Chapter 12

Teaching Geriatric Assessment:
A Hands-On Educational Experience

Patricia Gleason-Wynn, PhD

SUMMARY. This paper presents an experiential exercise that was used successfully to assist graduate social work students in integrating and applying knowledge about geriatric assessment. The experience was completed as a community service project for a local housing facility whose executive director used the data to support a grant for monies for an on-site social worker. This project provided students with a hands-on experience to interact with resident-volunteers, and apply the knowledge of geriatric assessment learned in the Direct Practice in Aging course. This exercise can be replicated in other communities between programs of social work and senior housing facilities. *[Article copies available for a fee from The Haworth Document Delivery Service: 1-800-HAWORTH. E-mail address: <docdelivery@haworthpress.com> Website: <http://www.HaworthPress.com> © 2002 by The Haworth Press, Inc. All rights reserved.]*

KEYWORDS. Geriatric assessment, social work, education

Patricia Gleason-Wynn is Adjunct Assistant Professor, The University of Texas at Arlington, School of Social Work, Arlington, TX 76019.

[Haworth co-indexing entry note]: "Teaching Geriatric Assessment: A Hands-On Educational Experience." Gleason-Wynn, Patricia. Co-published simultaneously in *Journal of Gerontological Social Work* (The Haworth Social Work Practice Press, an imprint of The Haworth Press, Inc.) Vol. 39, No. 1/2, 2002, pp. 195-202; and: *Advancing Gerontological Social Work Education* (ed: M. Joanna Mellor, and Joann Ivry) The Haworth Social Work Practice Press, an imprint of The Haworth Press, Inc., 2002, pp. 195-202. Single or multiple copies of this article are available for a fee from The Haworth Document Delivery Service [1-800-HAWORTH, 9:00 a.m. - 5:00 p.m. (EST). E-mail address: docdelivery@haworthpress.com].

10.1300/J083v39n01_16

INTRODUCTION

The population of America is getting older, and people are living longer (Administration on Aging, 2000). Zlotnik, Rosen, Green and Curl (2000) note that these demographic changes are going to create a demand for services to older adults as well as create new opportunities and challenges for social workers in health and social service settings.

Schools of social work and social work educators are also challenged to educate and supply qualified social workers to address and meet these increasing needs of an aging population (Choi & Dinse, 1998; Gleason-Wynn, 1995; Zlotnik, Rosen, Green and Curl, 2000; Zucchero, 1998). Special skills are needed for working with older adults and special attention needs to be given to training the professionals who work with older adults (Ivry, 1992; Schneider, Kropf & Kisor, 2000; Zucchero, 1998). It is especially important to understand the factors and interactions of biophysical functioning and psychosocial processes that are addressed in geriatric assessment (Schneider et al., 2000). Ivry (1992) notes that geriatric assessment is a complex, multi-faceted and multi-disciplinary process. Further, she states, "teaching geriatric assessment is not only an intellectual exercise, but, as in all social work, must relate to practice experience" (p. 19).

The integration of classroom teaching and the application of this knowledge in the practice setting or the natural environment of the client has always been a concern of social work educators (Haulotte & McNeil, 1998). Over the years social work educators have been challenged (Knowles, 1972; Memmott & Brennan, 1998) to attempt to do different things or to do things differently, in an effort to create a learning environment for students.

This paper describes a course assignment–conducting an in-depth assessment of the biopsychosocial functioning of an older adult living in public housing–for a graduate social work elective, Direct Practice in Aging. Students learned about geriatric assessment and conducted an assessment of an older adult outside the classroom. The assignment also allowed the instructor to enhance the students' understanding of the complexities of geriatric assessment in the client's environment. Taking the teaching out of the classroom and into the client's environment allowed for the integration of theoretical learning with the application of knowledge–learning by doing, and, "doing it" differently. In addition, the students were able to assess their own strengths and limitations, and to incorporate this knowledge into their practice.

PURPOSE OF THE COURSE

The purpose of this university course was to provide a foundation for social work practice with older adults and their caregivers. The students learned about engagement, assessment and intervention strategies that are related to the practice of social work with older adults and their families. Salient aspects of class, race, ethnicity and gender were presented. Lectures, class discussions, site visits, and an experiential exercise were the primary teaching methods used. Upon completion of the course, students were expected to demonstrate:

- Familiarity with the biopsychosocial and cultural aspects of aging,
- Knowledge of a suggested framework for assessment, intervention and evaluation of individual and family needs and services for older adults, and
- Ability to integrate these knowledge and practice skills into the completion of an assessment and the development of an intervention plan for an older person living in public housing.

THE SETTING

The setting was a seven story subsidized housing facility, with 234 units housing elderly and disabled low-income residents, located in the downtown area of a large Texas city. Over 2/3 of the population were female, over 2/3 of the population was over the age of 60, nearly 1/2 were minority (42% Black and 4% Hispanic), and a majority (93%) lived alone. Health conditions included arthritis, high blood pressure, heart disease, eye conditions, diabetes, hearing impairment, and stroke. Seventy percent rated their health as fair or poor. Current services utilized by residents included transportation services, homemaker, health aide, home delivered meals, and senior center services (located on-site).

There was no social worker employed in the building. The executive director was writing a grant to obtain monies to employ a full-time social worker. She planned to use the information collected by the students to demonstrate the need for a professional social worker.

THE PROJECT

The university instructor met with the executive director and the manager of the housing high-rise to discuss the community service project. The project would also serve as an experiential exercise for graduate social work students.

It involved graduate social work students conducting assessments of resident-volunteers, preferably over the age of 60.

The manager and executive director wanted help in finding residents in need of social services. The manager identified various residents who she believed would benefit from an assessment. These residents were invited to participate. In addition a written notice about the project was provided to all residents over the age of 60. An informative open meeting was scheduled for the residents to attend, to learn more about the project.

PREPARATION OUTSIDE THE CLASSROOM

The instructor conducted the open meeting with all interested residents to explain the project, the process and the desired outcome–to provide a practical experience for the students. The residents were assured that all information would be held in confidence unless it was determined that the resident was a danger to himself or others, or was being abused. It was also explained that the needs and services identified during this process would be presented in a non-identifying format to the manager, unless the resident gave permission for the information to be released.

Twenty residents agreed to participate. Prior to the actual experience, two weeks later, three dropped out for various reasons. There were 17 students and 17 volunteers.

These resident-volunteers understood that the students would meet with them either in the resident-volunteer's own apartment, which allowed for assessment of the person-in-environment, or in a private area downstairs until the volunteer felt comfortable enough to invite the student into the apartment. The instructor was to remain downstairs, available to consult with the students or provide direction if needed, and to answer questions or concerns of the volunteers.

PREPARATION INSIDE THE CLASSROOM

Prior to the students meeting with the resident-volunteers, two 3-hour lectures were devoted in the classroom to geriatric assessment including an overview of various assessment tools used to assess cognitive and functional capabilities. In the first 3-hour lecture, students were provided an intense look at geriatric assessment content: biological, psychological including probable causes of altered mental states, and social aspects, as well as an overview on the assessment form used for the assignment. They were introduced to screening tools relevant in geriatric assessment such as the Folstein Mini-Mental State Exam (MMSE) (Folstein, McHugh & McHugh, 1975), and the Geriatric Depression Scale (GDS)-Short Form (Sheikh & Yesavage, 1986) for mental functioning; the Activities of Daily Living scale (ADL); and the Instrumental Activities of Daily Living scale (IADL) (Kane & Kane, 1981) for physical functioning. The instructor demonstrated the administration of these tools.

The assessment form was developed by the instructor and included content based on recommendations from the literature (Bumagin & Hirn, 1990; Ivry, 1992; Schneider et al., 2000) as well as the instructor's personal experience. Content included

- Identifying information, including age, sex, class, ethnicity, culture, living arrangement, financial resources, physical appearance, grooming and dress.
- Assessment of social functioning: social history, coping methods (current and previous), patterns of interaction, living conditions, use of community services and satisfaction with current services, and informal support systems.
- Assessment of physical functioning: medical history, medications, functional capacities (observed and reported), and current medical and functional concerns.
- Assessment of psychological functioning: affect, cognitive abilities, and psychiatric history, if any, and treatment, if any, and relationship with student.
- Overall assessment of this person's functioning (strengths and limitations).

The students were asked to become familiar with the questions on the assessment and screening tools, and to be prepared to participate in role-playing in the next 3-hour lecture. Students were encouraged to practice with others outside class to help increase their comfort level with the content and their interviewing skills.

In the second 3-hour lecture, the instructor gave an overview of the physical, psychological and social aspects of geriatric assessment, and reminders on developing rapport and interviewing older adults (Bumagin & Hirn, 1990). The students learned about the setting in which the resident-volunteers lived, and the community resources currently utilized at the housing facility. The remainder of the time was spent role-playing a geriatric assessment including the administration of the Folstein MMSE, the GDS, and the ADL and IADL scales. The instructor provided feedback and answered questions in addition to offering reassurances to alleviate student anxiety about "doing the project right."

RESULTS

Benefits. A number of benefits were realized upon completion of this project. For the university there was the benefit of good public relations. For the school of social work there was an additional direct link to the community for student education. For the resident-volunteers, there was the opportunity to contribute to learning and, possibly, enhancement of self-esteem. In addition, several of the needs identified by the students were successfully addressed. For the non-participating residents, the executive director used the data collected and compiled to successfully obtain a grant to provide for an on-site professional social worker. For students, there was the benefit of a relevant and applicable learning experience.

Identified Needs. Students identified concrete needs, educational needs, prevention and safety concerns, and coordination of services need as concerns of the residents. The following needs were presented to the housing manager.

Concrete Needs:

- Screening programs for hearing, vision, and blood pressure,
- Exercise programs,
- Telephone contact/daily reassurance program,
- Assistance with heavy chores, and
- Financial assistance and resources available for residents on limited income (help with long-distance calls, medication).

Education-Related Needs:

- Information on advance directives (Medical Power of Attorney, Out of Hospital Do Not Resuscitate, and Living Wills),
- Information on nutritional needs and counseling, and
- Information related to various diseases: dementia, heart disease, and diabetes.

Prevention and Safety:

- Loose handrails in the hallways,
- Assistive and safety devices in bathrooms, and
- Low battery status on several smoke alarms.

Coordination of Client Services:

- Need of a person other than the manager to evaluate the resident's needs, make referrals, and monitor the implementation of services, and

• Need for a person to be a liaison with the mental health community center and ensure clients receive needed services.

DISCUSSION

Student Evaluation of the Project. The students had some concerns at first about the project such as how would they get there, did they have the necessary skills, what if the volunteer would not talk to them, and what if they asked a wrong question or asked the question in a wrong way. Directions to the housing project were easy to give and transportation easily arranged, while the other issues were addressed in class discussions and through role-play as noted above.

The primary purpose of the project was to provide a practical experience for the student. It appears that the purpose was achieved as noted in student comments: "this is the only direct practice class I have had in which we actually work with real people," "the assessment and evaluation were very relevant for future social work," "I like the techniques for assessment and intervention I learned," and "the assignments were the best . . . experience beats writing theory papers any day." One student stated that he would have rather used other clients, preferably someone known to him, for the assignment thus allowing for more contact with the person, and a more thorough assessment and intervention plan.

The Instructor's Evaluation. The desired outcome–experiential opportunity for students–was achieved. Preparation for the exercise was time consuming because effort was taken to ensure a successful venture for the students and the resident-volunteers. These tasks included meeting with resident-volunteers to explain the project; briefly interviewing volunteers to ensure they understood the project and were willing volunteers; being available to the students for task oriented (answering questions, suggesting approaches) and emotional support while in-house conducting the assessment; compiling the resident-volunteers needs as cited; following-up with the resident-volunteers and answering their questions about the project; and writing a brief final report on the outcome of the project for the executive director of the housing facility. Despite these tasks, it was challenging and exciting to introduce and complete this project with the students.

The primary focus of this exercise was on assessment skills, though students later used the information gleaned to develop a proposed intervention plan. The intervention plan was more of an intellectual exercise. Some students expressed frustration that they had only one visit with the resident-volunteer, and would have liked an additional visit to reassess some aspect, to follow-up on information provided in the primary interview, or to confirm the need for a community referral. In the future, the instructor will explore the option of additional structured visits, and structuring the development of an intervention plan. Additionally, for future students, it would be interesting to conduct a follow-up study on students who completed this assignment to see how it assisted them in their later practice with older adults.

Overall, this project was a successful learning experience. It was a different way to learn, and the students appreciated it. This hands-on educational exercise can be replicated in other communities between programs of social work and senior housing facilities.

REFERENCES

Administration on Aging. (2000). A profile of older Americans: 2000. Washington, DC: Author.

Bumagin, V. E., & Hirn, K. F. (1990). *Helping the aging family*. Glenview, IL: Scott, Foresman and Company.

Choi, N. G., & Dinse, S. (1998). Challenges and opportunities of the aging population: Social work education and practice for productive aging. *Educational Gerontology, 24* (2), 159-173.

Folstein, M. F., Folstein, S. E., & McHugh, P. R. (1975). Mini-mental state. *Journal of Psychiatric Research,12,* 189-198.

Gleason-Wynn, P. (1995). Addressing the educational needs of nursing home social workers. *Gerontology & Geriatrics Education, 16* (2), 31-36.

Haulotte, S., & McNeil, J. (1998). Integrating didactic and experiential aging curricula. *Journal of Gerontological Social Work, 30* (3/4), 43-57.

Ivry, J. (1992). Teaching geriatric assessment. *Journal of Gerontological Social Work, 18* (3/4), 3-22.

Kane, R. A., & Kane, R. L. (1981). *Assessing the elderly: A practical guide of measurement (5th ed.)*. MA: D. C. Heath.

Knowles, M. S. (1972). Innovations in teaching styles and approaches based upon adult learning. *Journal of Social Work Education, 8* (2), 32-39.

Memmott, J., & Brennan, E. M. (1998). Learner-learning environment fit: An adult learning model for social work education. *Journal of Teaching in Social Work, 16* (1/2), 75-96.

Schneider, R. L., Kropf, N. P., & Kisor A. J. (2000). Gerontological social work knowledge, service settings, and special populations (2nd ed.). Belmont, CA: Wadsworth Publishing.

Sheikh, J. I., & Yesavage, J. A. (1986). Geriatric depression scale: Recent evidence and development of shorter version. In T.L. Brink (Ed.), *Clinical gerontology: A guide to assessment and intervention* (pp. 165-173). Binghamton, NY: The Haworth Press, Inc.

Zlotnik, J. L., Rosen, A. L., Green, R. G., & Curl, A. L. (2000). The Sage-SW National Aging Competencies Survey Draft Report. Alexandria, VA: Council on Social Work Education.

Zucchero, R. (1998). A unique model for training mental health professionals to work with older adults. *Educational Gerontology, 24* (3), 265-279.

Chapter 13

Bridging the Gap Between Classroom and Practicum: Graduate Social Work Students in Health Care with Older Adults

Denice Goodrich Liley, PhD, ACSW

SUMMARY. In the wake of sweeping demographic change, health care services are in an ever-increasing state of flux, especially in the areas of technology, managed care, and availability to services. Social work literature indicates that it is incumbent upon social work educators to ensure that curriculum be particularly relevant to the fields of practice students will encounter. For this research report, thirteen second-year MSW students were interviewed at the beginning, mid point, and end of their field placements in a medical setting as to the appropriateness of their preparation for medical social work with an aged population. Additionally, a one-year follow-up was conducted with each student. *[Article copies available for a fee from The Haworth Document Delivery Service: 1-800-HAWORTH. E-mail address: <docdelivery@haworthpress.com> Website: <http://www.HaworthPress.com> © 2002 by The Haworth Press, Inc. All rights reserved.]*

Denice Goodrich Liley is Assistant Professor, Boise State University, School of Social Work, 1910 University Drive, E-716, Boise, ID 83725 (E-mail: Dliley@boisestate.edu).

[Haworth co-indexing entry note]: "Bridging the Gap Between Classroom and Practicum: Graduate Social Work Students in Health Care with Older Adults." Liley, Denice Goodrich. Co-published simultaneously in *Journal of Gerontological Social Work* (The Haworth Social Work Practice Press, an imprint of The Haworth Press, Inc.) Vol. 39, No. 1/2, 2002, pp. 203-217; and: *Advancing Gerontological Social Work Education* (ed: M. Joanna Mellor, and Joann Ivry) The Haworth Social Work Practice Press, an imprint of The Haworth Press, Inc., 2002, pp. 203-217. Single or multiple copies of this article are available for a fee from The Haworth Document Delivery Service [1-800-HAWORTH, 9:00 a.m. - 5:00 p.m. (EST). E-mail address: docdelivery@haworthpress.com].

10.1300/J083v39n01_17

KEYWORDS. MSW education, gerontological social work, medical social work, field placement

Health care in the United States continues to undergo change at breakneck speed. The key variables influencing the delivery of health care include the advent of managed care, the restructuring of social work departments in medical facilities, the movement toward increased outpatient-community based services, advances in medical technology, plus the fact that more people are living longer with chronic illnesses and the ensuing functional restrictions (Berkman, 1996, Kadusin & Egan, 1997, Long & Heydt, 2000). These changes in the aged population and in health care place medical social work at the focal point of social work educators.

Social workers in health care have long provided services and support to the aged, as well as having promoted the social functioning of those individuals. Recent social work literature calls attention to the need for social work educators to respond to these changes.

VARIABLES INFLUENCING THE NEED FOR CHANGE

Aging Population

The percentage of older adults in the United States has tripled since 1900, and the elderly population is expected to double between the years of 1999-2030. Not only are older persons greater in number, but they are also living much longer. The most rapidly growing group of older people in the United States today is that of adults 100 years and older. The U.S. Census Bureau (1996,1998) points to a doubling of people 100 years and older since 1990. Individuals who live longer are more likely to develop chronic illnesses and complex social and health care needs (Wacker, Roberto, & Piper, 1998). The primary concern of medical social workers is to work toward maintaining the health of and preventing further disability in the chronically ill and aging populations.

Field Work in Health Care

Thirty-three percent of National Association of Social Workers (NASW) members reported that their primary practice settings were in health, and 19.5% reported their secondary practice settings were in health care

(Gibelman & Schevish, 1997). Of 23,009 students in social work placements on November 1, 1997, 3,021 MSW students were in health placements, with another 4,421 not yet assigned placements (Lemmon, 1998). Additionally, sixty-two percent of NASW members reported the necessity for geriatric knowledge in their professional practices (Peterson & Wendt, 1990).

In addition to the increase in the size of the aging population and to the need for fieldwork within the health care community, the health care delivery system is undergoing dramatic changes. Managed care affects nearly every person in one way or another (Long & Heydt, 2000). Older health care consumers encounter new benefit status, new payment terminology, preferred providers, service restrictions (covered/authorized to non covered), while struggling to gain some understanding of their medical conditions. Professional social workers are confronted with organizational restructuring and the reshaping of professional expectations, which often results in the loss of social work defined positions to more universal positions of *care coordinators* and/or *discharge planners*.

Social work educators are called upon to be innovative and to forge new alliances within the social work practice field (Berkman, 1991; Berkman et al., 2000; Kadusin & Egan, 1997; Keigher, 1997; & Silverson, 2000). Unfortunately, social work educators are faced with already-burgeoning and overextended curriculae, thus making them wary of persistent calls to expand areas of content in attempts to model an ever-evolving, dynamic health care system (Vourlekis, Eli, & Padgett, 2001).

It appears to be a daunting task to meet the expectations of those who call upon social work educators to keep their curriculum apace of the perpetual change within the medical community and, therefore, to ensure that they prepare social workers for practice in today's health care world. While social work literature has advocated such a change for more than 20 years, the pressure to create that change has been top down, in effect, that of what practicing social workers perceive social work educators *should* do, or by examining *today's* (whenever that is) social work practice within the health care community to delineate the need for on-going change in social work curricula. What is missing from the literature appears to be the investigation of student perceptions about their preparedness for gerontological social work practice within the health care community. This study was designed to query the consumers of social work education (specifically, MSW students) during the course of their field practicum experiences in health care. Specific questions addressed were:

- In terms of knowledge and skills, how has your formal course work prepared you for your field work placement in health care with older adults?
- In the same way, what knowledge and skills do you feel your formal course work did NOT provide you with in preparation for this field work placement

SETTING

The site of this study is a Department of Veteran Affairs Medical Center located in the Intermountain West. The facility is an urban, academic teaching medical center serving as a major health care site to surrounding western states, a level one trauma center with 300 beds and census of over 80 percent. In 1999, the utilization by patients over the age of 60 was 72 percent. Social work services here provide high-risk screening of all hospitalized patients within 48 hours of admission. Medical crises, a myriad of psychosocial problems, and a large percentage of indigent patients, contribute to ongoing social work involvement with inpatient admissions, and a growing proportion of ambulatory patients. The facility's Department of Social Work has provided social work practicum training to Master Social Work Students for over 25 years, averaging 5 to 15 social work students annually.

METHODS

Upon the Institutional Review Board's approval, the researcher/author met on-site with a group of eight MSW practitioners who were designated to provide supervision to the upcoming class of masters of social work students. A list of questions was generated to probe student's learning experiences at beginning, middle, and end of their practicum experiences. The list of questions was formulated through review of the literature, through *practice wisdom* from field supervisor's experiences, and by reviewing the university's learning contracts and evaluation forms. Table 1 displays the eight categories probed. The researcher determined that a semi-structured interview process would be used at the three points of the study, and that a one-year, follow-up telephone interview would be implemented.

All MSW students were informed of the study prior to the start of their field practicum, and were asked to participate in the research. After meeting with their field supervisors, two students elected not to participate, stating that they were working in areas (psychiatry and substance abuse) with disproportionate numbers of younger patients, whereas the majority of the students would be

TABLE 1. Topical Probes

Topical Probes
Client Relationship
Collaboration
Hospital Setting
Medical Model
Policy
Professionalism
Program Development
Service Delivery
Social Work Practice
Treatment Approaches

working with older patients. Thirteen students agreed to participate in the study. Students were assigned to field placements in the following areas:

- Surgery service
- General medicine (2)
- Physical medicine–Rehabilitation
- Geriatrics Inpatient (2)
- Geriatrics–Outpatient
- Neurology
- Ambulatory Care (2)
- Home Care (2)
- Emergency Medicine Service

Two students were on block placements for 5 months; the other 11 students were in field practicums 20 hours a week for the entire academic year.

A semi-structured interview was held with each student: (1) at development of the learning contract at the beginning of semester (September); (2) at end of first semester, or prior to beginning second semester (December/January); (3) at the end of the final semester-evaluation (May); and (4) one year follow-up. All interviews were audio recorded and transcribed. The verbatim data was then analyzed into succinct categories by the researcher and two graduate assistants.

Subjects

Table 2 displays characteristics of this sample. The MSW field supervisors involved in this study expressed that this sample appeared similar to past students,

TABLE 2. Characteristics of the Sample

N = 13	Advanced Standing Students		2
	Second-year SW Students		11
Bachelor Degrees held	Social Science	5	
	Language Arts	3	
	Music Arts	1	
	Physical Education	1	
	Law Degree	1	
Universities represented	Out of state	2	
	Adjacent	8	
	45 miles away	3	
Gender	Female	9	
	Male	4	
Age	Median	29 years	
	Oldest	48 years	
	Youngest	22 years	

and that it was representative of a typical cross-section of former practicum field students. The students involved in this research came from three different universities: one located adjacent to the medical facility, another located 45 miles away, and the third located out of state. All universities had previously placed students within this medical setting for more than 5 years. The only difference in universities was that the out-of-state program offered a master's of social work degree by advanced standing, meaning students in their program had already earned bachelor's degrees in social work, and were completing their master's degrees in about 15 months, as opposed to the traditional two-year academic program for masters of social work degrees in which the other students were participating. All MSW students were in their final year of the masters program.

Findings

Originally, a comparison of learning contracts and evaluations was planned in order to expand the semi-structured interviews, but was not possible due to the distinct and varying evaluating models of each source university; therefore, a decision was made to evaluate only the transcriptions of the semi-structured interviews. Prior to beginning this research project, MSW field supervisors elected to use topical probes to gather information during their interviews with the students, rather than to use a questionnaire. Their rationale was that questionnaires tend to make use of closed questions that are likely to be Likert scaled, and thus limit students' thoughts and expressions. The field supervisors believed topical probes would also help to ground the interviews, as well as to allow for variations in students' experiences and meanings. Through the use of this process, the field supervisors believed the students would be responding to the very qualitative nature of their experiences and providing responses from which richer information could be garnered for this study.

Interviews at Beginning of Semester

From those interviews, the MSW field supervisors learned that the only field practicum area for which students felt unprepared was that of a medical social work environment. All thirteen students indicated that their course work had not prepared them for exactly what they believed they would be doing. None of the three participating universities had offered course work in medical social work. Ten students stated that this type of course work was offered as an elective only in the spring prior to graduation. All students felt they had developed strong practice skills and knowledge, but that they needed to learn how to apply knowledge and skills to the medical setting, specifically mentioning health care with older adults and the medicalization of the aging. Medicalization of aging as a knowledge category includes medical terminology and diagnosis, the trajectory of diseases, impact on functional ability, and the effect of medical health concerns on an older person and the family. All students felt that they were prepared for this practicum experience. Nine of the students stated that they felt assured that they would successfully complete this practicum based on the experiences of their first placement.

Interviews at End of First Semester

At the mid-point practicum evaluation, the practicum students cited four areas that they believed to be high levels of concern.

1. Medicalization of Aging

Twelve of the 13 students cited medicalization of the aging as an area for which they felt their formal course work failed to prepare them. This category resulted from the MSW field supervisors' use of the medical model probe. Students expressed their understanding of the medical model and problem orientation, but felt that much of the *aging* experience involved the need for medical care. The resulting medicalization of aging took precedence over the "normal" aging process. Twelve students shared a common concern–"What is normal aging?" This question arose for all thirteen students. None of the graduate social work students had taken any formal course work in gerontology. One student stated: "I have been around my family . . . that is my parents, aunts and my grandparents, but I am not sure now that they are all that old now." The various perspectives of what constitutes aging for an individual, as well as the impact of medical complications, created many questions for the graduate social work students.

2. Role Identification

Listed below are concerns students encountered in regards to identifying their roles as social workers within the medical community:

- What are the specific activities of the social worker?
- How do I differentiate my role from those of allied health care members?
- What does the social worker do?
- What is the *fit* of the social worker with other health care team members?
- What if I disagree with care decisions?

These questions dovetailed with initial concerns of all 12 students. Ten students expressed feeling unprepared, and eleven stated being very unprepared. Other questions that emerged include these:

- Who in the allied team does what?
- Is that a nursing role or concern?
- Why are others doing that? I thought the social worker did that!

3. Policy to Programs

All thirteen students expressed this as an area for which they felt unprepared; ten felt very unprepared, and three cited feeling *somewhat unprepared.*

Students expressed high levels of understanding of the historical perspective, legislation of programs, and the etiology of programs such as Social Security, Medicare, Medicaid, and Veteran Benefits. They claimed knowledge and understanding of benefits. However, the students expressed frustration with not knowing how to access resources, with being sure that clients were truly eligible (and what they were eligible for), and how to help clients gain access to services. Five students felt that patients and families knew more about services and eligibility than they did, and they indicated that they felt that, in the eyes of patients and patients' families, this detracted from their professionalism.

4. Communication Skills as to Loss

Nine students said that knowing what to say when patients and families received bad news was an area for which they felt ill prepared. Two of the youngest students expressed major concern in this regard, stating that they could listen, but did not have life experiences to adequately display empathy to older patients or their families. The following are the types of questions posed by four students:

- Can I cry in front of a patient?
- Just what do you say when they get news of dying?
- How do you acknowledge someone who is dying?
- Do I need to wait for the patient (or family) to say something first?

At mid point in their practicum experience, students listed the following as areas of strength in preparation for their field work:

(a) Interpersonal Skills

- Interviewing
- Listening
- Empathy
- Assessing individuals and families

All thirteen students expressed that they felt very confident and prepared in their skills.

(b) Understanding the client relationship

The MSW students expressed a clear understanding about *who* the patient was (all 13 expressed this), and felt that others in the health care arena lost sight of whom *the real* patient was. The students also indicated that they clearly understood the formulation of goals and objectives for patients. They felt confident in areas of the empowerment of client and client self-determination.

Interviews at End of Final Semester

At the end of their field experience, all the students expressed feeling *less* unprepared, but indicated they still had concerns related to some of the areas mentioned at the time of the entrance and mid term interviews. They felt that role identification was no longer a challenge, and that university course work could do little to help them in that regard, rather it was a learn-by-doing process. Five of the students thought variables such as personality of individuals, location of unit, type of patients, and field supervisor made up much of the differences.

In the areas of medicalization of aging and communication skills for loss, field practicum students indicated feeling they had improved significantly. They felt they had become more accomplished both by being in the agency, as well as from outside readings. All students had completed at least one research paper related to medical social work within the academic year for their university studies.

The area of policy to programs caused concern to the majority of MSW students (10). They expressed feeling unprepared to handle questions about where to obtain services for specific needs, and had second thoughts about suggesting services due to worrying whether the patient was eligible. They generally felt that programs contained subtleties about eligibility requirements that they did not understand. All students expressed that their class work did not prepare them for this.

The use of field seminars and supervision was explored as influencing students' preparation and as ways to obtain skills that course work could not teach. The more *connectedness* expressed by the students of classroom, practicum, field instructor, and field liaison, the more the students expressed feeling comfortable in their practicum settings. Students expressed varying opinions as to field affiliation. The only common factor appeared to be that the busier students perceived their field instructor to be, the less change they perceived in their skills. Students from one university met bi-weekly with a faculty liaison, and these students all stated that they found this helpful. The meetings were used to discuss specific topics, but they also provided a sounding board for events they encountered in the field. The students also felt that their university had a close relationship with the field agency and field instructors. The students from a University out of state and involved in block placements expressed a lack of connection, describing a lack of cohesiveness between practicum and course work, even though their programs required them to write an integrated thesis paper as part of the practicum experience.

One Year Follow-Up Interviews

All thirteen students participated in a one-year follow-up telephone interview. The calls lasted approximately one half-hour each, and were also taped and transcribed. Eight of the thirteen students were employed in health care or in case management settings. Two students were employed in programs for the aged. Two students were employed in state agencies, and one student was employed part time in home health services.

All students indicated increased competency in the areas of medicalization of the aging, role identification, and communication skills. Students felt that the more they did and experienced, the more that they learned. Seven stated they thought that, in part, they had confidence in what they were doing, and that, in itself, made them feel more confident. They stated that an increase in competency came by doing, reading, experience and time.

All of the participating social workers continued to feel challenged in the area of policy to program. Although the change in frustration appeared to be with the programs and policy, and not with themselves. Students stated that repeatedly programs changed or were terminated, making resource development a learning experience over and over again. Many students (5) said that knowledge by doing helped them push agencies harder to help. Acquiring the skill to be assertive became more important. One student stated, "I now know what advocacy is all about." All 13 students identified that gaining necessary knowledge of funded services, and eligibility restrictions and regulations, as a continuing challenge.

Initial Strength Areas

Both interpersonal and relationship skills, perceived as high at the first semester evaluation, continued to be viewed as strengths. Newly added to this was the value of *networking*. Knowing some one by name to call within the service agencies did help with program implementation.

At one year, half of the respondents also placed greater importance on co-workers and partnerships, and of learning and working together. Four of the students who did not express this stated having little support within their agencies and feeling frustrated. Two indicated that they were *most likely* to change positions.

For 11 social workers, a new area of concern had arisen in the first year of practice, that of empowerment and self-determination. Nine students felt agency policies did not always advocate for the patient or the family, but rather diminished their self-determination. The regulations within programs and services additionally detracted from patients' sense of empowerment.

Inquiry was made as to whether, after one year of employment as social workers, they perceived their preparation through formal course work for social work practice in health care to be different from what they had thought when they were a student. All thirteen students responded, "YES!" Seven students expressed that many of the courses now make more sense than when they had taken them, commenting on the interconnections between health care, poverty, and family relationships. Two students thought that the courses attempted to cover "too much"–"I would have liked more attention on treatment issues." The remaining four students stated that "time, experience, doing makes the skills more–I did not know I learned so much."

DISCUSSION

The MSW students perceptions are consistent with findings in the social work literature. Yet, it is interesting to note that there are also differences over time from the early stages of acclimation to the practice site in terms of knowledge and understanding of: (a) the uniqueness of the clients the MSW students serve; (b) the clients' world; (c) the vernacular of the medical model and terminology from that experienced in the social work curriculum and (d) making the "fit" of the medical model within the social environmental model, consistent with the model of generalist social work practice.

The area of communicating with those suffering loss is especially difficult. Social work beginning skills focus on strengths-based empowering forces for clients and their worlds. However, the reality that horrible situations do happen and words can not change that, is especially difficult. Most newly placed social workers express a sense of feeling at a loss and unprepared when dealing with the pain and loss of others. These students voiced the challenge of social work education–that is, knowledge and values of social work can be discussed and taught in the classroom, but the reality of the *practice* in a contextual setting is much more difficult and complex both for the social worker and the patient/client. Practice within the setting promotes confidence and enriches practice skills that "fit in the environment" for the entering social work student.

Toward the end of this study, the participants, while still not completely at ease, demonstrated less discomfort. Their experience supports the work of Holden, Cuzz, Spitxer, Rutter, Chernack, and Rosenberg (1997) that through experience in an actual working setting, social workers gain knowledge, and skills, as well as a respect for the initial difficulties of tasks in the setting. Workers become more confident over the years, even if not dramatically so.

Of interest is that ethical issues (self-determination and empowerment of clients) were not rated as concerns until the end of the field practicum experience. Ethical issues ranked even higher after one year. Corcoran and Vandiver (1996) discuss this ethical dilemma, which occurs throughout the health care system, in terms of the conflict between the worker's duty to provide quality care (beneficence), duty to contain costs (contractual), and the duty to allocate scarce and valuable resources fairly (social justice). Clearly, as the MSW students became more comfortable with their individual *fit* within their working environments, they in turn looked more closely at concerns in their environments (primarily, health care delivery) for their patients. The focus shifted from the individual level of the specific social work student and a client/family system to the larger context of the agencies' practices.

CONCLUSION

The students expressed confidence in their foundation content of social work practice, representing the core of social work knowledge, values, and skills. However, course work alone does not prepare students for the changing landscape of the health care environment and the roles of social workers within this environment.

There is a strong need for alliances within fieldwork. The social work educational arena and the field practice site must partner to assist social work students in their transition to professional practice. The reality of social work practice is strengthened by support and integration. Social work educators alone can not create the practice field that social work students will encounter. A partnership between the practice community and social work educators needs to be explored further to strengthen medical social work with older adults.

Long and Heydt (2000) claim that it is prime time for exploring non-traditional field arrangements for social work students. There is a critical need to assist students in the varying aspects of service delivery. Graduate social work students require experiences both in inpatient and outpatient care and careful attention needs to be placed on the continuum of care that patients, especially older patients, experience. Attention also needs to be given to the varying health care systems and an exposure to varying models of health care is necessary. Social workers need to understand health care in the arenas of for profit, not for profit, managed care, as well as the state and federal programs (Medicare and Medicaid). In today's world, schools of social work must prepare practitioners for a very different practice environment–one characterized by knowledge of finances and economics, as well as psychosocial interventions and work with-at-risk populations. The potential for the profession has never been greater.

REFERENCES

Aging Research & Training News. (1997). Business Publishers, Inc. 8737 Colesville Road, Sutie 1100, Silver Spring, MD 20910-3925.

Berger, C. S. & Ai, A. (2000). Managed care and its implications for social work curricula reform: Clinical practice and field instruction. *Social Work in Health Care, 31,* 83-106.

Berkman, B. (1981). Knowledge base needs for effective social work practice in health care. *Journal of Education for Social Work, 17,* 85-90.

Berkman, B. (1996). The emerging health care world: Implications for social work practice and education. *Social Work, 41,* 541-551.

Berkman, B., Kemler, B., Marcus, L., Silverman, P. (1985). Course content for social work practice in health care. *Journal of Social Work Education, 21,* 43-51.

Berkman, B., Silverston, B., Simmons, W. J., Volland, P. J., & Howe, J. L. (2000). Social work gerontological practice: The need for faculty development in the new millennium. *Journal of Gerontological Social Work, 34,* 5-23.

Caroff, P. & Mailick, M. (1985). Health concentrations in schools of social work: The state of the art. *Health & Social Work, 10,* 5-14.

Corcoran, K. & Vandiver, V. (1996). *Maneuvering the maze of managed care.* New York: Free Press.

Ell, K. (1996). Social work and health care practice and policy: A psychosocial research agenda. *Social Work, 41,* 583-592.

Gibelman, M., & Schervish, P. H. (1997). *Who we are: A second look.* Washington, DC: NASW Press.

Gottfried, K. S. (1997). The implications of managed care for social work education. *Journal of Social Work Education, 33,* 7-18.

Holden, G., Cuzzi, L., Sptizer, W. Rutter, S., Chernack, P., & Rosenberg, G. (1997). The hospital social work self-efficacy scale. *Health and Social Work, 22,* 256-263.

Hollis, E. & Taylor, A. (1951). *Social work education in the United States.* New York: Columbia University Press.

Kadushin, G. & Egan, M. (1997). Educating students for a changing health care environment: An examination of health care practice Content. *Social Work, 22,* 211-222.

Keigher, S. M. (1997). What role for social work in the new health care practice paradigm. *Health and Social Work, 22,* 149-160.

Lane, H. (1982). Toward preparation of social work specialists in health care. *Health and Social Work, 7,* 230-234.

Lemmon, T. (1998). *Statistics on social work education in the United States, 1997.* Alexandria, VA: Council on Social Work Education.

Long, D. D. & Heydt, M. J. (2000). Qualitative analysis of BSW field placement with a hospital owned physician practice in a skilled nursing facility. *Health & Social Work, 25,* 210-218.

Marshack, E., Davidson, K, & Mizrahi, T. (1988). Preparation of social workers for changing health care environment. *Health & Social Work, 13,* 226-233.

Netting, F. E., & Williams, F. G. (1997, March). Preparing the next generation of geriatric social workers to collaborate with primary care physicians. Paper presented at the Annual Program Meeting of the Council on Social Work Education, Chicago.

Raskin, M. S. & Blome, W. W. (1998). The impact of managed care on field instruction. *Journal of Social Work Education, 34,* 365-374.

Rehr, H. & Rosenberg, G. (1977) Today's education for today's health care social work practice. *Clinical Social Work Journal, 5,* 342-348.

Silverstone, B. (2000). The old and the new in aging: Implications for social work practice. *Journal of Gerontological Social Work, 33,* 35-50.

Spitzer, W., Holden, G., Cuzzi, L., Rutter, S., Chernack, P., & Rosenberg, G. (2001). Edith Abbott was right: Designing field work experiences for contemporary health care practice. *Journal of Social Work Education, 37,* 79-90.

U. S. Bureau of the Census. (1996). Population projections of the United States by age, sex, race, and Hispanic origin: 1995 to 2050. *Current Population Reports, pp. 25-1130.* Washington DC: U. S. Government Printing Office.

U. S. Bureau of the Census. (1998). *U. S. population estimates by age, sex, race and Hispanic origin: January 1, 1997.* Washington, DC: U. S. Government Printing Office.

Vourlekis, B. S., Ell, K., & Padgett, D. (2001). Educating social workers for health care's brave new world. *Journal of Social Work Education, 37,* 177-191.

Wacker, R. R., Roberto, K. A., Piper, L. E. (1998). *Community resources for older adults: Programs and services in an era of change.* Thousand Oaks, CA: Pine Forge Press.

Chapter 14

Incorporating Intergenerational Service-Learning into an Introductory Gerontology Course

Lorraine T. Dorfman, PhD
Susan Murty, PhD
Jerry G. Ingram, MSW
Ronnie J. Evans, MSW

SUMMARY. The service-learning approach in education, which integrates community service with academic classroom learning, is gaining national prominence. The goals of this project were to incorporate intergenerational service-learning into an undergraduate introductory gerontology course and to involve students and elders in meaningful in-

Lorraine T. Dorfman is Professor, School of Social Work and Aging Studies Program, Susan Murty is Associate Professor, School of Social Work, Jerry G. Ingram is a Doctoral Student, School of Social Work, and Ronnie J. Evans is a Doctoral Student, School of Social Work. The authors are all affiliated with The University of Iowa, Iowa City, IA 52242.

This project was funded by the Corporation for National Service, Learn & Serve Higher Education through a grant to The Association for Gerontology in Higher Education in partnership with Generations Together/University of Pittsburgh.

[Haworth co-indexing entry note]: "Incorporating Intergenerational Service-Learning into an Introductory Gerontology Course." Dorfman et al. Co-published simultaneously in *Journal of Gerontological Social Work* (The Haworth Social Work Practice Press, an imprint of The Haworth Press, Inc.) Vol. 39, No. 1/2, 2002, pp. 219-240; and: *Advancing Gerontological Social Work Education* (ed: M. Joanna Mellor, and Joann Ivry) The Haworth Social Work Practice Press, an imprint of The Haworth Press, Inc., 2002, pp. 219-240. Single or multiple copies of this article are available for a fee from The Haworth Document Delivery Service [1-800-HAWORTH, 9:00 a.m. - 5:00 p.m. (EST). E-mail address: docdelivery@haworthpress.com].

http://www.haworthpress.com/store/product.asp?sku=J083
10.1300/J083v39n01_18

teractions in a rural community setting. Thirteen of the 50 students in the class could be accommodated at nursing home and semi-independent living sites and were paired with elders for friendly visiting and oral history. Attitude scales (Pillemer & Albright, 1996) indicated that service-learning students showed more positive change at post-test in overall attitudes toward the elderly than did non service-learning students. Open-ended questions indicated that students valued the experience, felt it enhanced classroom learning, and gained knowledge about rural elders and communities. Follow-up interviews with elders were uniformly positive. *[Article copies available for a fee from The Haworth Document Delivery Service: 1-800-HAWORTH. E-mail address: <docdelivery@haworthpressinc.com> Website: <http://www.HaworthPress.com> © 2002 by The Haworth Press, Inc. All rights reserved.]*

KEYWORDS. Gerontology education, intergenerational, nursing homes, rural elders, service-learning

The service-learning approach in education, which integrates community service with academic classroom learning, is gaining national prominence. Utilizing this framework, intergenerational service-learning aims to connect older and younger generations in meaningful and productive interactions within a community setting, at the same time benefiting elders and students and meeting community needs (Larkin & Newman, 1997; Roodin, 2000). Fostering such intergenerational exchanges is particularly important because of the considerable geographic mobility of American families since the middle of the twentieth century, often resulting in infrequent contact between the generations (Newman, 1997). Intergenerational programs offer the promise of facilitating the kinds of intergenerational contacts and linkages that traditionally occurred spontaneously in geographically proximate families. Elders can develop a relationship with younger people and continue to contribute actively by sharing their life experiences, while students can learn about the older generation, have the opportunity to gain insights about their own aging, and develop a sense of community responsibility.

The goals of this intergenerational service-learning project were twofold: to incorporate intergenerational service-learning into an introductory social work gerontology course, and to involve students and elders in meaningful interactions in a rural community setting. The project was one of ten supported in 1999-2000 by the Association for Gerontology in Higher Education (AGHE)/Generations Together, University of Pittsburgh, with funds from the

Corporation for National Service. Service-learning programs may be particularly useful in addressing the human needs of rural communities because of the lack of available and accessible services in many of those communities (Krout, 1998; Watson, Church, Darville, & Darville, 1997). There may also be challenges in reaching client populations in rural communities (Watson et al., 1997). Yet, because of these characteristics, rural communities may also provide an excellent opportunity for student volunteers, and service-learning efforts utilizing students may serve to increase linkages between colleges and universities and rural communities.

Specific objectives of the current intergenerational service-learning project were: (1) students would interact with elders in rural nursing home and semi-independent living settings; (2) elders would help students learn about rural communities through friendly visiting, reminiscence, and oral histories; and (3) the model would be disseminated through University seminars and colloquia, a listserve, website, and a statewide conference. The project was co-directed by two faculty members from the University of Iowa School of Social Work, one of whom had primary responsibility for the classroom component of the project and the other who had primary responsibility for the field component. One of the faculty members also served as director of the University's interdisciplinary Aging Studies Program.

LITERATURE REVIEW

Student Outcomes of Intergenerational Service-Learning

Virtually all researchers report positive outcomes among students who participate in intergenerational service-learning. These include development of more positive attitudes toward elders, understanding the history and culture of elders, enhancement of classroom learning, and increased self-awareness and acceptance of one's own aging. The most prevalent theme is development of more positive attitudes toward and understanding of older people. In an analysis of 230 students who participated in the ten intergenerational service-learning sites supported by AGHE/Generations Together, Nichols and Monard (1999) report that at post-test significantly more students agreed that older people were healthy, productive, cooperative, and happy than at pre-test. Those students also said they found greater diversity among older persons than they had expected, and that all older people did not have negative personality traits, implying a reduction in negative stereotypes about elders. Similarly, Watson et al. (1997) found that at post-test, students working with rural elders were less likely to say that older people are pretty much alike or that most older people are isolated or lonely than at pre-test. Additionally, researchers have found more positive attitudes toward elders among students involved in visiting an older person than in a comparison group of students (Bringle & Kremer, 1993).

Students who experience intergenerational service-learning also report increased understanding and respect for the history and culture of elders. For example, Pine (1997) observed that a major theme in student responses to service-learning was gaining a sense of inspiration and respect for elders; students had a new understanding of elders and respect for their life experiences and the hardships they had endured. Likewise, students engaged in visiting programs with elders showed increased understanding of the culture, history, and survival mechanisms of elders after their service-learning experience (McCrea & Smith, 1997).

Other positive outcomes for students are enhanced classroom learning and commitment to community service (McCrea & Smith, 1997). Students report that applying concepts learned in class to service-learning helps change their career plans to include work with elders (Pine, 1997).

Finally, students commonly express better understanding of the aging process, less fears about their own aging, and increased self-understanding after participating in service-learning (Bringle & Kremer, 1993; McCrea & Smith, 1997; Newman, Lyons, & Onawala, 1985; Nichols & Monard, 1999). Another important personal outcome for students is developing a personal one-on-one friendship with an older person (McCrea & Smith, 1997) that often far outlasts the service-learning experience.

Elder Outcomes of Intergenerational Service-Learning

Elders are generally very positive about intergenerational service-learning experiences with college and university students. Several studies conducted in nursing home settings found overwhelmingly positive reactions from residents (Greene, 1998; Newman et al., 1985). In the former study, a large percentage (94%) of elders said they benefited from the experience. The largest percentage of those elders mentioned the value of companionship with students (64%); however, developing a new point of view through intergenerational interaction (38%), the enjoyment of meeting someone new (27%), and being able to express oneself and be more social (14%) were also outcomes (Greene, 1998). Further, all residents felt that the idea of having older adults teach younger ones was worthwhile. In the latter study (Newman et al., 1985), all nursing home residents said they enjoyed visits with students very much and gave reasons such as "I don't get many visitors" and "I like talking to someone other than sick folk" (p. 132).

Similarly, in telephone follow-up interviews with homebound and other older adults in a community setting, elders were overwhelmingly positive about visits from university-level students; elders described their visits with adjectives like "satisfying," "close," and "relaxing" (Bringle & Kremer, 1993). McCrea and Smith (1997) provide a nice overview of positive outcomes for elders in intergenerational programs by noting that these programs often result in increased self-esteem and reduced social isolation for the older person, with opportunities for friendship and companionship with a person of a younger generation providing a chance to share one's own story and life experience.

This review of the literature makes clear that there is considerable evidence to document the value of intergenerational service learning both for students and for elders. This study was undertaken to pursue the topic in two new directions that will add to our knowledge: the application of intergenerational service-learning in rural communities, and its integration into an existing social work gerontology course.

DESCRIPTION OF THE PROJECT AND METHODS

The Course and the Students

Intergenerational service-learning was integrated into the undergraduate introductory social work gerontology course at the University of Iowa, "Basic Aspects of Aging" (enrollment approximately 50 students each semester) in spring semester 2000. The course is open to social work and non-social work students and is highly interdisciplinary in nature. It is cross-listed with four academic units on campus: Social Work; Aging Studies; Health, Leisure, and Sport Studies; and Nursing. The course covers the biological, social, and psychological aspects of aging, and includes a broad variety of topics including health, economic status, social supports, and health and social services for elders. Previous to this time, there had been no fieldwork component of the course. By integrating service-learning into the course, we believed that students would gain valuable hands-on application of in-class learning and likewise would be exposed to possible careers in gerontological social work.

Students had the option of participating in the intergenerational service-learning experience in place of certain course requirements. Thirteen of the 49 students enrolled in the class elected the service-learning option; this was the maximum number that could be accommodated at the field sites.

The Community and Community Partners

The site of the service-learning experience was West Liberty, Iowa, a very small town (population 3,332) (U.S. Bureau of Census, 2001) with a largely underserved rural population approximately 15 miles from the University of Iowa in Iowa City.

There were three main community partners: the local nursing home, a semi-independent living apartment site located next door to the nursing home, and the local congregate meal site. The nursing home and semi-independent living apartments are managed by the same administrator. The nursing home is locally owned and managed and it is an important community institution in West Liberty. Many community members participate in activities and events at the nursing home. The congregate meal site provides meals and activities three days a week at the recently completed West Liberty Community Center, a focal point for many community activities. The meal site receives funding under the Older Americans Act through the local Area Agency on Aging and the State Department of Elder Affairs.

The Services Provided

The service-learning experience was semester-long and provided the opportunity for one-to-one student-elder relationships to develop over time (Pine, 1997). Students were recruited and trained for the service-learning experience after the project staff (the co-directors, the teaching fellow, and community partners) met for a period of two months prior to the beginning of the course to develop a strategy and schedule for the semester. The 13 students were divided into two teams, each of whom visited the field sites four times in sessions of approximately four hours each. Students met and received training as teams in sessions before the project started, midway in the project when they received oral history training from a staff member of the local historical society, and at the end of the project. Each student was paired with a resident selected by the nursing home staff on the basis of adequate cognitive and physical function to do friendly visiting, reminiscing, and oral history. Nursing home and semi-independent living elders with whom students were paired ranged in age from 68 to 98, but most elders were in their eighties or nineties ($n = 10$). All but one elder was female.

On one of their visits, the teams also observed and assisted the middle school Kid's Club After-School Program make puppets with the residents of the nursing home. Each team also visited the congregate meal site one time so that they had the opportunity to interact with elders who were more independent and higher functioning than those in the nursing home and semi-independent living facility. Most of the students traveled to West Liberty as a group in a University van, which helped develop the cohesion of each team and provided an opportunity for group planning and debriefing.

Students kept weekly reflective journals of their service-learning experiences that not only documented the activities they participated in, but addressed their personal growth and what they learned from their experiences. Students also completed evaluation forms at the beginning and end of the semester, and wrote a short paper summarizing their service-learning experience. The teams gave an hour-long presentation to the entire class at the end of the semester which included a video presentation, a description of what they had done in the field, and excerpts from the oral histories and their papers and journals. As a result, the entire class benefited from the service-learning experience. Finally, a celebration was held at the end of the semester at the West Liberty Community Center at which the service-learning students received certificates, said goodbye to their elder partners, and had their pictures taken together with a Polaroid camera.

Project results were disseminated through an e-mail listserve and web site (www. uiowa.edu~agingstp/intergen/index.html) developed on the University campus and through a mini-conference that was integrated into a three-day Geriatric Summer Workshop offered annually by the UI Aging Studies Program in June. The workshop was broadcast statewide over the Iowa Telecommunications Network, a fiber optics network. Finally, information about the project was disseminated in social work and aging studies newsletters and through University colloquia and seminars that reached substantial audiences.

Measurement of Outcomes

Student outcome measures. Student attitudes at the beginning and end of the service-learning experience were assessed by three attitudinal scales adapted from the Foundation for Long Term Care Service Learning Project (Pillemer & Albright, 1996). The scales include: (1) general attitudes toward the elderly; (2) attitudes toward community service work; and (3) attitudes toward working with older people (see Table 1). Each item on the scales was scored from 1 to 4 (1 = strongly disagree, 2 = mildly disagree, 3 = mildly agree, 4 = strongly agree). To reduce response set bias, some statements were reverse-scored. One item, "I fear getting really old," originally included in the Attitudes Toward Working with Older People Scale, was analyzed separately to assess whether the project helped reduce student fears of their own aging. Cronbach's alpha for the three scales ranged from .54 to .67 for the pre-test and from .60 to .72 for the post-test.

TABLE 1. Change in Attitudes Toward Aging, Service-Learning and Non Service-Learning Students: Pre- and Post-Test Scale

| | Service-Learning | | | | | Non Service-Learning | | | | |
| | Pre-test (n = 13) | | Post-test (n = 13) | | | Pre-test (n = 36) | | Post-test (n = 34) | | |
General Attitudes Toward the Elderly	Mean	SD	Mean	SD	t	Mean	SD	Mean	SD	t
Most old people are set in their ways.#	2.69	0.63	3.23	0.73	-2.21*	2.50	0.71	2.85	0.78	-2.24*
Most old people are not isolated.	3.08	0.76	3.54	0.78	-1.56	2.65	0.85	3.12	0.81	-2.77**
Old people are apt to complain.#	2.69	0.75	3.31	0.85	-2.31*	2.64	0.78	2.97	0.64	-2.07*
Old people can learn new things.	3.08	0.86	3.38	0.65	-1.76	3.26	0.79	3.21	0.88	0.32
People become wiser with old age.	3.08	0.76	3.54	0.52	-3.21**	3.44	0.70	3.41	0.74	0.22
Old people are against reform/hang on to past.#	2.46	0.66	3.15	0.90	-2.64*	2.91	0.67	2.94	0.69	-0.21
Most old people are in good health.	2.77	0.73	3.15	0.38	-2.13+	2.76	0.61	3.03	0.52	-2.06*
Most old people pry into other's affairs.#	3.54	0.52	3.69	0.63	-0.81	3.32	0.68	3.44	0.56	-1.28
Old people can perform as well as young people in jobs.	2.54	0.88	2.92	0.49	-2.74*	2.82	0.76	3.03	0.67	-1.31
Overall Score	2.88	0.29	3.32	0.29	-5.66***	2.91	0.36	3.11	0.38	-2.72**
Attitudes Toward Community Service Work										
It is the community's responsibility to take care of older persons.	3.38	0.51	3.54	0.66	-0.81	3.26	0.62	3.18	0.67	0.59
I am good at helping people.	3.77	0.44	3.77	0.44	0.00	3.71	0.46	3.59	0.50	1.16
I am NOT interested in community problems.#	3.31	0.63	3.62	0.65	-1.48	3.41	0.61	3.35	0.65	0.40
It is important to help people.	3.54	0.52	3.62	0.51	-1.00	3.68	0.47	3.65	0.49	0.30
It is hard to find time for other's problems.#	2.23	0.44	2.46	0.66	-1.00	2.38	0.85	2.50	0.93	-0.89
I want to work helping others.	3.69	0.63	3.69	0.63	0.00	3.68	0.59	3.65	0.60	0.57
Volunteering makes no sense due to no money.#	4.00	0.00	4.00	0.00	N/A	3.85	0.44	3.79	0.64	0.70
Careers in service can be rewarding.	3.54	0.52	3.54	0.88	0.00	3.62	0.49	3.65	0.49	-2.60
Overall Score	3.43	0.21	3.53	0.25	-1.64	3.43	0.33	3.42	0.35	0.60

TABLE 1 (continued)

Attitudes Toward Working with Older People	M	SD	M	SD	t	M	SD	M	SD	t
Working with older people is an interesting job.	3.15	0.56	3.62	0.51	-3.21**	3.14	0.59	3.24	0.61	-1.14
Working with older people is depressing.#	3.08	0.49	3.62	0.51	-3.74**	2.94	0.79	3.21	0.77	-1.79+
It would be stressful to work with older people.#	2.69	0.75	2.85	0.80	-0.56	2.61	0.65	2.74	0.86	-0.57
Working with older people is worthwhile.	3.46	0.52	3.62	0.51	1.00	3.33	0.68	3.41	0.70	-0.26
It is hard to make money working with older people.#	2.38	0.65	2.46	0.66	-0.43	2.22	0.80	2.38	0.92	0.96
Working with older people is prestigious.	2.69	0.75	2.92	0.64	-1.90+	2.67	0.72	2.65	0.95	0.19
I don't have the ability to work with older people.#	3.38	0.77	3.69	0.48	-2.31*	3.42	0.69	3.41	0.61	-0.24
Overall Score	2.98	0.27	3.25	0.31	-3.30**	2.90	0.44	3.00	0.48	-1.49

+$p < .10$. *$p < .05$. **$p < .01$. ***$p < .001$
= reverse scored

Service-learning students also completed a set of open-ended questions at the beginning and end of the project because we were interested in gaining more in-depth responses than are possible with standardized measures (Ward, 1997). The pre-test consisted of nine questions and the post-test consisted of ten questions. The open-ended questions elicited information regarding the value and challenges of the service-learning experience, experiences working with elders, and understanding of rural communities. The additional post-test question asked whether the service-learning students would recommend intergenerational service-learning to other students and why or why not (see Table 2).

Elder outcome measures. At the end of the semester, the elders were interviewed by a member of the project staff. They were asked to give both their general and specific thoughts about the project, what they perceived as their own and students' contribution to the project, and if they had suggestions or recommendations regarding future activities or improvements (see Table 3). These interviews were tape recorded and transcribed for analysis.

Data Analysis

Quantitative data. The pre/post-test design (Pillemer & Albright, 1996) allowed us to determine if the service-learning experience impacted students' attitudes toward older persons. We examined both between-groups change (service-learning vs. non service-learning students) and within-groups change

TABLE 2. Intergenerational Service-Learning Student Open-Ended Questions

Pre-test:

1. What do you expect to be the main value of the service-learning experience for you?
2. How do you expect service-learning to enhance what you learn in class?
3. What do you expect to be the main challenges of the service-learning experience?
4. What are the main things you hope to gain from working with elders?
5. How do you expect elders to contribute to your education?
6. When you think about nursing homes, what comes to mind?
7. What do you expect to learn about rural elders and communities?
8. How do you expect to meet community needs?
9. How do you feel about your own aging?

Post-test:
1. What was the main value of the service-learning experience for you?
2. How did service-learning enhance what you learned in class?
3. What were the main challenges of the service-learning experience?
4. What are the main things you gained from working with elders?
5. How did the elders contribute to your education?
6. When you think about nursing homes now, what comes to mind?
7. What did you learn about rural elders and communities?
8. How did you meet community needs?
9. Has the service-learning experience changed your feelings about your own aging?
10. Would you recommend intergenerational service-learning to other students? Why or why not?

TABLE 3. Intergenerational Service-Learning Elder Follow-Up Questions

Introduction: You are a valuable part of this project and your input is very much appreciated. We are very interested in your feedback in regard to the project so we can make improvements where they are needed.

1. In your opinion, was the matching of students and residents appropriate, or would you suggest some other way?
2. What did you particularly like and what did you dislike about this project?
3. What do you think you contributed to the student with whom you were working?
4. What do you think the student with whom you were working contributed to you?
5. What do you think might be different?
6. Would you suggest continuing this project? Why or why not?
7. Do you have any suggestions for next time?

from pre-test to post-test for both groups (service-learning students and non service-learning students). Data were analyzed using the Statistical Product and Service Solutions (SPSS) 10.0 software (Norusis, 2000). Analyses included both individual item analysis and summative scores for each scale. Between-groups analysis employed two-tailed independent-samples t tests; within-groups analysis utilized two-tailed paired-samples t tests.

Qualitative data. Answers to open-ended questions on student surveys and elders' follow-up interviews were completely transcribed and subsequently analyzed to identify major themes and categories using the method of constant comparison (Glaser & Strauss, 1967). Codes were developed for each theme and category. When agreement on themes and categories was reached by the research team (Glaser & Strauss, 1967), two independent raters coded the data. Inter-rater reliability was .87 for student open-ended pre-test responses and .88 for student open-ended post-test responses. Inter-rater reliability for elder follow-up interviews was .92.

A research assistant assigned the pre-determined codes to student and elder open-ended responses in the computer files. Codes and data files were entered into the program and were not altered once analysis began. The HyperResearch 2.0 (ResearchWare, Inc., 1999) data analysis software program was used to analyze the qualitative data.

RESULTS

Student Outcomes

Between-groups comparisons on pre-test. In order to determine whether the service-learning students and the non service-learning students were similar in attitudes prior to participating in the program, pre-test results of the two groups were compared. There were relatively few differences at pre-test on the three attitudinal scales. Because of the small sample size, marginally significant levels are reported (p between .05 and .10). On the General Attitudes Toward the Elderly Scale, only one item, *"old people are against reform/hang on to past,"* showed a marginally significant difference between the two groups at pre-test (t (49) = 1.75, p = .09). In this case, the service-learning students were slightly more likely to agree with the statement than the non service-learning students. On the Attitudes Toward Community Service Work Scale, differences between groups at pre-test (t (49) = -1.96, p = .06) were found on only one item: *"volunteering makes no sense due to no money."* Both the service-learning and non service-learning students disagreed strongly with the statement, but the service-learning students' disagreement was slightly stronger. On the Attitudes Toward Working with Older People Scale, there were no differences between the two groups on the pre-test, not even marginally significant ones. On the *"I fear getting really old"* item, which was analyzed separately, no significant differences were found between service-learning and non service-learning groups at pre-test; in fact, both groups had nearly identical means. Overall, the results of these analyses confirm that the two groups were quite similar in attitudes prior to participating in the project and provide some evidence that differences in attitudes at the time of the post-test cannot be attributed to initial differences between the two groups.

Between-groups comparisons on post-test. The effect of the service-learning project on students could be estimated by comparing the results for the two groups on the post-test. These results can be considered informative because the attitudinal ratings on the pre-test for the two groups were so similar. Therefore, it is reasonable to suggest that differences between the two groups on the post-test are due to one group's participation in the project.

On the General Attitudes Toward the Elderly Scale, a marginally significant overall mean difference between the service-learning and non service-learning groups was found at post-test (t (47) = -1.86, p = .07) with the service-learning students reporting more positive attitudes than the non service-learning students. As was discussed earlier, the service-learning students initially were more likely to agree that *"old people are against reform/hang onto the past"* on the pre-test. By the time of the post-test, however, the non service-learning students' level of disagreement had lessened and the service-learning students' level of disagreement had risen dramatically so that there was no longer even a marginally significant difference between groups.

There were no significant differences at post-test on the overall mean for the Attitudes Toward Community Service Work Scale. However, results on one single item are worth reporting. As was previously reported, on the pre-test the service-learning students had a very high level of disagreement with the item *"volunteering makes no sense due to no money,"* and their ratings were slightly higher than the ratings of the non-service-learning students. On the post-test, the service-learning students had maintained their extremely high level of disagreement with this item while the non service-learning students' level of disagreement decreased somewhat, making the difference between the two groups even greater (t (47)= $-1.87, p = .07$). This finding suggests that the service-learning experience confirmed the students' positive feelings about the value of volunteering.

More positive attitudes on the post-test were also found for the service-learning students on overall means on the Attitudes Toward Working with Older People Scale (t (47) = $-1.71, p < .09$). In particular, on this scale, two items showed marginally significant differences between the groups at post-test. The service-learning students were more likely to agree with the statement *"working with older people is an interesting job"* (t (47) = -2.01, $p = .051$) and to disagree with the statement *"working with older people is depressing"* (t (47) = $-1.77, p = .08$).

The *"I fear getting really old"* item, which was analyzed separately, also showed interesting results. Although there had been no significant differences at pre-test, a significant difference between the groups was found at post-test (t (47) = 2.27, $p = .03$). This finding suggests that the service-learning students became less fearful of their own aging as a result of participating in the service-learning experience.

Pre- to post-test change results. Table 1 reveals interesting pre- to post-test changes for both the service-learning and non service-learning groups. At post-test, service-learning students were significantly more likely than at pre-test to *agree* with the following items from the General Attitudes Toward the Elderly Scale: *"people become wiser with age,"* *"most old people are in good health,"* and *"old people can perform as well as young people in jobs."* They were also significantly more likely to *disagree* at post-test with the items *"most old people are set in their ways,"* *"old people are apt to complain,"* and *"old people are against reform/hang on to past."* Overall, service-learning students showed significantly more positive general attitudes toward elders at post-test than at pre-test t (13) = $-5.66, p < .001$.

Especially interesting are the findings that the non service-learning students' attitudes also changed. The overall mean change on the General Attitudes Toward the Elderly Scale for these students shows that on the post-test they had significantly more positive attitudes (t (34) = $-2.72, p < .01$), although the change was not as great as for the service-learning students (see Figure 1 for a comparison of the overall means). Four items on the General Attitudes Toward the Elderly Scale showed significant change among the non service-learning students at post-test (Table 1). Like the service-learning students, they were more likely to disagree with the items *"old people are apt to*

FIGURE 1. Attitude Change for Service-Learning and Non Service-Learning Students

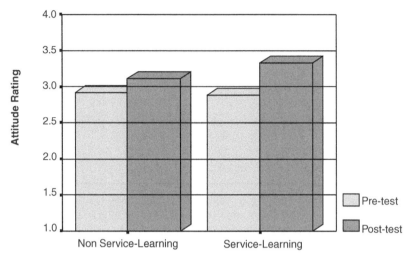

Non-service-learning pre-test N = 36; post-test N = 34
Service-learning pre-test N = 13; post-test N = 13

complain" and *"most old people are set in their ways."* Also like the service-learning students, they were more likely to agree with the item *"most old
people are in good health."* In addition, they were more likely to agree with the
statement *"most old people are not isolated."*

Although change between pre- and post-test scores was not found to be statistically significant on the Attitudes Toward Community Service Work Scale
for either service-learning or non service-learning students, significant differences were found on the Attitudes Toward Working with Older People Scale
(Table 1). Service-learning students exhibited a significant overall mean
change to more positive attitudes from pre- to post-test on the Attitudes Toward Working with Older People Scale (t (13) = −3.30, p < .01). Specifically,
service-learning students were more likely to *agree* at post-test with the following items: *"working with older people is an interesting job"* and *"working
with older people is prestigious."* They were also significantly more likely to
disagree at post-test that *"working with older people is depressing"* and *"I
don't have the ability to work with older people."*

Although the non service-learning students did not show a significant change in the overall mean on this scale, they reported a positive change on one item. Even though they had not experienced direct interaction with elders in the service-learning project, they were more likely at post-test to disagree with the statement that *"working with older people is depressing."*

With regard to the *"I fear getting really old"* item, a significant difference was found from pre- to post-test for the service-learning group only t (13) = 2.89, $p < .05$, indicating that at the conclusion of the service-learning experience they were less fearful of their own aging. In this case, the non service-learning students did not share the same positive attitudinal change.

Open-ended questions. We assessed the service-learning students' perceptions of intergenerational-service-learning in their own words in order to gain a better understanding of their service-learning experience. Responses to the questions listed in Table 2, asked both before and after the service-learning experience (Ward, 1997), reveal students' expectations and experiences during the semester. The majority of students expected the main value of the service-learning experience (Question 1) to be experiential learning. The following comments are illustrative:

"I expect the main value to be a greater appreciation for the elderly and a more interpersonal relationship with them. It's interesting to study and learn about aging but a hands-on experience should be more beneficial."

"I will be working with someone who has had many more life experiences than I have had and they will share some of their knowledge with me."

At the end of the service-learning experience, students had positive things to say about the value of experiential learning:

"It provided us with a great opportunity to apply the things learned in class to real people in a real-life context. Things discussed in class took on a new and deeper meaning. It was the difference between talking about "the elderly" in general and individual people who are aging."

"For me, it was nice to have the chance to converse with elderly people. This is something I enjoy but seldom get the chance to do on campus."

All but a few students said they expected service-learning to enhance what they learned in class through direct application of classroom learning (Question 2). Their actual experience confirmed this expectation. Typical student comments were: *"It showed me that the theories of aging about diversity and elders aging differently was very much true"* and *"Many things I learned in class I was able to apply in real life."*

Students also expected and experienced challenges in the service-learning experience (Question 3), the most common being in their relationship with elders. As one student put it: *"The main challenge for myself will be just starting communication to establish a relationship with the older person."* The actual challenges the students experienced, however, were somewhat different than they had expected. Eight students mentioned either the challenges in making arrangements for the project or the large time commitment needed for the project. Also, several students found it particularly difficult to say goodbye to their elders at the end of the semester even though they had been trained in termination issues by one of the project directors.

What the majority of students said they hoped to gain from working with elders (Question 4) was an increased understanding of older people. The students did report that they gained in understanding from working with elders; however, they were equally likely to report gains in knowledge about elders. As one student said: *"I feel more informed about the myths versus the realities of aging as well as [gaining] useful experience in dealing one-on-one with this population."* Students said elders contributed to their education (Question 5) primarily through experiential learning and through the intergenerational experience. *"Teaching real-life components that can't possibly be portrayed in textbooks"* is how one student put it.

Because the service-learning experience involved working with nursing home residents, we were interested in possible changes in students' attitudes concerning nursing homes. Student responses at the beginning of the semester reflected rather negative stereotypes about nursing homes: half of the students spoke negatively about characteristics of residents, whereas others perceived a lack of engaging activities, an unpleasant physical setting, and poor care. Students spoke of *"senile residents," "older people in wheelchairs relying on nurses to take care of them,"* and *"people in wheelchairs or with walkers and little mobility."* One student said that *"In my experience, they have been pretty closed, warm, kind of smelly, and depressing,"* and another viewed nursing homes as *"stinky, dark–unfortunately."*

Interestingly, by the end of the semester, there was an almost complete reversal of student attitudes regarding nursing homes. Nine of the students spoke of the pleasant setting they had found:

"I now think of [nursing homes] as clean, warm facilities, where people are taken care of and encouraged to participate in activities . . ."

"My new friend and the way she is respected, well treated, and well taken care of by the staff. Along with the cleanliness and welcoming atmosphere at the Memorial Home."

"It is still a place that people turn to, for the most part, as a last resort . . . but that doesn't mean it is a bad or depressing place."

Results for two questions that focused on student learning about rural elders and communities (#7 and #8) indicated students wanted to learn about characteristics of rural communities and gain a better understanding of them. These expectations were fulfilled by their learning about rural community and family values:

"Rural elders are very tied to their communities and most of them have been living there for a long time. This means that they have a lot of stories to tell."

"Rural elders value the family and meaning of the family higher than most other elements. I also learned that living on a farm was hard work and there were no excuses, only respect for all of those around you."

"These people are often very strong, independent, survivor types of people."
Most of the students felt they had met community needs by providing needed services and developing personal relationships with elders.

Question 9 addressed one of our major interests, whether service-learning had an effect on students' views of their own aging. Only five students expressed positive views of their own aging at the beginning of the semester, and some expressed fear or denial:

"I am concerned about the quality of life when I can no longer be as active as I am today and dread being viewed with the repulsion or fear that young people so often display toward the elderly."
By the end of the semester, however, the majority of students expressed positive, or at least more accepting, views of their own aging: They said: *"Aging isn't something you should fear, but a natural part of life that you just learn to deal with," "It has provided me with a more hopeful outlook on aging,"* or even *"Aging should be something to look forward to and not something to be scared of."*

Our final question at the end of the intergenerational service-learning experience asked students whether they would recommend it to others and why or why not. All of the students had positive things to say about the experience, as illustrated by these comments:

"I am lucky to have participated in service-learning because it has made me more secure and comfortable with my own aging process, and if I do have to go in a nursing home someday, I am going to be comfortable with it."

"It was an awesome experience. It taught me a lot about elders."

"I touched someone's heart, giving them a new friend."
The only negative comments that several students made about the experience centered on workload issues, because the service-learning experience was very time-consuming and was probably more work than many students had anticipated.

Elder Outcomes

In the follow-up interviews with nursing home and semi-independent living residents after the conclusion of the service-learning experience, elders were first asked their opinion about the way the students and elders were matched. All elders said that the matching was done well and that they had no suggestions for matching any other way. An eighty-two-year-old woman was effusive about the match with her student partner: *"Well . . . we just loved the kids you gave us. It worked out real well."* Her eighty-four-year-old husband concurred: *"I think most everyone that I talked to was real satisfied with the partner they received."*

Elders were next asked to discuss what they liked and disliked about the project (Question 2). No dislikes were mentioned by the elders. All of the elders, on the other hand, said they liked the personal interaction that the project offered them, as the responses of these two women, aged 94 and 84, illustrate:

"He was a very nice boy. He was very courteous. He seemed to be interested in everything that you said, and he was a good listener. Very, very nice. . . . He listened, and would ask about your experiences in life and different things."

"I thought it was very interesting. I looked forward to it each time. And my girl was a very nice girl. I've had a letter from her since. She wants me to write to her."

Two residents also commented positively on how the project was planned, as indicated by the remarks of this 86-year-old woman:

"Well, I was flattered to have been chosen as one of the people. . . . I thought the project was well planned and I would think it turned out very well."

The qualitative data confirm that the experience was perceived as reciprocal. When elders were queried about what they felt they had contributed to the students with whom they were paired (Question 3), all but one responded that they felt it was sharing their life experiences with the students. Two women, aged 84 and 94, respectively, expressed their thoughts this way:

"Well, she couldn't believe some of the things that happened in my life years ago, you know. How we grew up so poor. I think it gave her encouragement that you can get farther ahead in life. That's the way I kind of felt she felt, because I told her we started out with nothing."

"I know she was especially interested in that I really had started teaching and taught for a while, decided that wasn't what I wanted, then I made a change and was much happier with the change that I made. I know she was interested in that, and maybe that she could see it could be done. You didn't have to stick to one occupation."

What elders said students contributed to them (Question 4), conversely, was a greater understanding of young people today and the opportunity to develop relationships with them (Question 4). The words of this 90-year-old reflect the responses of the majority who said they learned more about young people from the project: *"I think it gave me a lot of insight on the people in college."* The comments of her even older (aged 94) fellow resident provided a touching tribute to the students:

"Well, a lot of the people today are very conscientious and try hard to do what's right. There's still a lot of good boys and girls in the world. That's right." The only male elder participating in the project spoke of the advantages to elders of developing relationships with students: *"Well, it entertained us. And took up our time. Here there's days we get a little bored, and we enjoy people just coming and talking to us."*

The last three questions in the interview schedule asked elders what might be done differently, whether they thought we should continue the project in the future, and specific suggestions for next time. All elders felt that we should continue the project. The words of this 84-year-old expressed the generally positive reaction of elders to continuing the project: *"I think it would be nice. I know [the administrator] asked us that, and we told him we wouldn't mind doin' it another year. In fact, I'd kinda feel left out if we didn't get asked again. I thought it was fun, and real interesting. Looked forward to it."*

And the 84-year-old male said: *"I think it's very nice for the people here and for them both. I think they both learned from it."*

With regard to what might be done differently and suggested changes for next time, elders had only one recommendation: two women residents suggested that a greater number of elders be given the opportunity to participate in the project, thus creating greater inclusiveness for residents and a greater variety of life experiences for students to learn from. As a 94-year-old woman put it: *"Probably you'll choose different people here. Get a broader view. I think it would be a good idea, because I think you'll get a lot of different ideas. You'll run into different occupations, you know. I think probably most of the people they interviewed, their occupations were mostly farming."*

DISCUSSION

The findings of this study confirm previous research on the value of intergenerational service-learning. The experience was especially effective in its impact on attitudes and affective learning. Student attitudes toward the elderly, toward work with the elderly, and toward their own aging had all improved by the end of the service-learning experience. The qualitative comments made by service-learning students provide convincing and persuasive evidence of the positive change associated with this learning experience. Especially important were the responses that indicated how much they valued the relationship with an elder, their increased interest in a career working with the elderly, and their more positive attitudes toward their own aging. The elders, in their turn, expressed appreciation for the opportunity to engage in the service-learning project and confirm that the benefits were reciprocal.

The only negative feedback from several students concerning workload will be addressed in the future as this project is continued. The students who participated in the first service-learning experience were not required to take one exam that the other students were required to take. In the future, additional academic credit will be offered to the students who participate in the service-learning experience to more completely compensate them for the additional time and work commitment.

Some aspects of this project suggest future directions for intergenerational service-learning. For one thing, it documents the value of rural communities for intergenerational service-learning projects. Although about one-fourth of all elders reside in rural areas, many students are not familiar with rural communities and the life experience of rural elders. The rural community as a context for service-learning experiences adds valuable learning opportunities for students and is appreciated by rural elders who may not have as many opportunities to relate to students as do their urban counterparts. In this project, non-social work as well as social work students were exposed to possible careers working with elders in rural settings, hopefully helping to prepare them to move into social work with elders. At least one non-social work student declared her intention of pursuing an M.S.W. degree at the end of the service-learning experience.

Another innovative aspect of the project was the use of teams of students who traveled to the rural community together. Although this approach presented scheduling problems for some students who would have liked to participate, it had very positive effects. It allowed for the development of a cohesive team spirit, discussions that allowed students to compare and reflect on their experiences, and for the teaching fellow who facilitated the service-learning project to guide and enhance the learning experiences of the students and follow up on any problems they might encounter at the service-learning sites.

The most significant contribution of this study was the incorporation of the service-learning component into an existing social work gerontology course. This made it easy to recruit students interested in intergenerational service-learning and provided excellent application of the content of the course to the real life situation of rural elders. More importantly, it set the stage for the service-learning experience to affect all the students in the class, both those who participated in service-learning and those who did not. Because the professor was one of the faculty who developed the project and the graduate teaching fellow who supervised the service-learning students served as teaching assistant for the course, the service-learning project was well integrated into the content of the course. Because the service-learning students shared their experiences with other students in class discussion and in a class presentation at the end of the semester, all students in the class benefited from the intergenerational service-learning project. As the quantitative results show, the non service-learning students improved significantly in attitudes towards the elderly and toward working with elders, although the changes were not as great as for the service-learning students.

Limitations of the study include the small number of cases, especially for service-learning students. Because this intergenerational service-learning project has been continued, data are being gathered on additional cohorts of students, which will increase the number of cases. The established quantitative instruments were useful, but limited in their content. Additional measures of the impact of service-learning would be helpful. Qualitative data were gathered only for the service-learning students. A comparison of qualitative data between service-learning and non service-learning students would add to the findings by documenting the attitudes of the both groups of students in their own words. Further research could also gather information on ways in which group process enhances service-learning experiences, and could compare urban and rural service-learning projects. It would be valuable to explore the use of intergenerational service-learning options in other social work gerontology classes and how they can add to the curriculum. Finally, since the study was carried out for only one class and only in one rural community, it is limited in generalizability. Further research should continue the process of replicating the results in a variety of contexts.

Despite these limitations, this study makes an important contribution by confirming and extending the results of prior research on intergenerational service-learning, by demonstrating the value of such projects in rural communities, and by showing the value of integrating service-learning into existing social work gerontology courses. The student benefits from such educational experiences include better understanding of the life experiences of rural elders, improved attitudes toward the elderly, greater interest in a career working with the elderly, and more positive attitudes toward their own aging. Elder benefits include opportunities to interact with students, to contribute to their learning, and to receive recognition for their worth and life experience.

REFERENCES

Bringle, R. G., & Kremer, J. F. (1993). Evaluation of an intergenerational service-learning project for undergraduates. *Educational Gerontology, 19*, 407-416.

Glaser, B. G., & Strauss, A. L. (1967). *The discovery of grounded theory: Strategies for qualitative research.* New York: Aldine de Gruyter.

Greene, D. (1998). Reciprocity in two conditions of service-learning. *Educational Gerontology, 24*, 411-424.

Krout, J. A. (1998). Services and service delivery in rural environments. In R. T. Coward & J. A. Krout (Eds.), *Aging in rural environments: Life circumstances and distinctive features* (pp. 247-266). New York: Springer.

Larkin, E., & Newman, S. (1997). Intergenerational studies: A multi-disciplinary field. *Journal of Gerontological Social Work, 28*, 5-16.

McCrea, J. M., & Smith, T. B. (1997). Types and models of intergenerational programs. In S. Newman et al., *Intergenerational programs: Past, present, and future* (pp. 81-93). Washington, DC: Taylor and Francis.

Newman, S. (1997). Rationale for linking the generations. Publ. No. 130, Generations Together, University of Pittsburgh, University Center for Social and Urban Research.

Newman, S., Lyons, C. W., & Onawala, R. S. T. (1985). The development of an intergenerational service-learning program at a nursing home. *The Gerontologist, 25*, 130-133.

Nichols, A., & Monard, K. (1999). Implications for measuring changes in attitudes toward aging and the elderly among students in intergenerational service-learning courses. Paper presented at the 52nd Annual Scientific Meeting of the Gerontological Society of America, San Francisco, CA (November).

Norusis, M. J. (2000). *SPSS 10.0 guide to data analysis.* Upper Saddle River, NJ: Prentice Hall.

Pillemer, K., & Albright, B. (1996). Evaluation. In B. M. Westacott & C. R. Hegeman (Eds.), *Service learning in elder care: A resource manual* (pp. 99-106). Albany, NY: The Foundation for Long Term Care.

Pine, P. (1997). Learning by sharing: An intergenerational college course. *Journal of Gerontological Social Work, 28*, 93-102.

ResearchWare, Inc. (1999). *HyperResearch 2.0.* Randolph, MA: Author.

Roodin, P. (2000). Intergenerational service-learning: Between older adults and college students. Paper presented at the Annual Meeting of the Association for Gerontology in Higher Education, Myrtle Beach, SC (February).

U. S. Bureau of Census (2001). *Profiles of general demographic characteristics: 2000 census of population and housing, Iowa.* Washington, DC: Author.

Ward, C. R. (1997). Intergenerational program evaluation. *Journal of Gerontological Social Work, 28*, 173-181.

Watson, J. B., Church, C., Darville, R., & Darville, S. (1997). University-community college partnership development for eldercare service-learning: A model for rural community impact. *Building Civic Responsibility in Higher Education, 2*, 59-64.

Chapter 15

The Family Study:
A Useful Gerontological Tool

Denise Eldemire-Shearer, PhD
Chloe Morris

SUMMARY. The Caribbean, although classified as a developing country has been experiencing an ageing of its population over the past two decades. Faced with the lack of a well-developed social service infrastructure for seniors and economic challenges, care of the elderly is predominantly by families and in the community. Training institutions have had to develop new programs and new approaches to aid those caring for seniors.

A course for community based social workers of varying backgrounds has been developed to enhance their skills in promoting good health as well as maximum independence in all aspects of life among seniors. Health as defined by the World Health Organization is all embracing including physical, mental, social and spiritual aspects. The course uses several innovative approaches one of which the paper discusses.

A key component of the course is the use of the "Family Study" which exposes teams of students to a family, which includes a senior for the du-

Denise Eldemire-Shearer and Chloe Morris are affiliated with the World Health Organization Collaborating Centre on Ageing & Health, Department of Community Health & Psychiatry, University of the West Indies, Mona, Kingston 7, Jamaica W.I.

[Haworth co-indexing entry note]: "The Family Study: A Useful Gerontological Tool." Eldemire-Shearer, Denise, and Chloe Morris. Co-published simultaneously in *Journal of Gerontological Social Work* (The Haworth Social Work Practice Press, an imprint of The Haworth Press, Inc.) Vol. 39, No. 1/2, 2002, pp. 241-261; and: *Advancing Gerontological Social Work Education* (ed: M. Joanna Mellor, and Joann Ivry) The Haworth Social Work Practice Press, an imprint of The Haworth Press, Inc., 2002, pp. 241-261. Single or multiple copies of this article are available for a fee from The Haworth Document Delivery Service [1-800-HAWORTH, 9:00 a.m. - 5:00 p.m. (EST). E-mail address: docdelivery@haworthpress.com].

10.1300/J083v39n01_19

ration of the 20-week course. Seniors are chosen for study based on their social, physical complaints and desire for assistance.

Using a modified version of the social compass and other quality of life assessment tools, students are required to not only identify the problems but how the problem affects the senior and the family and to plan and implement an intervention based on the strengths and weaknesses of the senior and the support system. The paper describes the process and the evolution of the use of the family study since 1992 and the students' evaluation of it.

The family study also exposes the students to other aspects of theories and practices associated with ageing, including the importance of effective communication and how to work in teams.

The inclusion of a practical approach involving seniors and their families has strengthened the academic program while benefiting the client so satisfying the needs of both. *[Article copies available for a fee from The Haworth Document Delivery Service: 1-800-HAWORTH. E-mail address: <docdelivery@haworthpress.com> Website: <http://www.HaworthPress.com> © 2002 by The Haworth Press, Inc. All rights reserved.]*

KEYWORDS. Ageing, community based social work, family study, teaching tool

INTRODUCTION

The elderly (60+) are a growing percent of the Caribbean population and there has been increasing recognition of their needs including the need for services (PAHO, 1999). There has also been increasing awareness of the contribution the seniors are making in maintaining the family unit and contributing to communities (Tout 1989). At the same time there have been changes in the social and economic environment, which have reduced the ability of the family to adequately support itself emotionally and economically (HelpAge, 1999). Any additional burden created by a sick or dependent elder is unwanted and a challenge to the coping capacity of the existing situation of family and community.

Social services for at-risk individuals and families are still not well developed in the developing world and Jamaica is no exception. The existing services have concentrated on the vulnerable group of children and these are the most developed. The importance of seniors as a vulnerable group has only just been recognized and, as such, social services for them are few and very basic. There is not even universal pension coverage.

It is important that social workers understand the relationship and interactions taking place in family units in helping either a senior or a family to cope with a problem. A family study has proven a useful way to demonstrate this and is an effective learning tool for the gerontological students who implement the study.

Rationale for a Community-Based Course

Because of the growth of the elderly population and the increasing recognition of the role of the senior in families and communities as well as the influence of social relationships on the quality of life, a twenty-week course for Community Workers with the Elderly by the Department of Community Health & Psychiatry, University of the West Indies, and an age care organization, Action Ageing in 1992 was developed with the family study as the main component. The course is intended to enhance the theoretical knowledge base of the participants and increase their practical skills in caring for older persons.

Didactic methods and role-play are used to teach how to build relationships and communication skills. The course includes a significant practical component and wherever possible students are involved in "hands on" learning.

In order to meet its stated objectives the course is taught in eight modules (Table 1) which although taught separately are all integrated especially through Module D.

The importance of two concepts is fundamental to the family study and gerontological students–family and ageing.

BACKGROUND TO THE FAMILY STUDY

Aspects of Ageing

The fundamental principle of ageing as a life course event encompassing a normal sequence of changes and events influencing subsequent stages of life underlies all teaching (Figure 1). Life is examined as a series of age linked transitions.

Ageing is defined as a concept with many interrelated dimensions; the physical which people are usually familiar with, but also the less familiar social and psychological changes (Figure 2). The impact of adapting to these changes and the subsequent influence on attitudes and perceptions both positive and negative is discussed. The course stresses the quality of life issues and the importance of such to seniors (Figure 3). The underlying principle driving all the above, remains Maslow's Hierarchy of Needs (Figure 4).

TABLE 1. Course Content

Module A	**The need of elderly people in the Caribbean:** On completion of this module, participants will have an understanding and awareness of the needs of elderly people in the Caribbean.
Module B	**Home care skills and rehabilitation:** On completion of this module, participants must be able to perform basic skills in home care and re-habilitation.
Module C	**Self-care skills among the elderly:** On completion of this module, participants must be able to help elderly people develop self-care skills.
Module D	**Family and community care resources:** On completion of this module, participants will be able to utilize family and community care resources.
Module E	**The development of interpersonal skills:** On completion of this module, participants must be able to demonstrate a minimum level of interpersonal skills in the management of their relationships with elderly people and their carers.
Module F	**Self-evaluation skills:** On completion of this module, participants must know how to perform and respond to self-evaluation exercises.
Module G	**Meetings, reports and recommendations:** On completion of this module, participants must be able to produce effective reports and recommendations.
Module H	**Field work and practicals:** On completion of this module, participants will have put into practice all the material and principles taught in this course. It will consist completely of fieldwork and practicals.

FIGURE 1. Life Course and the Transitions

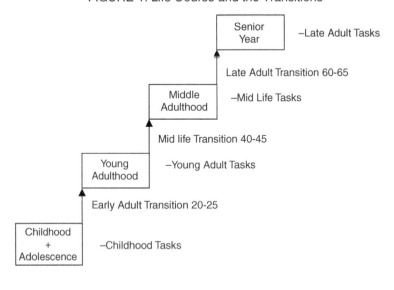

FIGURE 2. AGEING

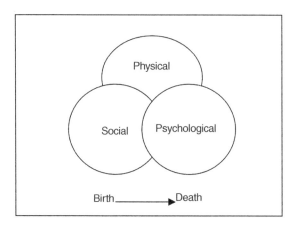

FIGURE 3. Factors Influencing Seniors

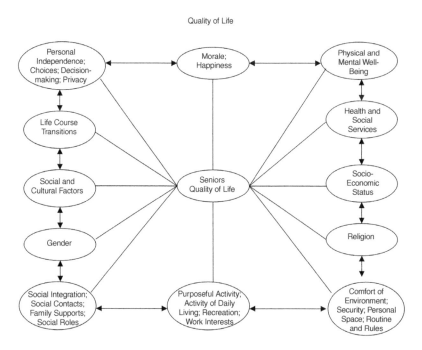

FIGURE 4. Maslow's Hierarchy of Needs[1]

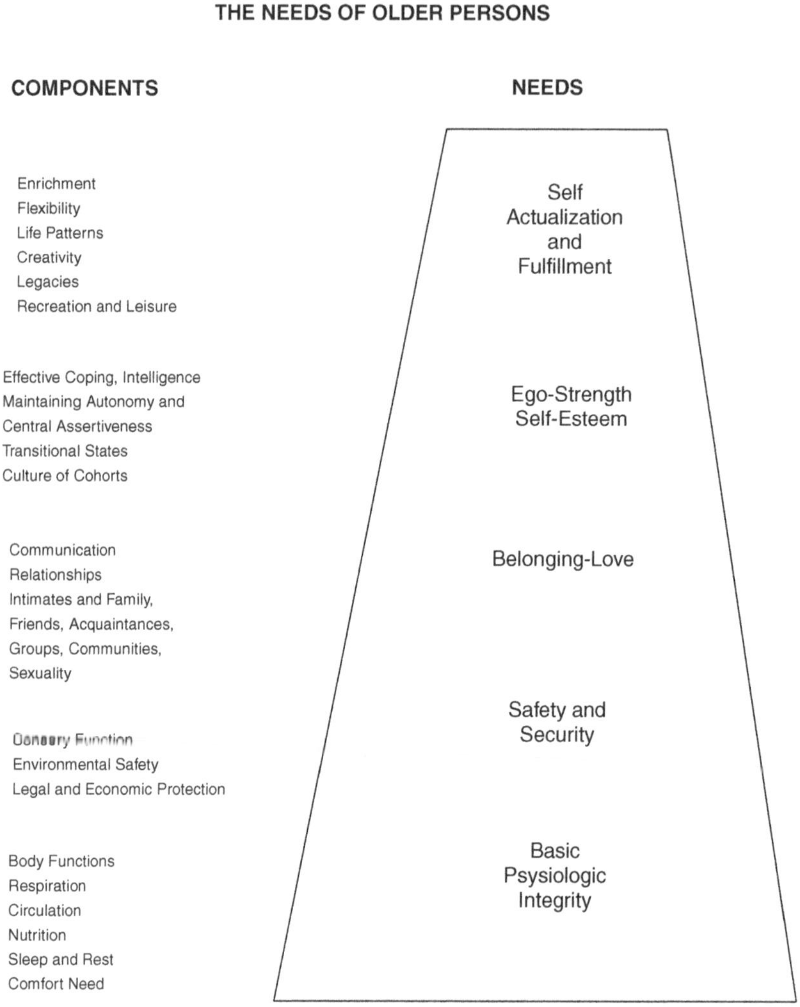

THE NEEDS OF OLDER PERSONS

COMPONENTS   **NEEDS**

Enrichment
Flexibility
Life Patterns   Self
Creativity   Actualization
Legacies   and
Recreation and Leisure   Fulfillment

Effective Coping, Intelligence
Maintaining Autonomy and   Ego-Strength
Central Assertiveness   Self-Esteem
Transitional States
Culture of Cohorts

Communication
Relationships   Belonging-Love
Intimates and Family,
Friends, Acquaintances,
Groups, Communities,
Sexuality

Sensory Function   Safety and
Environmental Safety   Security
Legal and Economic Protection

Body Functions   Basic
Respiration   Psysiologic
Circulation   Integrity
Nutrition
Sleep and Rest
Comfort Need

[1]Adapted from Maslow, A.: 1954, Motivations and Personality, Harper and Row Publishers, Inc., New York

How an individual has negotiated the changes has many dimensions, social, behavioral and developmental. In addition how the change is affected by outside factors such as community events influences the final outcome.

Students are encouraged through open discussions to examine their own attitudes to ageing, to their older relatives and to identify their fears.

These discussions are usually very revealing and necessary, as individuals working with elderly clients must also be comfortable with the ageing process.

Such discussions lead into the concept of what is "healthy ageing" and how one achieves such a state. Healthy ageing is defined as the maintenance of maximum functional capacity through physical, mental, social and spiritual well-being over the life course (WHO, 1999). It is much more than the absence of disease and disability, it is the cumulative product of life's experiences, the environment and lifestyle.

Finally, there is an emphasis on ageing taking place in an environment that promotes and facilitates the rights of the senior (UN, 1992). These include the right to participation, choice, self-fulfillment, care, and dignity. The intention is to expose the gerontological student to a new concept of ageing. One that differs from a disease dependency oriented model and introduces the student to the idea that the senior and family can and should be actively involved in solutions to problems rather than simply having "things" done for them and that any intervention should aim at promoting maximum independence and reducing disability whether physical, psychological or social (Figure 5).

FIGURE 5

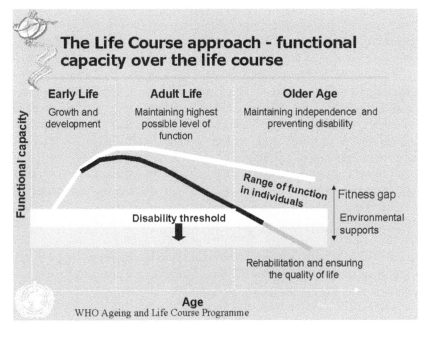

Aspects of Family

The family is still recognized as the fundamental unit of society. Several studies have supported conventional wisdom that the family is the most important source of support for seniors (Eldemire, 1993; SLC, 1995; Barrow, 1996). Fears that the family is disintegrating are not supported by all of the current research (Eldemire 1993; Barrow 1996) but it is changing. The decrease in fertility rates has led to smaller families. Industrialization and urbanization with their modern technology such as telephones and computers have meant that families can stay in touch without living together (Morris, 2000). In such situations remittances are the major form of support. The research also indicates that there are still multi-generational families living together (Eldemire, 1993; Dilworth-Anderson & Burton 1999). Whichever view one subscribes to, the endpoint is the same, fewer available family members as social supports and or caregivers, will impact on social work approaches. The research (Eldemire, 1993) has highlighted the gender differences as women maintain social supports throughout the life span but are often compromised financially. Men, especially older men, may not identify a caregiver but may have the money to pay for one. Social work interventions have to take such findings into consideration.

In addition many seniors remain as head of the household and the majority of these are female. The family is a major support to its members in meeting the developmental tasks of each age. The importance of satisfying personal needs have been well documented (Eldemire, 1993; Mendes de Leon et al., 2001) as have the problems of unmet needs (SLC, 1999). The needs of seniors differ from those of younger members and are unique. The impact of unmet or unfulfilled needs by one member is however felt by the family and can affect all members causing stress and dislocation if not resolved. Similarly a happy satisfied senior can have a positive impact on the family and be a resource for problems among other generations.

As stressed by Silverstone (1999), the family study and practical exposure stresses the importance of seeing "the client" in their environment and the importance of direct work with individuals, families and communities. In order to ensure correct ethical practice, the family study has an intervention component after the investigation. WHO (2000) reminds that families remain the major providers of long term care but they cannot shoulder the burden of care alone as family resources are decreasing. Well-managed and adequately supported home care can improve the quality of life of the recipient and their caregivers. The burden of caregiving is usually borne by women who have less access to resources with which to get help. Family studies are basic for evaluation of the need for home care services because the ability of the family determines whether or not such services can succeed.

APPROACH

The family study is based on the principles of family and ageing as previously discussed.

Aims

The family study:

1. Gives students a practical experience of working with the family, enabling them to apply what they have learnt in class in relationship to themselves, the elderly, and the community both in sickness and in health.
2. Encourages positive student interventions, as they affect the senior, the caregiver and the other members of the family who interact regularly with the senior.
3. Is the pivot around which the modules come together as all the information and skills can be used during the study.

Change and adaptability along the life course have been identified as important concepts. Illness of a member especially a dependent member such as a senior is one such change and is a very important consideration in looking at family interactions. The use of the family study recognizes that care providers need to understand the changes and individuality of each family member and of the family as a whole and its reactions, before planning interventions, so as to improve their appropriateness for a particular family and so improve the chances of success.

Role of Illness

The family study of a senior very often involves the presence of illness whether physical or mental. The importance of paying attention to and supporting the caregiver has been stressed in recent times (Shaibu, 2000; Burgio et al., 2001). Features of the impact of illness of the elderly in the family are stressed in the lectures orienting the students.

Illness precipitates many stressful feelings and reactions for the family members including anxiety, anger, denial, shame, guilt, uncertainty and role reversal. If the illness is prolonged or causes dependency, the family reactions also move through stages and change, requiring different approaches from care providers. These include:

1. *The Patient Role Implications.* Becoming ill or dependent means that an individual is assigned a new and special role in which freedom, autonomy and control may be lost temporarily or permanently. Persons will have differing reactions to these losses depending on their previous experiences and personality. Maslow's hierarchy of needs is used to direct the investigation and suggest possible interventions.

2. *Role Dislocation.* The illness of the individual also changes the roles of the other family members. In the case of the senior, someone becomes the caregiver and decision-maker often dislocating other aspects of the family. The reallocation of power and roles can cause a state of disequilibrium.

3. *Disruption of Family Functions.* The functions of the family need to be maintained and illness can create problems. In many cases the senior is not only an economic contributor but is actively involved in providing emotional support and security to members, helping with child rearing and helping in the transfer and preservation of culture. Inter-generational relationships and conflict are important.

4. *The Other Factors Involved.*

   a. Details of the illness such as nature, severity, contributing factors, duration.
   b. The socio-economic circumstances. Family finances are often an important factor in a family's decision whether or not to use health services. Considerations include the cost of the medical services, transportation and income lost by caregiver.
   c. Community support services. The family lives in a community and the interrelationships are important. The cultural and social norms play an important role in influencing decision and acceptance of certain services.

5. *What Is Available.* Intervention is an essential component of the family study so a review of the available resources is undertaken. The study of resources is broken down into family, community and state. The students are encouraged to do some self-investigation as each community is unique and has its own ways of helping its members. The church in particular usually has programmes to help even nonmembers. As the students are drawn from several areas they are often their own best sources of information about available resources.

METHODOLOGY

Having been taught the specifics with regard to the ageing process and the family, the students are given a framework, including definitions, which utilizes the points above and a modified Desmond Connor Compass (Connor 1969) for use in their investigation *and* home visits.

The framework has 13 areas (Figure 6); a profile of the senior and a description of 12 factors that will influence the social, psychological, economic and total well being of the present status of the elderly and the family. These are assessed in relation to the illness, its consequences and actions to be taken and in some instances as to whether they are available or not.

- History: Specific and significant experiences of past events e.g. births, deaths, illnesses, family life problems, traditions, social and economic, factors that would affect the elderly and promotion and prevent them attaining their life goals.
- Space Relations: Immediate environment of family, and social activities, available transportation, distances and time to travel to capital town. Relations within the community, overcrowding and/or under population with the negative and positive effects on the life of the elderly.
- Resources: *Human*–the number of people (friends social network) and their capabilities to function and help, skills of returning migrants and the distribution of remittances from migrant children, assets and pension. Educational, medical, recreational and spiritual facilities available.
  Man-made–such as roads, communication: television, radio, etc.
  Natural–land, water, minerals: coal.
  Resources are therefore what the family members, inclusive of the elderly, need to satisfy their individual and/or shared needs.
- Technology: The tools, skills and techniques used by the families, and in this case what the elderly persons had used to make a living. The kinds of "know how" that they used to solve problems, and the ways in which they adapted to their circumstances and environment. Technology also takes into account the introduction of modern technological devices (vacuum cleaners, fridges, gas and electric stoves as compared with traditional methods of sweeping, food storage and cooking). These modern instruments point to adaptability of the elderly, and where the traditional methods are still practiced there can be risks to the elderly. To be noted also is the impact of advances in technology on family life in nutrition, types of shelter, cleanliness, health and education.

- Knowledge and Belief: This element covers what is known and thought about life, the awareness of healthy lifestyles and the possession of positive health attitudes. Belief is a personal conviction. It is easier to change knowledge than belief, although an education programme based on a person's belief has a firmer foundation than one, which is based upon items of information.
- Values and Sentiments: These values are essentially "ideals of the desirable" which are held by elderly. Many values are shared by most of the people in the community and form the basis for their pattern of behaviour, e.g., pride in home, family and community; loyalty to family and community. Sentiments consist mostly of what people feel about certain ideas. Both sentiments and values are resistant to change. For example, an elderly woman who will never be seen going out without a hat or a tie head, or a man who, while clutching his walking stick in one hand, still insists on opening the door for a woman.
- Goals and Felt Needs: Specific and concrete targets or goals that people set for themselves. Some goals will be shared by most people while others will be limited to sub-groups, and others to an individual. Elderly persons who feel that they have not achieved their life's goals tend to be miserable and unfulfilled (Cook, 1983). Felt need, especially in the elderly, is most often perceived only by the elderly individual. The worker must be aware of this and also recognize that the felt need is very real to the individual. Felt needs will be under constant review and change. Transitions and adaptation to change are reviewed.
- Norms: These are the standards of what is right, good or bad, appropriate or inappropriate that are specific to each family including, conduct of family and its members, expected roles of in-laws and grandparents, and child rearing practices. Size of family, typical age for marriage, type of behavior to non-family members warm or reserved. Clearly, identifying the norms is critical in planning interventions.
- Position and Roles: Position and role of each person in the family with specific reference to the elderly. This can be determined by observing behaviors and responses.
- Power Leadership and Influence: Who are the natural leaders in the family and who will influence for good or bad? Who emerges as the family leader during an emergency, the shifting role of leadership, how the power invested in the leader will influence other members of the family and the community. Many times the senior, not the breadwinner, is the leader.

- Sanctions: The rewards and punishment for performance, or lack of, by individuals within the family.
- Social Rank: How the family is rated in the community and why as well as the influence of family background on this rating. For example, (1) Great grandfather was a lawyer, children professionals; (2) Great grandfather went to prison for murder. How do factors such as these affect the status of the family? Does this affect how the elderly person is treated in the family and in the community.

Having provided the students with a method for study, they are then introduced to their family. The Course Coordinator who accompanies them on the first visit introduces clients to students and helps to establish acceptance by the senior and their family.

CHOOSING THE FAMILY

The Process

1. Families for the study are selected through the National Council for Senior Citizens and the Coordinator of the Course in Community Care of the Elderly in the Caribbean.
2. Families include an elderly member and permission is obtained both from the elder and significant family members to conduct the study. An elderly person living alone may also be included as a study although the family interactions will be different. The percentage of seniors living alone will dictate the need to include such cases.
3. Number of visits is dependent on the assessed needs and complexities, but not less than 6. (Note: students are free to do other visits, in their own time.)
4. Students work in pairs but no two foreign students work together.

In some instances an elder who is coping successfully with ageing and life is chosen so as to identify what contributes to positive experiences.

Guidelines for Visits

Bearing in mind that the students are from different agencies, it helps to pool resources. The two caseworkers learn how to work together, recognizing their individual differences but working toward the common goal of helping the client. The students also learn from the elderly and this is encouraged.

FIGURE 6. Matrix for Assessing Seniors

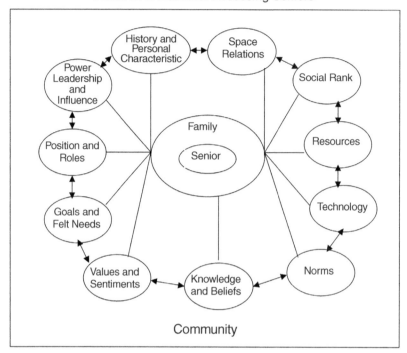

The study involves group dynamics as different person's work together which in itself is a learning process. The value of teamwork is stressed.

Before each session the students set objectives for each visit and, at the end of the visit they will revisit these to see if all were met. If this was not done they will carry forward the objectives. A running daily diary helps the process as it identifies barriers and keeps the students on track.

Students are taught how to formulate a basic questionnaire using the outline described. With the advent of the telephone, the coordinator is able to stay in touch with the client and monitor the process. The questionnaire covers the twelve areas identified earlier. It is used only as a guide for the discussions on the visits, and students are advised to keep writing to a minimum so as to maintain eye contact with the senior especially in the early stages before trust has been established.

Students are also introduced to a number of possible interventions and communication skills. It is recognized that at times there will be difficulty establishing a relationship and the coordinator may have to intervene.

Guidelines for the Study

1. Be professional, friendly, caring and considerate throughout.
2. Much information can be gained from simply observing and listening to what goes on around.
3. A helpful approach and answering questions and/or giving assistance with simple tasks will usually break down barriers, encourage trust, and build confidence.

The first visit should be to get acquainted and establish rapport, to give a statement about the course, and to explain the purpose of the visiting which is to learn from the elderly member.

Subsequent visits are organized around specific objectives to be met at each visit. Recording is completed immediately after each visit.

Students are also taught how to enter a community and establish rapport with their family. Techniques on obtaining information are also shared with the student. Observation is emphasized and students are encouraged to document nonverbal findings. Active listening is emphasized as a skill to be developed.

Assessment of the Study

There are two oral presentations and a written submission.

First Presentation

After the first four visits, a half-hour presentation is made to the class with the tutor being the facilitator, to help guide students' focus and clarify questions. This session is interactive with all other members seeking clarification and making suggestions. The presenters share the challenges they are experiencing and solicit the help of the group.

Second Presentation

At this time, twelve weeks of working with the family would have been completed. Students now present the challenges they faced and how they were resolved. What interventions they were able to put in place, to make the life of this elderly client better and more manageable for the family. This presentation is done with all members of the class, the tutor and other invited persons and may include the clients themselves. What the caseworker gained personally is also identified. After this process the case is written up by the student. It is to include:

- Sketch of the home (not to scale) to show the bathroom, yard space and other spatial arrangements.
- Family tree.
- Problems and selection of interventions.
- Interventions undertaken.
- Lessons learnt and experiences of the students.
- Recommendations for follow-up.

Before handing in the written report there is a three-day period to allow for modifications based on the oral presentation.

EVALUATION

Over 100 students from 13 Caribbean countries have participated in the family study module since the inception of the course in 1992. In an evaluation done five years later, 80% said it was very useful, 17.1% said useful and 2.9% said not useful. Ninety percent said the family study had contributed to an increase in confidence as it built their communication skills and increased their knowledge. Ninety-four percent reported that it had a positive impact on their feelings about older persons, due mainly to a better understanding of their feelings and recognition of their need for independence. Eighty-five percent reported an improvement in their ability to communicate effectively and credibly with seniors and their families as well as their own. Eighty-eight reported an improvement in their ability to teach older persons new ideas especially in health matters.

The majority reported a change in work practices since the course specifically encourages in-depth involvement of family members and volunteers. Fifty percent reported a change in behaviour in the home and an improvement in inter-family relationships resulting from a better understanding by family members of the senior living with them.

Eighty percent of the supervisors also reported that the persons they supervised showed improvement in their knowledge and understanding of seniors while 60% reported an improvement in work attitudes and 69% an increase in communication skills. Based on the formal evaluation and the annual end of course evaluation, the family study is a useful teaching tool for several reasons. It helps the students to understand seniors by working with them while being exposed to new thoughts on the ageing process. It allows the students, while being taught communication techniques, to practice classroom teachings and then discuss with tutors any difficulties or misunderstandings and try again. Also it helps to build team spirit through working with others.

The family study is also used in two other settings with modifications in emphasis. Medical students are exposed to an abbreviated version over a two-week period to study the impact of illness on the family and the sick persons chosen can be any age. This has been very helpful for the young students in studying topics such as HIV/AIDS and the devastation to a family socially and economically.

Further, it is used as a teaching tool in the Masters of Public Health Programme where emphasis is placed on how public health problems affect the family. This study is done over a ten-week period and includes an intervention component. So there is scope for the family study to be modified and applied to other areas. The wheel used to guide the detailed investigations can be adapted to represent the important areas of study. The one presented here highlights the areas that are important to older persons but could be changed to represent those important to children or any other chosen population in public health.

Initially, difficulties were encountered. The first was administrative and involved a lack of proper transportation for making weekend visits. However students who had their own means of transportation were encouraged to use them and claim for gasoline. A second difficulty involved seniors becoming weary and this, sometimes, made it difficult for relationships to be established even though the seniors met with representatives from the National Council for Senior Citizens and the course tutor prior to the student's visit to help them become comfortable with the process they were to encounter. At other times, a spouse or other member of the family expressed suspicion of the visits. Students were encouraged to persevere and the course tutor paid another visit to reassure the family. In all but one case, the perseverance was rewarded. In cases where the senior and family were willing participants it usually took two or three visits to establish trust and obtain real insights into the issues. Students are generally prepared for this during their preliminary teaching sessions.

A third difficulty is one commonly seen in social work practice–the breaking or ending of the interactions. This is addressed and attempts are made to prepare the students for termination but even so tears may be shed and some students and families have remained in contact over the years.

CONCLUSION

The family study has been used as a teaching tool since the inception of the course and has evolved to include new and changed concepts of the ageing process. Students continue to evaluate its usefulness highly as a learning tool and, more significantly, report that the contact with the family was an invaluable experience. Learning outcomes include increased knowledge about the community and how to mobilize resources at a personal level, strengthening of interviewing and communication skills, and a growth in the individual student's awareness of their own value and capability as case workers. In addition the family study provides a human face to theory. Several graduates remain in contact with their family after several years.

For the participating seniors and their families, the intervention component ensures that they both benefit from what is essentially a teaching tool.

REFERENCES

Barrow, C. (1996). Family and Community Breakdown in Barbados: Myth and Reality. Paper prepared for the Health Rationalization Study, Barbados.

Burgio, L., Corcoran, M., Lichstein, K., Nichols, L., Czaja, S., Gallagher-Thompson, D., Bourgeois, M., Stevens, A., Ory, M., Schultz, R. for the REACH Investigators. (2001). Judging Outcomes in Psychosocial Interventions for Dementia Caregivers: The Problem of Treatment Implementation. The Gerontological Society of America. The Gerontologist 41 (4): pp. 481-489.

Connor, D. M. (1969). Understanding your Community. 2nd. ed., rev. Ottawa, Development Press, 8-9, 25.

Cook, A. S. (1983) Contemporary Perspectives on Adult Development and Ageing. Colorado State University. Macmillan Publishing Co., Inc. New York: 8-9, 347-353.

Dilworth-Anderson, P., Burton, L. (1999). Critical Issues in Understanding Family Support and Older Minorities. Full-Color Ageing: Facts, Goals, and Recommendations for America's Diverse Elders. The Gerontological Society of America, 93-102.

Eldemire, D. (1993). An Epidemiological Survey of the Elderly in Jamaica. A thesis submitted in fulfillment of the requirement for the degree of Doctor of Philosophy in public health, university of the West Indies, Jamaica.

HelpAge International (1999). The Ageing and Development Report, Poverty, Independence and the World's Older People. Earthscan Publications Limited, London, 71-81.

Maslow, A. (1954). Motivations and Personality. Harper and Row Publishers, Inc., New York.

Mendes de Leon C. F., Gold, D. T., Glass, T. A., Kaplan, L., George, L. K. (1986-1992). Disability as a function of Social Networks and Support in Elderly African Americans and Whites. The Duke EPESE. The Journals of Gerontology, Series b, Psychological Sciences and Social Sciences, The Gerontological Society of America, 2001: 56B: 3, 179-190.

Morris, C. (2000). A Tribute to Grandparents. Unpublished.

Pan American Health Organization. (1999). Plan of Action on Health and Ageing: Older Adults in the Americas, 1999-2002. Pan American Health Organization, Washington, 6-17.

Planning Institute of Jamaica and the Statistical Institute of Jamaica (2000). Jamaica Survey of Living Conditions, 1999.

Planning Institute of Jamaica and the Statistical Institute of Jamaica (1999). Jamaica Survey of Living Conditions, 1998.

Planning Institute of Jamaica and the Statistical Institute of Jamaica (1998). Jamaica Survey of Living Conditions, 1997.

Planning Institute of Jamaica and the Statistical Institute of Jamaica (1995). Jamaica Survey of Living Conditions, 1994.

Shaibu, S. (2000) Caregiving on the edge: The situation of family caregivers to older persons in Botswana. Department of Nursing Education, University of Botswana. Southern African Journal of Gerontology, 9 (1): 15-19.

Silverstone, B. (2000). The Old and the New in Aging: Implications for Social Work Practice, Journal of Gerontological Social Work, The Haworth Press, Inc. 33: (4), 35-50.

Tout, K. (1989). Ageing in Developing Countries. Oxford University Press, London, 3-10, 39-47.

United Nations (1992). Declaration of the Rights of Older People.

World Health Organization. (2000). Towards an International Policy for Long Term Care of the Ageing, World Health Organization, Geneva 2000: 6, 9, 10-12.

World Health Organization (1999). A Life Course Perspective of Maintaining Independence in Old Age, World Health Organization, Geneva, 3-4.

World Health Organization (1999). The Life Course Approach–Functional Capacity over the Life Course. Reprinted, with kind permission, from: A Life Course Perspective of Maintaining Independence in Older Age, World Health Organization, Geneva.

APPENDIX

Questionnaire

Profile of the Subject   Age

Date of Birth   Religion
Gender
Single   Married   Divorced   Separated   Widow
Address
With whom do you live?
How long has this arrangement been in place?
What were the main reasons for the arrangement? (Social, economic, physical, other).

Family History

Births   deaths   marriages   migrations
Significant experiences of past.
Number of children/grandchildren alive.
How often do you see them/hear from them?
Present family structure–How many members live in the house?
Type of family: Extended/nuclear/yard setting.

Family Tree (represent the family members who impact directly or in directly on the elder under study)
How many dependent members and ages?

Location of house

In community.
Distance from social network: Church, market/shop, post office, clinic/hospital
How near is the main road?
What kind of transportation system?

Type of structure

Wood/concrete.
Sanitation, garbage disposal, running water, electricity.
Size of house with basic floor plan?
Size of land (is there room for gardening?)
Is it fenced?
Who owns the land—rented/leased?

Technology

Does the house have modern equipment: Television, microwave, refrigerator, telephone, etc.?

Health and Education

How was your health as a child?
How was your health as an adult?
What is your health status now?
What is wrong?
What kind of medication is being taken, for how long—Compliance?
Have you ever been hospitalized? Why? How long?
Note any disabilities (Observe for this, as this could be a sensitive area).
Do you use any traditional medicines (home remedies)?
In what church activities are you involved?
Does the family make provisions for subject to worship according to belief?

Schools

How far did you go in school?
Query for beliefs and how these affect what they practice.

Position and Role in Family

Who is the head of the household?
Who pays the bills?
What is your source of income?
Who is your main source of financial support?
Who is your main source of emotional support?
Do you receive a pension?
Who gives the orders?
What sanctions are given—Measure of discipline?
Who is the leader of the household?
What is the perceived influence of the elder in the family?

Social Network

Who is your closest friend?
Do you see them as often as you would like?
Are you involved in any community group?
What are they?
What is most valued in the family, e.g., education, manners, church, etc.?
What does this elderly teach the children/grandchildren?
What are the goals (dreams) not met?
Are they still attainable?
What is expressed as a need (felt need) by the elderly?
What is identified as a need (real) by the student?
What standard of behaviour was imparted?
What is now being practiced?
Students should identity how the experience impacted on them, inclusive of feelings.
Student with this information, using all the knowledge gained from all the lessons in all modules will now do the write up of:

The problems/challenges that they have identified
What is considered the problem that you will attempt to address during your time of interaction with the family?
What are the planned interventions?

Index

intergenerational service-learning
approaches and, 220-221
service-learning approaches and,
183,220-221
student interest strategies and, 64
Attitude enhancement issues. *See*
Practice-related knowledge
and attitude enhancement
Attitudes Toward Community Service
Work Scale, 230-232
Attitudes Toward Working with Older
People Scale, 232-230
Awareness-building issues, 75-76

Bachelor of Social Work (BSW)
programs
basic competencies for, 26-30,
34-35
grantmaking programs and, 76-79
practice-related knowledge and
attitude enhancement and,
159-175
student interest strategies and, 59
Bakalar, H., 91-110
Basic competencies. *See* Competencies
(basic)
Bibliographies. *See* Reference and
research literature
Biopsychosocial domains, 40-41,
196-202
BSW programs. *See* Bachelor of Social
Work (BSW) programs
Bures, R. M., 111-127

Campbell, R., 91-110
Capacities (functional), 247
Care coordinators, 205
Career guidance (academic), 151-152
Caribbean countries (family studies),
241-261
Class and field curriculum programs

for family studies, 241-261. *See
also* Family study-related
issues
for geriatric assessment training,
195-202. *See also* Geriatric
assessment training
gerontological social work
education issues, relationship
to. *See* Gerontological social
work education issues
graduate-level, 203-217. *See also*
Graduate-level class and field
curriculum programs
for intergenerational
service-learning approaches,
219-240. *See also*
Intergenerational
service-learning approaches
introduction to, xvii-xviii,1-3,
157-158
for practice-related knowledge and
attitude enhancement,
159-175. *See also*
Practice-related knowledge
and attitude enhancement
school-based initiatives and. *See*
School-based initiatives
for service-learning approaches,
177-194,219-240. *See also*
Service-learning approaches
Clients/patients
assessment and outcome measures
for, 222-223,226-228,
235-237
relationships with, 211
service-learning approaches, impact
of, 189-190
CNS. *See* Corporation for National
Service (CNS)
Cohort-related issues
doctoral fellowship programs, 152,
154
grantmaking programs, 80-81
student recruitment, 95

reference and research literature
    about, 258-259
selection processes for
    assessment and outcome
        measures, 255-256
    introduction to, 253
    study guidelines, 255
    visitation guidelines, 253-254
United Nations (UN) and, 247
World Health Organization (WHO)
    and, 241-242,247-249
Fellowship programs. *See* Doctoral
    fellowship programs
Field practicum rotations
    assessment and outcome measures
        for, 136-137,141-142
    Council on Social Work Education
        (CSWE) and, 130
    future perspectives of, 142-143
    Hartford Foundation and, 129-144
    at Hunter College, School of Social
        Work, 129-144
    impact of, 137-139
    importance of, 130-131
    introduction to, 129-130
    models of, 131-134
    reference and research literature
        about, 143-144
    summer internships and
        activities and tasks, 135
        field instructor experiences,
            134-136,139-142
        student experiences, 134,
            137-139
FIPSE. *See* Fund for the Improvement
    of Post Secondary Education
    (FIPSE)
Folstein Mini-Mental State Exam
    (MMSE), 199
Fortune, A. E., 111-127
Foundation for Long Term Care
    (FTLC), 177-194
Frameworks (professional). *See*
    Professional frameworks
    (common)

FTLC. *See* Foundation for Long Term
    Care (FTLC)
Functional capacities, 247
Functioning (biopsychosocial), 40-41,
    196-202
Fund for the Improvement of Post
    Secondary Education
    (FIPSE), 183
Future perspectives
    of basic competencies, 35
    of common professional
        frameworks, 20-21
    of doctoral fellowship programs,
        154-155
    of family study-related issues,
        257-259
    of field practicum rotations,
        142-143
    of geriatric assessment training, 202
    of graduate-level class and field
        curriculum programs, 215
    of graduate-level training programs,
        124-125
    of grantmaking programs, 83
    of interdisciplinary practices, 50-52
    of intergenerational
        service-learning approaches,
        239
    of practice-related knowledge and
        attitude enhancement,
        171-172
    of service-learning approaches, 191
    of student interest strategies, 65
    of student recruitment, 108-110

Galambos, C., 7-23
GDS-Short Form. *See* Geriatric
    Depression Scale
    (GDS)-Short Form
General Attitudes Toward the Elderly
    Scale, 230-232
Generations Together program. *See*
    Association of Gerontologists
    in Higher Education (AGHE)